Introduction to Cross-Border E-Commerce Ecosystem

Xiaheng Zhang

Introduction to Cross-Border E-Commerce Ecosystem

西安交通大學出版社
XI'AN JIAOTONG UNIVERSITY PRESS

Springer

Xiaheng Zhang
School of Business
Northwest University of Political Science
and Law
Xi'an, China

ISBN 978-981-96-1164-5 ISBN 978-981-96-1165-2 (eBook)
https://doi.org/10.1007/978-981-96-1165-2

Jointly published with Xi'an Jiaotong University Press.
The printed edition is not for sale in China Mainland. Customers from China Mainland please order the print book from Xi'an Jiaotong University Press.

The original submitted manuscript has been translated into English. The translation was done using artificial intelligence. A subsequent revision was performed by the author(s) to further refine the work and to ensure that the translation is appropriate concerning content and scientific correctness. It may, however, read stylistically different from a conventional translation.

This Springer imprint is published by the registered company Springer Nature Singapore Pte Ltd.
The registered company address is: 152 Beach Road, #21-01/04 Gateway East, Singapore 189721, Singapore

Contents

Chapter 1
Introduction

1.1 Background of Cross-Border E-Commerce

1.1.1 Deepening Development of Global Economic Integration

Since the 1970s, with the global expansion of multinational corporations, the elements and activities of production began to reorganize on a global scale. The globalization of production organization activities brings about the synchronicity of global economic development, and at the same time, it brings about a global demand for corresponding productive services. The service industry begins to globalize, pushing globalization into a new stage. After a certain stage of rapid development, emerging economies have improved their production and consumption capabilities and have begun to develop in reverse to developed areas. This is first manifested as an increase in demand for consumer goods in developed areas, making the trend of global production, consumption, and market integration more apparent. International organizations and governments are also promoting the formulation of related policies, and a large number of free trade agreements between countries or regions have been signed to promote trade facilitation and improve efficiency in the trade process. The flow of global information and goods is becoming more free, trade globalization and borderless trade are further developing, and cross-border trade is becoming increasingly frequent.

1.1.2 Traditional International Trade Showing Weakness

The outbreak of the global financial crisis in 2008 dealt a heavy blow to the economies of all countries. In the post-financial crisis era, the domestic economic growth of

X. Zhang, *Introduction to Cross-Border E-Commerce Ecosystem*,
https://doi.org/10.1007/978-981-96-1165-2_1

Table 1.1 Total amount and growth rate of China's goods imports and exports (2012–2021)

Year		2012	2013	2014	2015	2016	2017	2018	2019	2020	2021
Export of goods	Total amount (trillion yuan)	12.94	13.71	14.39	14.12	13.84	15.33	16.41	17.24	17.93	21.73
	Growth rate (%)	—	5.62	4.73	−1.91	−2.02	9.72	6.58	4.81	3.85	21.19
Import of goods	Total amount (trillion yuan)	11.48	12.11	12.04	10.43	10.5	12.48	14.08	14.33	14.29	17.36
	Growth rate (%)	—	5.49	−0.58	−13.37	0.67	18.86	12.92	1.78	−0.28	21.48

major countries is weak, and traditional international trade on a global scale is showing a sluggish growth trend. Taking China as an example, compared with previous years, China's economic growth has slowed down in recent years. As shown in Table 1.1, China's traditional goods import and export growth has been weak in recent years. China's goods exports experienced negative growth in 2015 and 2016; China's goods imports also experienced negative growth in 2014 and 2015, especially in 2015 when the growth rate reached −3.37%, and China's goods imports also experienced negative growth in 2020. Not only that, from the data from 2012 to 2020, the growth trend of China's traditional goods imports and exports contrasts significantly with the rapid growth of the cross-border e-commerce industry. Although China's economic growth has slowed down, the structural adjustment under the new normal of the economy has provided opportunities for the development of cross-border e-commerce.

1.1.3 Policy Dividends from Various Countries Are Continuously Emerging

The push of government and policy is huge, and it can even play a guiding and decisive role. After cross-border e-commerce became a global hotspot, governments of various countries have introduced a series of policies to promote its development, and the drive of policy dividends has further accelerated its development pace. Taking China as an example, according to incomplete statistics, the government has introduced many policies aimed at promoting the development of cross-border e-commerce. In June 2015, during the St. Petersburg Economic Forum, Russia proposed to shift the source of economic growth from energy (oil, natural gas, nuclear power) to the Internet economy, logistics, and cross-border trade. In Australia, the government encourages small and medium-sized enterprises to explore overseas markets through cross-border e-commerce channels, and has conducted promotional trials through the Chinese e-commerce platforms "JD.com" and "Yihaodian", fully verifying the driving effect of cross-border e-commerce on Australian goods exports.

1.1.4 Continuous Improvement of Related Infrastructure

Infrastructure is the cornerstone of cross-border e-commerce development. The construction and improvement of infrastructure and resources related to networks, technology, logistics, payments, etc., promote the rapid development of cross-border e-commerce. The construction of network infrastructure associated with the Internet and mobile networks has promoted the increase in Internet penetration, opening up the medium for the realization of cross-border e-commerce; the layout of infrastructure in terms of payment tools and technology, financial networks and facilities, etc., has improved the payment carrier needed for cross-border e-commerce; the vigorous development of logistics infrastructure represented by logistics outlets and transportation, has met the commodity circulation needs of cross-border e-commerce. With the improvement of PC equipment performance and the decrease in prices, the popularity of smartphones, especially those priced around a thousand or even a few hundred yuan, has promoted the development of e-commerce networks and mobile networks, with a particularly significant push in emerging markets for the development of cross-border e-commerce.

1.2 Concept of Cross-Border E-Commerce

Cross-border e-commerce, or simply cross-border e-commerce, refers to the activities of trading entities belonging to different countries or borders, carrying out all activities of commodity transactions through e-commerce platforms, and realizing the flow of goods from sellers to buyers through cross-border logistics, as well as other related activities. It is a new type of e-commerce application model. Cross-border e-commerce extends from e-commerce, belongs to the category of e-commerce, and is a new application model of e-commerce. Cross-border e-commerce includes overseas shopping, purchasing agents, cross-border retail, and cross-border B2B models, etc. Other business activities that cross national or border boundaries through e-commerce models can also be classified as cross-border e-commerce.

1.3 Features of Cross-Border E-Commerce

1. Entities Cross Borders

The most typical feature of cross-border e-commerce is that the trading entities belong to different countries or borders, and the transactions cross different countries or borders. Compared with domestic e-commerce, its trading entities are generally in the same country, such as domestic enterprises to enterprises, domestic enterprises to individuals, or domestic individuals to individuals. The trading entities of cross-border e-commerce break through the boundaries of the same country or border, emphasizing that they are located in different countries or borders, and may be domestic enterprises to foreign enterprises, domestic enterprises to foreign individuals, or domestic individuals to foreign individuals. Due to the characteristic of crossing borders, cross-border e-commerce is also affected by this typical feature in terms of payment, logistics, business environment, etc.

2. Distinct Network Attributes

Cross-border e-commerce extends from e-commerce and has typical Internet attributes. Cross-border e-commerce supports commodity trading activities with the Internet and information technology, and cannot exist independently of the Internet. Cross-border e-commerce is also seen as Internet + foreign trade. With the healthy and rapid development of cross-border e-commerce, "Internet + foreign trade" is conducive to expanding consumption, promoting the development and upgrading of an open economy, and creating new economic growth points. Cross-border e-commerce transaction activities have realized the Internetization of commodity display, exhibition, sales, after-sales, etc., all these transaction activities are completed with the support of the Internet. Therefore, cross-border e-commerce presents distinct network attributes.

3. Complex Associated Activities

The cross-border e-commerce transaction chain is complex. In addition to the commodity trading activities involved in cross-border e-commerce platforms, it also involves cross-border payments, cross-border logistics, customs inspections, and other main links. The transaction entities are spread all over the world, with different consumption habits, cultural psychology, and lifestyle customs. This requires cross-border e-commerce to have a deeper understanding of traffic introduction in various countries, promotion and marketing in various countries, foreign consumer behavior, international brand building, etc. The environment involved in cross-border e-commerce is far more complex than domestic e-commerce, and the political, technological, economic, cultural, social, and other aspects of the countries between the transaction entities will affect cross-border e-commerce. Domestic companies have a weak awareness of intellectual property rights, and a large number of unbranded, low-quality goods and counterfeit goods flood the cross-border e-commerce market, and infringements of intellectual property rights occur from time to time.

4. Risks Are Intertwined

Cross-border e-commerce transactions are complex and business risks are numerous. In the context of global economic integration, companies involved in cross-border e-commerce increasingly face many new, hidden, and not to be underestimated business risks in their transnational operations, such as credit risks, cross-border logistics risks, information risks, and other inherent risks, as well as legal risks, political risks, natural risks, infrastructure risks, and other external risks. As for the risk of cross-border e-commerce service supply chain, it includes credit risk, cross-border logistics risk, and information risk, as well as legal risk, political risk, and natural risk. Taking exchange rate risk as an example, cross-border e-commerce cannot escape the impact of exchange rate changes. Exchange rate changes directly or indirectly affect cross-border e-commerce, bringing many business risks.

1.4 Cross-Border E-Commerce Process

The transaction entities of cross-border e-commerce belong to different countries or borders. When the country where one of the transaction entities is located is fixed, according to the different directions of commodity flow, cross-border e-commerce can be divided into cross-border e-commerce exports and cross-border e-commerce imports. From the perspective of cross-border e-commerce exports, the producer directly supplies the produced goods to the cross-border e-commerce platform, or supplies the goods to the cross-border e-commerce platform through the supplier, realizing the display and exhibition of the goods on the cross-border e-commerce platform. When consumers browse the goods on the cross-border e-commerce platform, decide to place an order to purchase and complete the payment, the goods will be spatially displaced through offline cross-border logistics, go through two customs and commercial inspections, and finally be delivered to the buyer through the logistics and distribution of the buyer's country, thus completing the entire cross-border e-commerce transaction process. The process of cross-border e-commerce imports is basically the same as the content and links of cross-border e-commerce exports, the only difference is the direction of the process, as shown in Fig. 1.1.

1.5 Cross-Border E-Commerce, Domestic E-Commerce and International Trade

The emergence of cross-border e-commerce stems from the integrated development of international trade and domestic e-commerce. Driven by the rapid development of e-commerce, traditional international trade has incorporated many elements of e-commerce; domestic e-commerce development is becoming saturated, and the domestic market growth is sluggish. Under the impetus of the internet and information

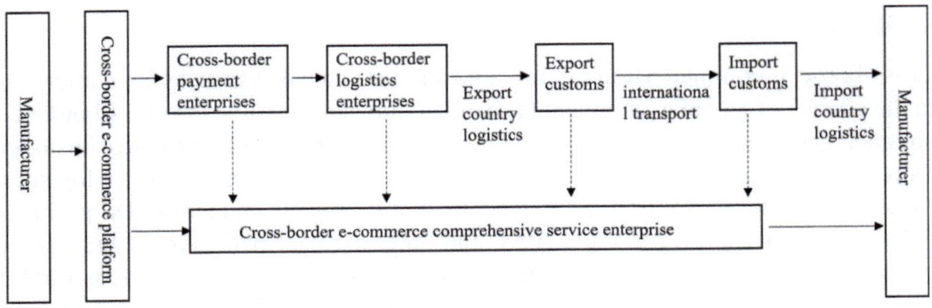

Fig. 1.1 Cross-border E-commerce process

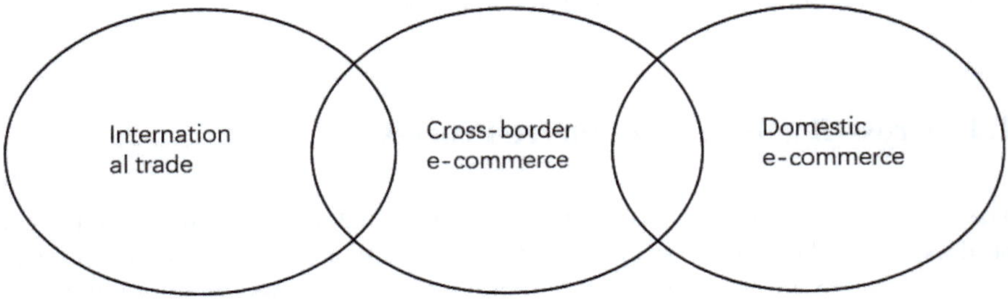

Fig. 1.2 Cross-border e-commerce, domestic e-commerce, international trade

technology, domestic e-commerce has extended its reach to foreign markets, thereby providing momentum for the emergence of cross-border e-commerce. Cross-border e-commerce bears traces of international trade and domestic e-commerce, but it is not entirely equivalent to international trade and domestic e-commerce. As shown in Fig. 1.2, we can clearly understand the relationship between the three.

1.5.1 Cross-Border E-Commerce and International Trade

Compared with international trade, cross-border e-commerce has both similarities and significant differences. Both are business activities between different countries or regions, involving the circulation of commerce, logistics, capital flow, and information flow between two or more countries or regions; both involve import and export customs clearance and commercial inspection activities, and are affected by political, economic, cultural and other environmental factors due to different countries. Cross-border e-commerce is not equivalent to international trade, and the differences are mainly reflected in the following aspects.

1. The nature of the trading entity. The trading entity of international trade generally appears as an organizational paradigm; the trading entity of cross-border e-commerce includes both organization-to-individual and individual-to-individual.

2. Trading medium. Although international trade has introduced modern internet and information technology, the trading medium is still mainly traditional modes, such as official websites, trade platforms, emails, communication tools, etc.; cross-border e-commerce uses e-commerce platforms dominated by the internet and information technology as the trading medium, whether it is a self-built e-commerce platform or a third-party e-commerce platform, all belong to the category of e-commerce platforms.
3. Logistics. International trade mostly uses international transportation modes, especially international multimodal transport, and does not involve terminal distribution in the importing country, etc.; cross-border e-commerce not only needs to realize cross-border transportation of goods, but also needs to provide logistics and distribution services in the importing country.
4. Payment. International trade involves large amounts of money, mainly offline payments, using methods such as telegraphic transfer (T/T), collection (D/P, D/A), letter of credit (L/C), Western Union, etc.; cross-border e-commerce payments are mainly online and electronic payments, especially through third-party payment intermediaries, involving smaller amounts, more scattered objects, and higher frequency.

1.5.2 Cross-Border E-Commerce and Domestic E-Commerce

Compared with domestic e-commerce, although cross-border e-commerce belongs to the large category of e-commerce and has many common points with domestic e-commerce, because it crosses national boundaries, it shows some significant differences. Cross-border e-commerce emphasizes the spatial location of the trading entity, which must be in different countries or regions, thus forming characteristics different from domestic e-commerce in many aspects of e-commerce, with more links and more complex operations. The main manifestations are as follows.

1. The spatial location of the trading entity. The trading entity of domestic e-commerce is located in the same country or region; the trading entity of cross-border e-commerce breaks through the boundaries of countries or regions and belongs to different countries or regions.
2. Payment. Domestic e-commerce does not require cross-border payment; cross-border e-commerce uses cross-border payment, especially involving financial policies of different countries and exchange rate issues of different currencies, etc.
3. Logistics. Domestic e-commerce only involves logistics and distribution within the same country; cross-border e-commerce requires cross-border logistics to be implemented. Because it involves different countries or regions, cross-border logistics need to go through the customs and commercial inspections of the exporting country, the customs and commercial inspections of the importing country, and extend to the logistics and distribution of the importing country. Reverse logistics caused by returns and exchanges is a serious challenge.

4. Environment. The environment involved in cross-border e-commerce is far more complex than domestic e-commerce because it involves different countries or regions. The political, technological, economic, cultural, and social environments of the trading entity's country will all have an impact on cross-border e-commerce, and its complexity is far higher than domestic e-commerce.

1.6 The Evolution of Cross-Border E-Commerce

The prototype of cross-border e-commerce originated from overseas shopping and personal purchasing. Under the stimulation of various factors, the Chinese cross-border e-commerce market gradually developed. The form of cross-border e-commerce is no longer limited to overseas shopping and personal purchasing, and it has gradually developed on a large scale and corporatized. More and more companies are constantly entering the cross-border e-commerce market. Overseas shopping and personal purchasing have many prominent problems, so cross-border e-commerce companies have gradually replaced them and become the main force in the cross-border e-commerce market. From the appearance of overseas shopping and purchasing, the development of cross-border e-commerce has been more than ten years.

According to the industry life cycle theory, the industry life development cycle refers to the time an industry experiences from its emergence to its complete withdrawal from social economic activities. The industry life development cycle mainly includes four development stages: introduction, growth, maturity, and decline. Before the industry enters the decline stage, it may enter the innovation stage and then enter the next life cycle.

The life cycle of cross-border e-commerce refers to the evolution process of cross-border e-commerce from growth to decline, which is the time from the appearance of cross-border e-commerce to its complete withdrawal from social economic activities. Chinese cross-border e-commerce has gone through the industry introduction, growth, and maturity stages, and is currently in the innovation stage. Each stage shows different characteristics. Globally, cross-border e-commerce originated in the late 1990s, marked by Amazon (1998) and eBay (1999) stepping out of the United States and entering the European market. In China, Alibaba International Station appeared as a symbol of domestic cross-border e-commerce in 1999. Entering the twenty-first century, domestic cross-border e-commerce companies in China have emerged in large numbers, and the development of cross-border e-commerce has gradually advanced.

1.6.1 Introduction Stage of Cross-Border E-Commerce

The introduction stage is the first stage of the industry life cycle theory. The market is not yet mature at this time, the industry profit rate is low, the market growth rate is high, the demand growth is fast, the technology change is large, and the pioneers in the industry are mainly committed to opening up new users and occupying the market. However, there is a lot of uncertainty in technology, and there is a lot of room for strategy in products, markets, services, etc. There is not much information about industry characteristics, industry competition, user characteristics, etc., and the barriers to entry are low.

From 1999 to 2007 was the introduction stage of cross-border e-commerce, this stage has 2 landmark nodes, namely: the establishment of Alibaba International Station in 1999, and the launch of Dunhuang Network and Amazon China in 2004. In the introduction stage, cross-border e-commerce often provides information services for both parties of the transaction through information platforms, and other links of cross-border trade are mostly completed offline, which is an attempt to combine traditional trade with the Internet. Subsequently, some cross-border e-commerce platforms began to get involved in online commodity trading activities, but such a proportion was small.

Before 2007, with the dramatic increase in the number of students studying abroad, the first batch of personal purchasing agents represented by these students emerged, mainly manifested as overseas personal purchasing models recommended by acquaintances. In addition to the purchasing agent model, the main business model during the import period of cross-border e-commerce was the foreign trade information service model of online display and offline transactions. The main function of the third-party platform at this stage is to provide a network display platform for enterprise information and products, and does not involve any transaction links on the network. At this time, the profit model is mainly to charge membership fees (such as annual service fees) to companies that display information. During the development process of this stage, a one-stop information flow value-added service for suppliers gradually derived from bidding promotion, consulting services, etc. During the import period of cross-border e-commerce, Alibaba International Station and Global Resources Network are typical representative platforms. Among them, Alibaba was established in 1999, with online information services as the main and offline transactions as the auxiliary, and is one of China's largest foreign trade information yellow page platforms. Global Resources Network was established in 1971, formerly known as Asian Source, is an early provider of trade market information in Asia, and was listed on the NASDAQ Stock Exchange in 2000, with the stock code GSOL. During this period, a large number of cross-border e-commerce platforms mainly for supply and demand information transactions, such as China Manufacturing Network, South Korea EC21 Network, Kellysearch, etc., also appeared. Although the Internet has solved the problem of trade information facing global buyers, it still cannot complete online transactions, and the integration of the foreign trade e-commerce industry chain stops at the information flow integration link.

During this period, many people, to be precise, a group of people studying abroad, sold game coins on eBay and Amazon, and made their first pot of gold in life. After 2006, online games were not so popular. In 2007, eBay announced that it would no longer engage in virtual game currency transactions, and this stage also ended. In 2004, Wang Shu Tong left Joyo.com and founded Dunhuang.com, focusing on small online wholesale. In 2006, Dealextreme, which started with eBay (later DX), went online, mainly focusing on electronic products. In 2007, Lanting Collection was launched, which was the first foreign trade e-commerce platform in China with venture capital participation and self-operation. The platform e-commerce began to be active during this period.

1.6.2 Cross-Border E-Commerce Development Period

The development period is the second stage of the industry life cycle theory. During this period, the market growth rate is very high, the demand is growing rapidly, the technology is gradually becoming fixed, the industry characteristics, industry competition conditions and user characteristics are relatively clear, the barriers to entry for enterprises are increasing, and the variety of products and the number of competitors are increasing.

From 2007 to 2014 was the development period of cross-border e-commerce. During this stage, cross-border e-commerce companies were continuously established in China, such as eBay China, Lantingji and Taobao Global Shopping launched in 2007, Yangmatou and Dalong.net were established in 2009, AliExpress launched in 2010, and Haitao.com launched in 2013. In 2007, Taobao launched "Global Shopping". In the same year, eBay.cn (eBay China) was launched, mainly engaged in B2C cross-border e-commerce in foreign trade. At that time, cross-border e-commerce was just a concept, and companies like Dunhuang Network and Lantingji were just starting. Obviously, eBay hoped to use its first-mover advantage in the international market to attract the interest of Chinese merchants again. As it turned out, eBay made the right choice. Almost at the same time as Taobao seized the domestic online retail market, eBay seized the cross-border e-commerce market, making a comeback. Subsequently, websites focusing on purchasing agents emerged one after another, developing and expanding the market for overseas purchasing agents, especially the "poisonous milk powder incident" that swept the country in 2008 stimulated the development of overseas purchasing and forwarding services, and the categories of Haitao expanded from maternal and child products to health products, electronic products, clothing and hats, cosmetics, luxury goods, etc. The global financial crisis in 2008 fully fostered and achieved the Chinese foreign trade B2C industry. That year, the market share of the largest 3000 importers in the United States in the Chinese market dropped by 10%. At the same time, more and more importers began to try small amounts and frequent forms to avoid risks. But the deeper reason is that with the Internet eliminating information asymmetry and world flattening, the popularity of online payment tools PayPal, and the improvement of express delivery channels, the global barriers to online trade were quickly broken. And unlike the domestic e-commerce still in its infancy, the e-commerce environment in developed countries in Europe and America is quite mature. There are many small and medium-sized enterprises of online trade types, providing excellent soil for foreign trade e-commerce. In September 2010, China adjusted the management policy of inbound and outbound personal postal items, tightening the Haitao and purchasing agent market, and the cost and risk of Haitao and purchasing agents increased dramatically.

More and more people are beginning to believe that cross-border e-commerce represented by small cross-border transactions is more attractive and explosive. The most obvious reason is that low-priced Chinese-made goods are often sold abroad at several times the price. This undoubtedly provides sufficient profit space for online trade that bypasses many intermediate links. Of course, compared with China's huge export volume, the transactions of these e-commerce websites are just a drop in the bucket. It is clear that e-commerce platforms are becoming a new window for Chinese companies to face the world. After the traditional foreign trade market was hit by the financial crisis, a large number of surplus products in China are looking for various new sales channels. At this time, cross-border e-commerce just filled this gap, it mainly has two forms: one is to become a big seller of Amazon or eBay, and the other is to establish an independent website. These two forms have their own advantages and disadvantages. The former is more suitable for small and medium-sized enterprises and entrepreneurs, but with the growth of scale or the intervention of capital, some more ambitious foreign trade B2C sellers directly leave eBay and Dunhuang Network and establish independent websites for wholesale and retail, such as Lantingji, Chinavasion, etc. These websites usually require sufficient financial support and rich online marketing experience, but their advantages are also obvious. First, they no longer need to pay transaction fees to the platform, and it is easy to integrate procurement, logistics and other links, generate scale effects, and have higher profit margins; second, after reducing the platform link, it is easier to win the trust of buyers. For example, once there is a dispute over the goods, the buyer and the seller can communicate directly, which is more convenient and faster than the three-party communication through the trading platform. During this period, in addition to a large number of third-party platform sellers, a number of relatively well-known Chinese cross-border e-commerce platforms also appeared.

During the development phase of cross-border e-commerce, more and more cross-border e-commerce companies are emerging, conducting online trading activities through cross-border e-commerce platforms, and using digital technology to reduce transaction costs and improve transaction efficiency. Various cross-border e-commerce models, such as B2B, B2C, C2C, etc., have emerged during this stage. Cross-border e-commerce activities are becoming increasingly active, and related links such as payment and logistics are gradually moving online.

1.6.3 Cross-Border E-Commerce Maturity Period

The maturity period is the third stage of the industry life cycle theory. The market growth rate is not high during this period, the demand growth rate slows down, the technology is mature, the industry characteristics, competition conditions, and user characteristics are very clear and stable, a buyer's market is formed, the industry's profitability declines, and the development of new products and new uses for products becomes more difficult. The industry enters a high barrier.

From 2014 to 2020 was the maturity period of cross-border e-commerce. During this stage, some cross-border e-commerce companies continued to grow and become stronger, and mainstream companies have emerged, such as Tmall International, Xiaohongshu, Mia, No.1 Overseas Shopping, Suning Global Purchase, Vipshop Overseas Shopping, Jumei Overseas Shopping launched in 2014, and JD Global Shopping launched in 2015. With the development of digital technologies such as artificial intelligence, big data, cloud computing, and the increasing personalization of consumer demand, cross-border e-commerce transactions are becoming more mature, the proportion of cross-border e-commerce transactions is increasing, and the scale of the cross-border e-commerce market is continuously rising. At this stage, China launched the pilot cities for cross-border e-commerce services, opening the fast track for the development of cross-border e-commerce. After 2011, the term "cross-border e-commerce" began to be known to us, and the country also began to pay great attention, with a series of related policies being introduced, local government support strengthened, and of course, competition became increasingly fierce. There are traditional industries transforming and entering, more and more offline suppliers, logistics providers, service providers, and domestic e-commerce sellers are pouring into AliExpress. After a round of wild growth, Chinese cross-border e-commerce began to experience intense competition. Since July 2014, including the 56th and 57th documents of the General Administration of Customs, various favorable policies have been introduced, involving customs, commodity inspection, logistics, payment, etc., stimulating the development of cross-border e-commerce, and thus cross-border e-commerce companies have emerged continuously and gradually entered the normal development track. 2014 was an important year of transformation for cross-border e-commerce, and the business models of the entire cross-border e-commerce industry chain have changed. In 2015, NetEase Koala, JD Global Shopping, and Alibaba International Station's credit insurance business were launched one after another. The scale of the cross-border e-commerce market has been rising year by year, breaking through the 10 trillion mark in 2019. By the end of 2020, China has successively established five batches of cross-border e-commerce comprehensive pilot zones, and the 9710/9810 customs supervision models have been introduced, all of which have promoted the development of China's cross-border e-commerce. Not only that, the sudden epidemic has stimulated the development of cross-border e-commerce, and some new cross-border e-commerce models have emerged, such as the emergence of cross-border social e-commerce.

With the transformation of cross-border e-commerce, the "big era" of cross-border e-commerce has arrived, characterized by the online presence of large factories, the scaling of B-class buyers, the increase in the proportion of medium and large orders, the joining of large service providers, and the explosion of mobile users. At the same time, cross-border e-commerce services have been fully upgraded, with stronger platform carrying capacity, and the online service of the entire industry chain has also become an important feature of the maturity of China's cross-border e-commerce industry. In the mature stage of cross-border e-commerce, the user group has shifted from "grassroots" entrepreneurship to factories and foreign trade companies, with extremely strong production design management capabilities. The platform's sales products have shifted from online merchants and second-hand sources to first-hand sources. The main seller group at this stage is in the difficult transition period from traditional foreign trade business to cross-border e-commerce business, the production mode has shifted from large production lines to flexible manufacturing, and the demand for operation and industry chain supporting services is high. In addition, the main platform model at this stage has also shifted from C2C, B2C to B2B, M2B mode, and the medium and large transactions of wholesale buyers have become the main orders of the platform.

1.6.4 Cross-Border E-Commerce Innovation Period

According to the industry life cycle theory, the industry will enter a decline period after the maturity period. When stimulated by some factors, the industry may not necessarily enter a decline period, but may also undergo some new changes, or re-enter a new cycle of the industry life cycle, entering an innovation period. In the global Internet economic environment, stimulated by various policy dividends and internal and external favorable factors, China's cross-border e-commerce has entered an innovation period.

Cross-border e-commerce has undergone more than ten years of development, whether it is the market transaction scale, cross-border e-commerce model, or cross-border e-commerce participating enterprises have reached a new height. What follows is a surge of potential problems, the first of which is the increasingly stringent international resistance to counterfeits and fakes. Restrictions from foreign governments and consumer boycotts have put China's cross-border e-commerce in a "comprehensive blockade" situation. Amazon's platform, starting in 2021, has comprehensively rectified its platform's online stores involving intellectual property issues, and a wave of store closures has swept the Amazon platform. The sharp increase in costs has also become a difficult problem to solve. Doing B2C, the ranking of search engines is quite important. In recent years, the price of Google's keyword optimization search has become more and more expensive, foreigners are accustomed to using PayPal, each transaction also generates about 4% of the transaction fee, which is a considerable amount under the background of profit compression. The appreciation of the RMB has also directly led to an increase in product costs. The vicious competition among peers has further worsened the market environment of cross-border e-commerce. For example: a wedding dress, the past cost of 300 yuan, sold to Americans for 300 dollars; now the cost of 800 yuan, but sold for 200 dollars. This kind of vicious price competition has squeezed the survival space of the industry. The last is the pressure from the lack of talent.

After 2020, China's cross-border e-commerce has entered an innovation period, with many new formats and models gradually emerging, and cross-border e-commerce has begun to enter the stage of compliance operation from wild growth. For example: in 2021, the independent site of cross-border e-commerce has heated up, and the cross-border live e-commerce model represented by TikTok has begun to exert its strength; in 2022, the cross-border social e-commerce represented by Pinduoduo has continued to increase its efforts. During this period, the field of cross-border e-commerce is full of innovation and breakthrough.

1.7 Cross-Border E-Commerce Development Overview

1.7.1 China Cross-Border E-Commerce Development Overview

Since 2012, China's cross-border e-commerce has entered the fast track of development. Data from the Ministry of Commerce in 2013 showed that there were more than 5000 cross-border e-commerce platform companies in China, and more than 200,000 companies in China were engaged in cross-border e-commerce activities through various platforms. According to data from Tianyancha, as of November 2022, there were more than 14,000 related companies in China's cross-border e-commerce; looking at the establishment time, 58.1% of the related companies were established within 1–5 years. As shown in Fig. 1.3, the scale of China's cross-border e-commerce transactions broke through 30 trillion in 2013, reached 42 trillion in 2014, with an annual growth rate of 35%, and the scale of China's cross-border e-commerce industry transactions is expected to be 157 trillion in 2022. The annual growth rate of the scale of China's cross-border e-commerce transactions has exceeded two digits in recent years.

In 2012, the scale of China's import and export trade surpassed the United States for the first time, ranking first in the world. 2012 was also the first year of the development of China's cross-border e-commerce, with a transaction volume of 21 trillion yuan, a year-on-year growth rate of 32%. However, compared with the scale of China's overall import and export trade market, the proportion of cross-border e-commerce is relatively low, accounting for only 9.6%. According to data from the Net Economy Society E-commerce Research Center, the scale of China's cross-border e-commerce transactions will continue to develop rapidly, and its proportion in China's import and export transactions will become larger and larger, reaching 38.83% of the total import and export trade volume in 2020. After the first batch of

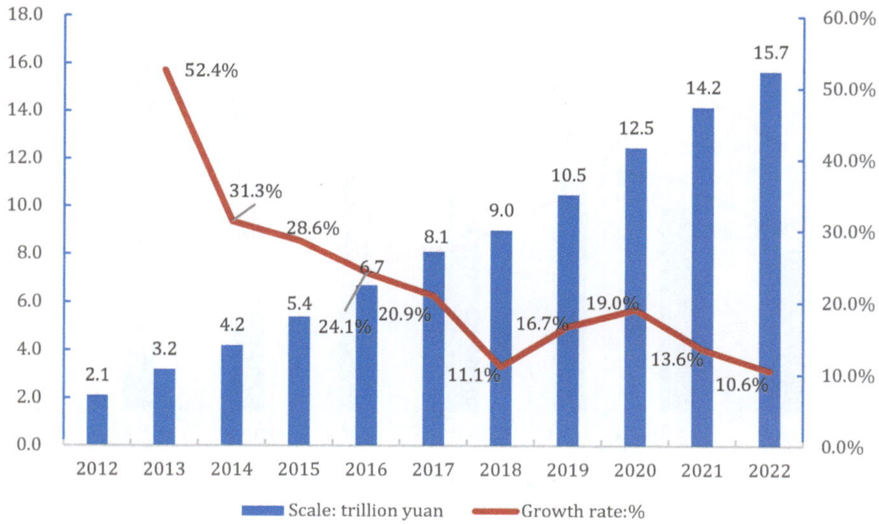

Fig. 1.3 Scale and growth rate of China's cross-border e-commerce industry transactions (2012–2022)

cross-border e-commerce pilot cities in Zhengzhou, Hangzhou, Ningbo, Shanghai, and Chongqing, the state has successively approved pilot cities such as Suzhou, Shenzhen, Pingtan, Changsha, Yinchuan, Mudanjiang, Qingdao, Harbin, Yantai, and Xi'an. On March 7, 2015, the Chinese government approved the establishment of the China (Hangzhou) Cross-Border E-Commerce Comprehensive Pilot Zone. By the end of 2022, China has established 165 cross-border e-commerce comprehensive pilot zones, covering all provinces, autonomous regions, and municipalities directly under the Central Government, and even achieving full coverage of prefecture-level cities in Guangdong Province, Jiangsu Province, Zhejiang Province, and Shandong Province. China's growth rate is higher than the global average. Judging from the leading position of China's import and export trade in the global market, the future development potential of China's cross-border e-commerce market is huge, and its impact on the global cross-border e-commerce market will also increase day by day. Although cross-border e-commerce has experienced a short development history, from the perspective of the number and scale of participating companies, market capacity, market regions, market environment, related links, etc., the heat wave of cross-border e-commerce is not diminishing, showing a dramatic increase trend, heralding the full arrival of the era of China's cross-border e-commerce.

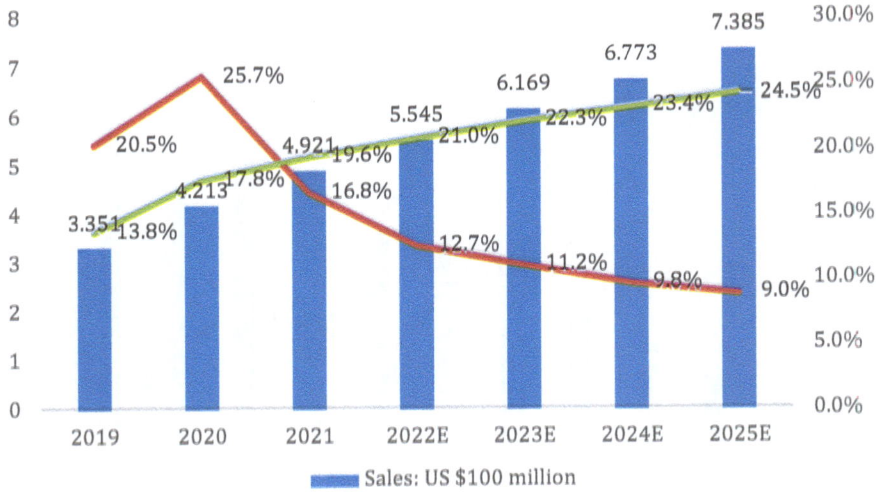

Fig. 1.4 Global retail e-commerce sales (2019–2025)

1.7.2 Global Cross-Border E-Commerce Development Overview

According to the "Global Retail E-commerce Sales (2019–2025)" data released by eMarketer, as shown in Fig. 1.4, the global retail e-commerce sales in 2021 were 4.921 trillion US dollars, and it is expected to reach 7.385 trillion US dollars by 2025; the proportion of e-commerce sales in total retail sales will also rise from 19.6% in 2021 to 24.5% in 2025. This will mean that the global e-commerce penetration rate is constantly increasing, cross-border e-commerce is also increasing year by year, and will have huge market opportunities.

Cross-border e-commerce has attracted global attention since its inception, from developed regions such as Europe and North America to developing regions such as Asia–Pacific, and then to relatively backward regions such as Latin America and Africa, cross-border e-commerce generally shows a rapid growth trend and quickly spreads globally. From a global market perspective, although cross-border e-commerce is developing rapidly as a whole, its performance varies in different regions. The specific performance of cross-border e-commerce is in line with the economic, technological, and infrastructure development levels of various places. The North American region led by the United States and the Western European region led by the United Kingdom, Germany, and France, as traditional economically developed regions, have relatively mature markets and are also mature markets for cross-border e-commerce.

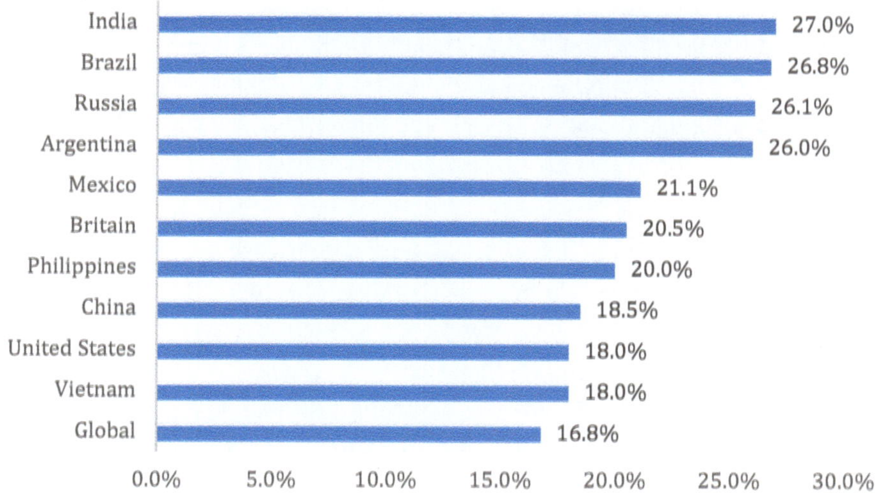

Fig. 1.5 Top ten countries in global e-commerce sales growth rate in 2021

According to eMarketer data, the top ten countries in global e-commerce sales growth in 2021 are India, Brazil, Russia, Argentina, Mexico, the United Kingdom, the Philippines, China, the United States, and Vietnam, their growth rates all exceed the global average, as shown in Fig. 1.5. India, ranked first, will continue to maintain a high growth rate, followed by major Latin American economies such as Brazil, Argentina, and Mexico. The Asia–Pacific region is the largest e-commerce retail market to date and is also the region where emerging countries maintain high growth rates; the Latin American region is also a high-growth area that cannot be ignored.

Globally, the regional differences in cross-border e-commerce are also reflected in best-selling products. This difference is manifested as differences between different regions, differences between different levels of economic development, differences between countries with different languages within the same region, and differences between different countries within the same region. For example, there are different best-selling items between countries such as North America, Europe, Asia–Pacific, and Latin America, differences between developed countries such as North America and Europe and developing countries such as Latin America, the UK, France, and Germany in Europe value different best-selling items, and the best-selling items in the United States and Canada in North America are also different.

Chapter 2
Cross-Border E-Commerce Ecosystem

2.1 Theoretical Basis of Cross-Border E-Commerce Ecosystem

2.1.1 Evolution Path of Cross-Border E-Commerce Ecosystem

The concept of the ecosystem was first proposed by Tansley (1935), who believed that the ecosystem is an inseparable whole formed by the interconnection and mutual influence between organisms and the environment. In an article titled "The Use and Abuse of Vegetation Concepts and Terms" published in Ecology, Tansley mentioned: "The more fundamental concept… not only includes the synthesis of organisms, but also the whole system of the synthesis of physical factors that become the environment… They cannot be separated from their specific environment, they form a natural system with the specific environment… This is the case, the system formed constitutes the basic unit of the natural world on the surface of the earth… We call these ecosystems." The definition of the ecosystem in the Convention on Biological Diversity (CBD) is generally recognized, that is, a dynamic, complex functional unit composed of plant, animal and microbial communities and their inorganic environment. Some scholars have proposed that the description of the ecosystem should also include its spatial relationship, the investigation of its natural features, its habitat and ecological niche, its basic stock of organisms and energy substances, the nature, energy and behavior of its input substances, and the trend of its entropy level. From the perspective of constituent elements, some scholars emphasize the three types of elements and the exchange of matter, energy, and information with the external environment, including producers, consumers, and decomposers; some scholars propose that the ecosystem is composed of six components, namely inorganic substances, organic compounds, climatic factors, producers, consumers, and decomposers.

X. Zhang, *Introduction to Cross-Border E-Commerce Ecosystem*,
https://doi.org/10.1007/978-981-96-1165-2_2

With the help of the ecosystem viewpoint and theory, James F. Moore (1993) first proposed the business ecosystem, believing that the business ecosystem is an economic union based on organizational interaction. Later, Moore (1996) detailed the theory of the business ecosystem in his work (The death of Competition: Leadership and Strategy in the Age of Business Ecosystem), believing that the business ecosystem is an economic union based on the interaction of organizations and individuals (organisms in the business world), and produces products or services of value to consumers; the business ecosystem includes core enterprises, consumers, market intermediaries (agents, sales channels, etc.), suppliers, risk bearers and powerful members (government, legislative bodies, etc.), and to a certain extent also includes competitors.

The business ecosystem is a complex system, and its members face a complex and changing environment, especially in the big data environment, the competition between enterprises is no longer individual competition, nor is it competition between supply chain links, but has evolved into competition between business ecosystems of enterprise alliances. In order to cope with dynamic and uncertain environmental changes, the co-evolution mechanism formed in the business ecosystem is more important. While each member improves itself, it must pay attention to other members in the system and actively cooperate with them. At the same time, other members should also make self-efforts to achieve the goal of transformation, among which the role of the backbone and core members is more critical.

The e-commerce ecosystem is proposed based on the concepts of the ecosystem and the business ecosystem. The business ecosystem is a type of ecosystem, and the e-commerce ecosystem is a type of business ecosystem. Under the theoretical background of the ecosystem and the business ecosystem, as a manifestation of the constituent species, that is, various enterprises or organizational structures, the focus should be shifted from improving the internal capabilities of the organization to increasing the overall capabilities of the business network in which the organization participates. The competition of the future is no longer between individual organizations, but is evolving into a contest between business ecosystems. Therefore, it is necessary to explore the cross-border e-commerce ecosystem from the evolution trajectory of the ecosystem-business ecosystem-e-commerce ecosystem.

2.1.2 Theoretical Basis of Cross-Border E-Commerce Ecosystem

1. Ecological Niche Theory

Ecological Niche (ecological A niche refers to the position occupied by a population in an ecosystem, as well as its functional relationships and interactions with related populations over time and space. The niche, also known as the ecological niche, represents the minimum threshold of habitat necessary for the survival of each species in an ecosystem.

The content of the niche includes the regional range and the function and role of the organism itself in the ecosystem. It was first proposed by J. Grinnell in 1924, emphasizing its spatial concept and regional significance. In 1927, Charles Elton further developed its connotation, adding the functional role and status of the species in its community, and mainly emphasizing the nutritional relationship of the organism with other species. In the natural environment, each specific location has different types of organisms, their activities and relationships with other organisms depend on their special structure, physiology, and behavior, hence they have their own unique ecological niche. For example, each species occupies its own space, has its own function and nutritional position in the community, and the position it occupies in the gradient of environmental changes such as temperature, humidity, and soil. The ecological niche of a species is determined by its food and habitat. For example, starfish occupy the niche of the main predator along the Pacific coast of North America. According to the principle of competitive exclusion, any two species generally cannot occupy the same ecological niche. The winner in a specific ecological environment is the species that can most effectively use food resources and living space, and its population grows faster with a high birth rate and low death rate. Several closely related species with similar food or space requirements do not compete with each other because they occupy different ecological niches.

Whittaker and others suggested: At each point on the multi-dimensional body of the ecological niche, a quantity representing the species' response, such as population density, resource utilization, etc., can be added. Thus, one can imagine a cloud permeating the multi-dimensional space, with the intensity of each point indicating the accumulated quantity, further depicting the situation at each point within the multi-dimensional body. In addition, by adding a time axis, the instantaneous ecological niche can be transformed into a continuous ecological niche, so that two species using the same resources at different times each occupy different multi-dimensional bodies in the same multi-dimensional space; if further competition of other species are included in the multi-dimensional space coordinate system.

2. Ecosystem Architecture Theory

Although the concept of an ecosystem is defined from different perspectives by different scholars, it is generally recognized as a loosely coupled domain set, which includes the environment where species live together, and species will actively adapt to their own interests and integrate with the environment. An ecosystem has two components, namely complex species and the environment on which they depend for survival. Moreover, the ecosystem also provides the services needed by the social system, such as movable matter, energy, and social system information suitable for human needs. The ecosystem has distinct characteristics, and from many definitions of the concept of the ecosystem, it is found that it has five characteristic manifestations.

(1) The ecosystem is a major structural and functional unit in ecology, and it is the highest level of ecological research. According to the levels of ecological research from low to high, they are individual, population, community, and ecosystem (see Fig. 2.1);

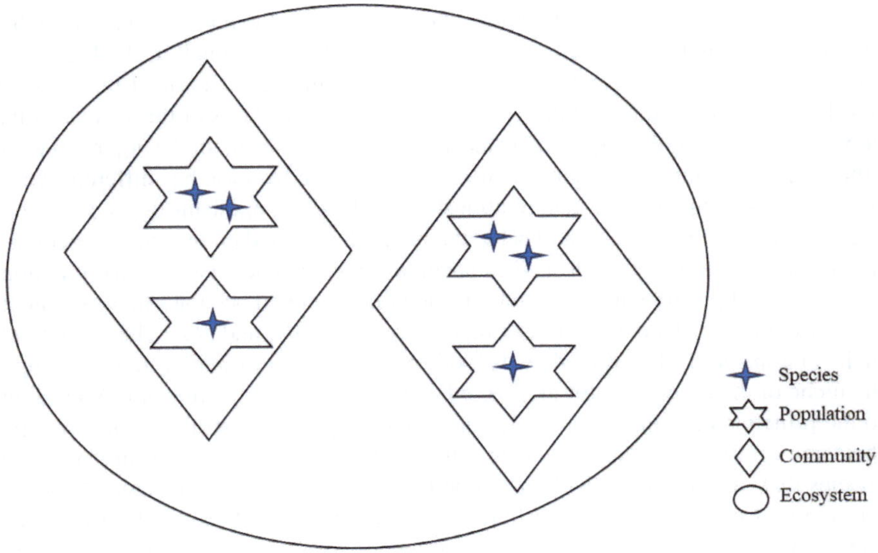

Fig. 2.1 Schematic diagram of ecosystem structure

(2) The ecosystem has self-regulation ability;
(3) Energy flow, material circulation, and information transmission are the three major functions of the ecosystem;
(4) The number of trophic levels in the ecosystem is limited by the maximum energy value fixed by the producers and the huge loss of this energy during the flow process;
(5) The ecosystem is a dynamic system, going through a development process from simple to complex, from immature to mature.

3. Synergy Theory

Synergetics originates from Greek, meaning the science of synergistic action. H.I. Ansoff proposed the concept of synergy in 1965, aiming to emphasize a way to make the overall benefits of a company greater than the combined benefits of each independent part. Herman Haken published "Synergetics: A Science of Cooperation" in 1971, introducing the concepts of synergy and synergetics, and in 1976, he systematically discussed the theory of synergy and established synergetics. He believed that the systems or parts within the entire environment cooperate with each other, forming new qualitative structures and characteristics that do not exist at the micro-individual level. Haken's research shows that all open systems, whether they are cosmic systems, macro systems, or micro systems, whether they are natural systems or social systems, can present non-equilibrium ordered structures under certain conditions, which may apply to the theory of synergetics.

The purpose of synergetics is to establish a concept and method for dealing with complex systems from a unified perspective. Haken summarized that synergetics studies a composite system composed of a large number of subsystems interacting in complex ways. Under certain conditions, the subsystems generate synergy phenomena and coherent effects through nonlinear actions, forming a self-organizing structure of space, time, or spacetime with certain functions.

A system is a complex collection composed of many subsystems. As Haken discussed, all systems can be divided into subsystems. The observed system behavior is not a simple superposition of subsystem behaviors. Due to the contribution of all subsystems interacting with the total system, the behavior of the total system seems to be regulated and purposefully self-organized. The stability of a system structure depends on the order of the system, and the order of the system depends on the synergy between the elements. Synergy emphasizes that there is a relationship of mutual influence and cooperation between the systems in the environment.

Synergistic thinking is the idea of coordination and synchronization between the elements or subsystems that make up the system. Tim Hindle (2004) summarized Campbell and others' ways of implementing corporate synergy, pointing out that companies can achieve synergy through sharing skills, sharing tangible resources, coordinating strategies, vertical integration, negotiating with suppliers, and joint forces.

Synergy emphasizes the coordination of two or more different individuals or resources, and these individuals or resources are regarded as a whole environmental system. The concept of synergy is quite broad, not only including synergy between people, but also full-scale synergy between different subsystems, resources, equipment, application scenarios, people and machines, technology and tradition. Through synergy, people, objects, machines, information, funds and other resources can be linked to cooperate for the realization of common goals. By maximizing the development and utilization of limited resources, the maximum benefit of the entire system can be achieved, and various obstacles in the cooperation process can be eliminated or minimized as much as possible.

2.2 Concept and Features of Cross-Border E-Commerce Ecosystem

2.2.1 *Concept of Cross-Border E-Commerce Ecosystem*

Cross-border e-commerce is derived from e-commerce and is a new application mode after the mature development of e-commerce. The cross-border e-commerce ecosystem is derived from the e-commerce ecosystem, but it is not exactly the same as the e-commerce ecosystem. Its complexity far exceeds the e-commerce ecosystem, which not only includes the complexity of species but also contains the complexity of the environment.

The cross-border e-commerce ecosystem is composed of individuals, enterprises, organizations, or institutions related to cross-border e-commerce activities as species, with cross-border e-commerce platforms as the medium and channel for communication and interaction. Through various forms of complementary advantages and resource sharing, it realizes the dynamic flow, communication, sharing, and circulation of goods, funds, logistics, capabilities, and information between species and between species and the environment, forming a multi-dimensional, multi-angle, multi-level, multi-faceted e-commerce ecosystem. The cross-border e-commerce ecosystem not only includes species such as cross-border e-commerce platform companies and consumers, but also includes species such as customs departments, commercial inspection departments, suppliers, payment companies, cross-border logistics companies, information support institutions, as well as the internal environment of each species and the political, social, economic, technological, and natural environmental factors of the countries where the trading entities are located. Combining the structure of the e-commerce ecosystem, according to the positioning of the species, the elements of the cross-border e-commerce ecosystem can be divided into core species, key species, supporting species, parasitic species, and environment. Combined with the business ecosystem structure proposed by Moore, a structure diagram of the cross-border e-commerce ecosystem is constructed, as shown in Fig. 2.2.

1. Core Species

The core species are cross-border e-commerce companies or platforms. The core species are the leaders of the entire cross-border e-commerce ecosystem, undertaking the role of resource integration and communication coordination through the trading platform and information, supervision and other services they provide.

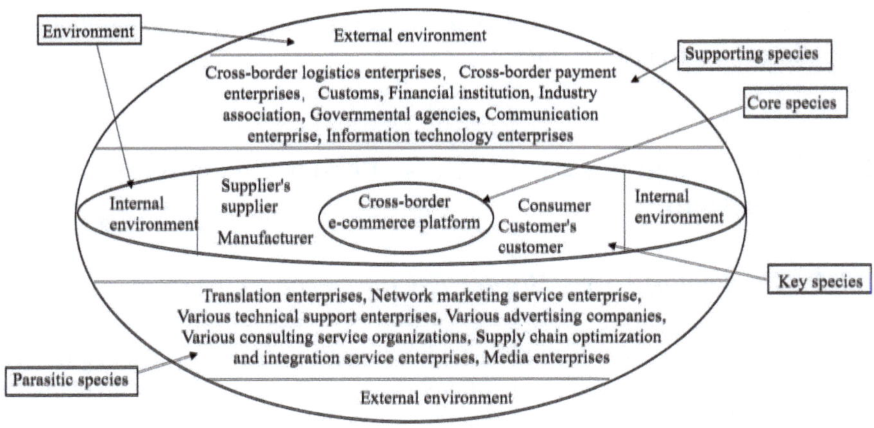

Fig. 2.2 Structure of the cross-border e-commerce ecosystem

2. Key Species

Key species are the trading entities of cross-border e-commerce, including suppliers, consumers, investors, producers, and even suppliers' suppliers and customers' customers, together constituting the object of service for other species in the cross-border e-commerce ecosystem.

3. Supporting Species

Supporting species are enterprises, organizations, or institutions that cross-border e-commerce transactions must rely on, including cross-border logistics companies, cross-border payment companies, customs institutions, commercial inspection institutions, financial institutions, industry associations, government institutions, communication service companies, information technology institutions, etc. These species all revolve around the core and key species of the cross-border e-commerce ecosystem, supporting the normal operation of the cross-border e-commerce system.

4. Parasitic Species

Parasitic species are service providers that provide value-added services for cross-border e-commerce transactions, including language translation companies, online marketing service providers, various types of technology outsourcing service providers, e-commerce consulting service providers, supply chain optimization and integration service providers, logistics value-added service project providers, various types of advertising service providers, etc.

5. Environment

The environment includes all types of environments contained in the cross-border e-commerce ecosystem, including the internal environments of various enterprises, organizations, and institutions, as well as the external environments they face, and the external environments faced by the system. From a category perspective, the environment can be divided into political, economic, legal, technological, socio-cultural, and natural environments.

Characteristics of the Cross-Border E-Commerce Ecosystem

1. Ecological Niche Separation

The establishment of the cross-border e-commerce ecosystem is based on the separation of corporate ecological niches. When two species in the cross-border e-commerce ecosystem share the same resource or jointly occupy a certain environmental variable, ecological niche overlap will occur, resulting in competition. The result is that these two species cannot occupy the same ecological niche, resulting in ecological niche separation.

In the business world, the more similar the demand for resources among companies, and the closer their products and market bases, the greater the overlap of their ecological niches, and the more intense the competition. Therefore, companies must develop survival skills and techniques that are not entirely the same as other companies, find the position where they can best play their role, and achieve the separation of corporate ecological niches. Successful companies will be those that can find their own ecological niches. The separation of corporate ecological niches not only reduces competition. More importantly, it provides conditions for the formation of a super cycle of functional coupling between companies.

2. Species Diversity

The concept of diversity originates from ecology. Various types of organisms in the ecosystem each play an important role in the environment. Through the feeding dependency relationships between species and between organisms and the environment, nature forms multiple complete food chains and constitutes a complex food web, carrying out the benign circulation of material flow and energy transmission within the ecosystem. The break of the food chain will greatly affect the functioning of the system. Like natural ecosystems, diversity is also very important for cross-border e-commerce ecosystems. Firstly, diversity plays a buffering role for companies to deal with uncertain environments. Secondly, diversity is conducive to the creation of value in the business ecosystem. Finally, diversity is a prerequisite for the business ecosystem to achieve self-organization.

3. System Dynamics

As a complete whole, members within the system will constantly update, and there will be external forces continuously participating in expansion. These endogenous and exogenous forces mean that the e-commerce ecosystem has dynamic characteristics, with the system's constituent elements constantly being eliminated and updated, ultimately achieving the joint development of all parts of e-commerce and the perfection of the entire system.

The cross-border e-commerce ecosystem believes that the operation or driving force of the system does not come from outside the system or the top of the system, but from the interaction between various elements within the system or between various subsystems. It autonomously and spontaneously generates system rules through the interaction of subsystems. This is the most fundamental thought and method of synergy. This idea tells us that the emergence of complex patterns is actually produced through the competition and synergy of lower-level (or lower-level) subsystems, not external commands. The various subsystems within the system compete and cooperate, thereby making one or several trends in the competition dominant, and thus leading the entire system from disorder to order. The business ecosystem is a complex adaptive system, under certain rules, the low-level interactions of different types of self-managed individuals drive the system towards higher-level, orderly evolution.

4. Network Structure

The cross-border e-commerce ecosystem, especially the virtual business ecosystem, has fuzzy boundaries and presents a network structure. This is mainly reflected in two aspects. Firstly, each business ecosystem contains many small business ecosystems, and at the same time, it is part of a larger business ecosystem, that is, its boundaries can be determined according to actual needs. Secondly, a certain company can exist in multiple business ecosystems at the same time.

5. System Openness

Only an open system can have the strongest self-regulation and self-repair functions, to ensure that the system can continuously absorb the best members and freely exchange information with the outside world. Openness allows companies to establish strategic partnerships to the greatest extent, form a good system cycle, and achieve optimal allocation and effective use of resources. The cross-border e-commerce ecosystem is also an open system, and species such as cross-border e-commerce platforms, cross-border logistics, and cross-border payments also enter or exit this system. In the practical field, every year, many companies of different species types enter the field of cross-border e-commerce, and some companies exit. This embodies the system openness of the cross-border e-commerce ecosystem.

2.3 Synergy Mechanism of Cross-Border E-Commerce Ecosystem

2.3.1 Synergy Principle of Cross-Border E-Commerce Ecosystem

Gereffi et al. (2003) proposed a relatively rigorous and complete analytical framework based on the production network theory proposed by Powell and Sturgeon, combined with value chain theory, transaction cost economics, technological capabilities, and corporate learning theories. They first summarized five typical global value chain governance methods. According to the degree of coordination and power asymmetry between the main bodies in the chain, they are arranged from low to high as market type, modular type, relational type, captive type, and hierarchy. Then, they explained these five types of value chain governance methods through three variables: the complexity of inter-firm transactions, the degree of reducing transaction costs with standardized contracts (standardization ability of transactions), and supplier capabilities.

1. Market Type

When contracts can reduce transaction costs, the product is relatively simple, the supplier's capability is strong, the buyer does not need to invest too much, and the asset specificity is low, market governance will occur. At this time, the transaction is relatively simple, and both parties can control the uncertainty of the transaction well through price and contract, without too much coordination.

2. Modular Type

The product is more complex, the supplier's capability is strong, its asset specificity is high, and although the number of buyers and sellers is limited, there is still some market flexibility, and it is easier to change partners. The amount of information exchanged between the two parties is larger and more complex than the market type, but it can be reduced well through standardized contracts, so the coordination cost required is not high.

3. Relational Type

The complexity of the product leads to complex transactions, and the amount of information that both parties need to exchange is large and complex. The supplier's capability is strong, and there is a strong mutual dependence between the leading manufacturer and the supplier. However, both parties can reduce transaction costs through reputation, spatial proximity, family or ethnic relations. Both parties can often negotiate and exchange complex information through face-to-face communication, requiring more coordination, therefore, changing trading partners is more difficult.

4. Captive Type

The product is complex, the supplier's capability is low, and a large amount of investment and technical support is needed. In order to prevent competition from other suppliers, the supplier specializes its assets. The supplier's dependence on the leading manufacturer is very strong, and it is difficult to change the trading object, becoming a "captive supplier". The leading manufacturer achieves governance by highly controlling the supplier, and at the same time makes the supplier willing to maintain the cooperative relationship by providing various supports.

5. Hierarchy

When the product is very complex, the cost of external transactions is high, and the supplier's capability is low, the leading manufacturer has to adopt a vertically integrated internal governance method. Because the transaction may involve the leading manufacturer's core capabilities (such as tacit knowledge, intellectual property rights, etc.), the leading manufacturer cannot control opportunistic behavior through contracts, and can only adopt internal production.

In addition, Griffith also studied the dynamics of value chain governance. Over time, the three variables that determine the governance model of the value chain will change, and the governance model of the value chain will change accordingly. This dynamic change exists in reality, such as in the bicycle industry, due to the improvement of economies of scale, standardization, and supplier capabilities, the governance mode has shifted from hierarchical to market governance; in the clothing industry, due to the reduction in transaction complexity and the enhancement of supplier capabilities, it has developed from a leadership type to a relational type; in the U.S. electronics industry, the development of division of labor and specialization has shifted the governance mode from hierarchical (vertical integration) to modular.

The reasons for the changes in the three variables mainly come from three aspects: First, the increase in procurement requirements by leading manufacturers has relatively reduced the capabilities of suppliers, while increasing the complexity of transactions; second, innovation and standardization are contradictory, innovation will reduce standardization capabilities; finally, the capabilities of suppliers will change over time, learning can improve corporate capabilities, the introduction of new supplier competition, new technological revolutions, and changes in procurement requirements by leading manufacturers will all affect the relative capabilities of suppliers.

Taking cross-border e-commerce and cross-border logistics as examples, their synergy mechanism is shown in Fig. 2.3.

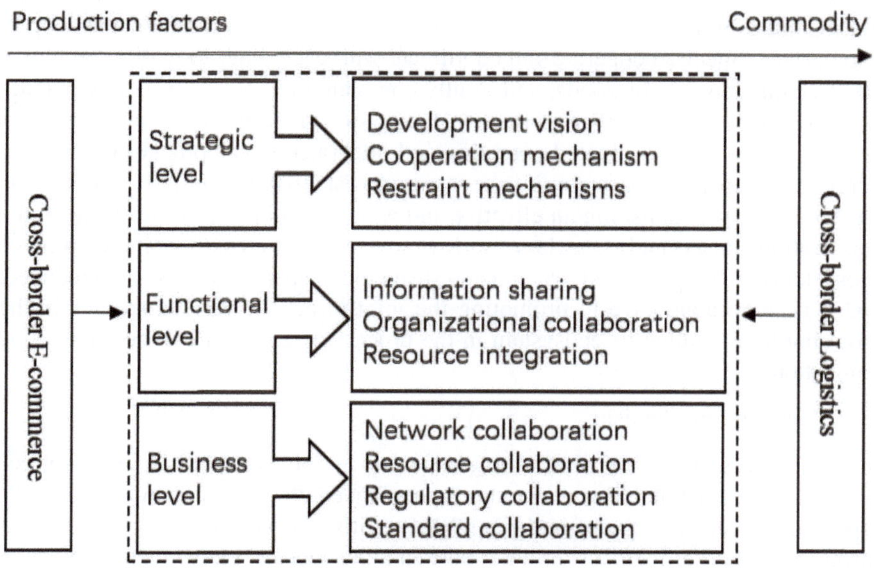

Fig. 2.3 Synergy approach of cross-border e-commerce ecosystem

2.3.2 *Cross-Border E-Commerce Ecosystem Synergy Path*

1. Strategic Synergy

(1) Strategic planning

The related species of the cross-border e-commerce ecosystem coexist in a global value chain, and the species depend on and influence each other. The participating species of the cross-border e-commerce ecosystem have the same development goals and strategic planning. They should, based on the division of labor and position in the global value chain, maximize the value brought by this value chain, expand and strengthen the cross-border e-commerce market, and seek their own value maximization on this basis. The formulation and implementation of strategic planning need to fully consider the factors of relevant stakeholders in the global value chain, and more importantly, incorporate the respective strategies of cross-border e-commerce platforms and cross-border logistics. Under the constraint of unified goals, establish and improve each other's strategic planning. The various species of the cross-border e-commerce ecosystem, through strategic alliances, aim at the development plan reflected by common interests, implement their own corporate activities on the global value chain, optimize resource allocation, and then pursue common corporate value.

(2) Cooperation mechanism

The various related species of the cross-border e-commerce ecosystem, as important links in cross-border e-commerce transactions, have many coordination and cooperation points. Species cooperate and coordinate with each other to realize the global value chain activities of goods, and jointly complete the process of goods circulation and value transfer from production factors to final consumption. In order to better promote the coordinated operation and integrated development of the cross-border e-commerce ecosystem, it is necessary to establish a long-term cooperation mechanism. By establishing an effective and win–win cooperation mechanism, the cooperation barriers and obstacles of various species in the cross-border e-commerce ecosystem can be eliminated, friction and suspicion in specific work can be reduced, and it is more conducive to promoting the joint efforts of various species in the cross-border e-commerce ecosystem in the process of goods circulation and value realization.

(3) Constraint mechanism

In the process of cooperation among species in the cross-border e-commerce ecosystem, it is inevitable to encounter "speculative behavior" and "moral hazard", especially under the drive of interests. Whether it's cross-border e-commerce platforms, cross-border logistics, or other participating species, there is a possibility of self-serving behavior, transferring individual risks to others or outside the individual through actions that harm the overall interest or value. To promote long-term cooperation among species in the cross-border e-commerce ecosystem, it is necessary to establish an effective constraint mechanism. This constraint is not limited to the form of paper contracts, but more of a mechanism or concept, a standard for all species in the cross-border e-commerce ecosystem. In the constraint mechanism, it should also fully reflect the punishment and enforcement measures for violations. The formalism of the constraint mechanism should be avoided, making it an application of the concept of "law". In cross-border e-commerce activities, there should not only be "law" to rely on, but also "law" must be followed, law enforcement must be strict, and violations must be investigated. Through the establishment of the constraint mechanism, regulate the behavior of all species in the cross-border e-commerce ecosystem, crack down on and eliminate possible "speculative behavior" and "moral hazard", and make it an invisible industry entry and exit threshold.

2. Functional Synergy

(1) Information Sharing

The relationship between species in the cross-border e-commerce ecosystem is actually a relationship of interest game. This game relationship is due to the lack of efficient exchange and communication of information among the species in the cross-border e-commerce ecosystem. Because of the information asymmetry in practice, it not only weakens the enthusiasm of the species in the cross-border e-commerce ecosystem to work together, but also is not conducive to their long-term integrated development. Although each species in the cross-border e-commerce ecosystem has its own independent information database, many small and medium-sized enterprises have weak database system resources and cannot effectively dock with the databases of some large enterprises. Moreover, even if each species in the cross-border e-commerce ecosystem has its own information database, it still cannot effectively integrate the huge information flow on the global value chain. In addition, the information system of customs agencies still mainly serves traditional international trade and has not effectively matched with cross-border e-commerce. Based on the pursuit of their own interests, many cross-border e-commerce platforms and cross-border logistics companies do not provide or provide inaccurate or biased data, making the cross-border e-commerce information system at China's customs ports still imperfect. To solve this shortcoming, it should be based on major organizations such as cross-border e-commerce platforms, cross-border logistics, customs agencies, relying on information technology such as big data and cloud computing, to build a cross-border e-commerce information system and information platform, to achieve real-time upload and seamless docking of information related to cross-border e-commerce activities. Through information sharing, eliminate communication barriers, connect commodity buying and selling, ensure real-time monitoring, promote commodity transportation, coordinate the operation between various links of cross-border e-commerce activities with cross-border e-commerce, cross-border logistics, and customs as the main nodes, and improve the timeliness of transportation, customs clearance, and distribution in cross-border logistics activities.

(2) Organizational Collaboration

The carrier of corporate activities is the organization, so the coordination, matching, and mutual adaptation of organizational structure, job setting, personnel arrangement, etc., should be emphasized in the cooperation of all species in the cross-border e-commerce ecosystem. For an organization, in addition to organizational goals, it also includes organizational activities, organizational elements, organizational members, etc., all of which together constitute the basis and support for the activities of all species in the cross-border e-commerce ecosystem. From the perspective of organizational cooperation, each species in the cross-border e-commerce ecosystem should set up an organizational structure that serves each other within their own enterprises and arrange corresponding positions and personnel. The setting of organizational goals should also fully consider the needs of the specific activity content involved by all species in the cross-border e-commerce ecosystem, and comprehensively consider the needs of the overall activities of cross-border e-commerce, as well as the activities and value creation required by the corresponding global value chain. The organizational activities involved are specifically manifested as the demand for goods circulation and instructions generated by the cross-border e-commerce platform, including time, cost, location, services, etc. Cross-border logistics includes sorting, packaging, transportation, customs clearance, commodity inspection, distribution, etc. When setting up and implementing specific activities, the inclusiveness and commonality of each other should be considered, and the relevant activity content of the organization should be organized from the perspectives of cost, efficiency, etc., to achieve the organizational cooperation of all species in the cross-border e-commerce ecosystem.

(3) Resource Integration

From the perspective of the global value chain, cross-border e-commerce activities involve various resources related to the entire industrial chain from production factors to final consumption. The cross-border e-commerce platform and cross-border logistics, as two important links in the circulation of goods in cross-border e-commerce activities, will especially involve many resources upstream and downstream. Cross-border e-commerce platforms and cross-border logistics belong to different economic categories and industrial categories, and they have different resource advantages. From the purpose of maximizing overall value and benefits, all species in the cross-border e-commerce ecosystem should systematically integrate resources, including tangible and intangible resources, as well as resources of different levels and types, aiming to achieve optimal allocation and full utilization of resources, and achieve value optimization and maximization. All species in the cross-border e-commerce ecosystem should pay more attention to the direct resources required for the circulation of goods, as well as the indirect resources required, and even more to the key resources that play a core role. Through resource integration, the effects of connecting supply and demand of goods, optimizing transportation networks, enhancing circulation efficiency, reducing circulation costs, and improving service quality can be achieved.

3. Business Collaboration

(1) Network Collaboration

From the perspective of the global value chain and commodity supply chain, all species in the cross-border e-commerce ecosystem form a complex logistics network due to the circulation of goods. The operation of the logistics network requires the support of the information network, attracting elements of different work links, different geographical areas, and different organizational individuals to this network system. The collaboration of all species in the cross-border e-commerce ecosystem (such as cross-border circulation of goods) needs to focus on the logistics network collaboration based on the information network, improve the coverage of the logistics network, establish and improve the cross-border logistics information sharing network, and include the upstream and downstream of cross-border e-commerce activities, cross-border e-commerce platforms, cross-border logistics, financial institutions, customs and other departments into this information network, and effectively connect related activities through the Internet.

(2) Resource Collaboration

The operation of various activities in the cross-border e-commerce ecosystem relies on corresponding resources. These resources include people, materials, finances, information, etc. Cross-border e-commerce platforms and cross-border logistics should pay more attention to the resources they own, the resources they need, and the resources they lack. Through strategic alliances, organizational cooperation, resource integration, information sharing, etc., they can strengthen cross-enterprise cooperation and achieve synergistic advantages of resources. For example, setting up the packaging of goods in advance from the perspective of cross-border goods transportation and terminal distribution, through the synergy of this information resource and production factor resource, can reduce cargo damage and secondary packaging during transportation, and also help to reduce costs and improve logistics efficiency. In addition, cross-border e-commerce platforms and cross-border logistics can jointly reduce the software and hardware equipment facilities required for cross-border logistics through joint ventures, equity participation, cooperation, alliances, etc. Cross-border e-commerce platforms externalize internal logistics resources, and while meeting their own logistics service needs, they can also dock with professional cross-border logistics trunk lines and branches, and effectively connect warehousing, transportation, and distribution links.

(3) Regulatory Synergy

In cross-border e-commerce activities, the virtual network environment is prone to many security risks and transaction risks. Regulating the behavior of trading entities can effectively prevent and avoid these risks. In the process of the coordinated operation of various species in the cross-border e-commerce ecosystem, attention should be paid to the synergy of both parties in terms of regulatory content, regulatory measures, and regulatory calibers. For example, the cross-border e-commerce platform sets a reasonable and moderate penalty amount based on the potential deception risk of cross-border logistics, which encourages cross-border logistics to actively cooperate and reduces the regulatory cost and potential loss of the cross-border e-commerce platform to cross-border logistics. Cross-border e-commerce platforms should also study the size of the private benefits obtained by cross-border logistics, and choose the appropriate regulatory probability based on this, which not only achieves effective regulation of cross-border logistics, but also helps to reduce blind regulation, thereby reducing regulatory costs.

(4) Standard Synergy

Cross-border e-commerce activities involve different industries and countries. There are differences in industry norms and standards between different industries, and there are also differences in standard norms between different countries. Various species in the cross-border e-commerce ecosystem should strive to formulate and implement unified business operation standards, service quality standards, and even detailed to product packaging and labeling, warehousing norms, etc. Standard synergy is conducive to promoting the network synergy, resource synergy, and regulatory synergy of various species in the cross-border e-commerce ecosystem, and it also helps to reduce communication barriers, reduce communication costs, and improve communication efficiency. In addition, various species in the cross-border e-commerce ecosystem should also formulate rules and standard systems applicable to cross-border transactions or internationalization based on the relevant guidelines of different countries in terms of commodity circulation and return and exchange, after-sales service, etc.

Cross-border e-commerce provides an opportunity for our country's enterprises to enhance their position in the global value chain. From the perspective of the global value chain, our country's cross-border e-commerce platform companies are not a single link and cannot survive in isolation in the value chain. To promote the healthy development of cross-border e-commerce and the synergy of all species in the cross-border e-commerce ecosystem is imperative. Some differentiated features of cross-border e-commerce, especially the fact that the main bodies of cross-border e-commerce transactions are located at different borders, making the cross-border logistics link more complex, have become an important link restricting and influencing the development of cross-border e-commerce platforms. Against this backdrop, the synergy between cross-border e-commerce platforms and cross-border logistics is not just about synergistic operations, but more about functional integration and development. Although the development of cross-border e-commerce platforms and cross-border logistics is fast, they have not yet formed a mutually adaptive and cooperative development trend. Although this problem changed slightly in 2016, it still needs mutual adjustment to achieve true synergistic operation. Specifically, from a global perspective to our domestic market, the rapid expansion of cross-border e-commerce has outpaced the expansion of cross-border logistics in the short term. This problem was very prominent in 2014 and 2015. The traditional international postal parcels, international express delivery, and other cross-border logistics models have not yet adapted to the development of cross-border e-commerce, exacerbating the low degree of synergy between cross-border e-commerce and cross-border logistics in these two years. In 2016, the cross-border e-commerce market was somewhat consolidated, with cross-border e-commerce companies represented by AliExpress, Amazon, Tmall International, JD Global Purchase, Koala Sea Purchase, Lanting Collection, Dunhuang Network, etc., gradually exerting their strength, and promoting overseas warehouses, border warehouses, international logistics dedicated lines, free trade zone logistics and other new cross-border logistics application models, to some extent alleviating the problem of lack of synergy between cross-border e-commerce platforms and cross-border logistics. Overall, promoting the synergistic development of cross-border e-commerce platforms and cross-border logistics, achieving their organic combination, can not only promote the upgrade of the cross-border logistics industry but also help promote the further take-off of cross-border e-commerce.

Chapter 3
Cross-Border E-Commerce Platform

3.1 Concept of Cross-Border E-Commerce Platform

3.1.1 Concept of E-Commerce Platform

An e-commerce platform is a virtual network space for conducting business activities established based on the Internet and a management environment that ensures the smooth conduct of related business activities; it is an important place to integrate and coordinate the orderly, related, and efficient flow of information, goods, and funds. The network infrastructure, payment platform, management platform, and security platform provided by the e-commerce platform enable enterprises and merchants to share resources, enabling them to effectively reduce costs while conducting business activities. The initial goal of establishing an e-commerce platform was to strengthen customer contacts, improve transaction efficiency, and make market transactions more convenient.

3.1.2 Definition of Cross-Border E-Commerce Platform

Cross-border e-commerce platforms have evolved from e-commerce platforms, referring to virtual venues where transaction entities belonging to different borders or customs exchange information, reach transactions, make payment settlements, and complete cross-border logistics. Cross-border e-commerce is a great innovation based on traditional international trade and domestic e-commerce, which greatly reduces the cumbersome intermediate links of traditional international trade and significantly improves the transaction efficiency of cross-border trade. In the entire transaction activity of cross-border e-commerce, the cross-border e-commerce platform, as the bridge and link for communication between various transaction entities, plays a core and central role. The construction level, function realization, and service

X. Zhang, *Introduction to Cross-Border E-Commerce Ecosystem*,
https://doi.org/10.1007/978-981-96-1165-2_3

quality of the cross-border e-commerce platform directly affect the intention of enterprises, consumers, and governments and other transaction entities to participate in cross-border e-commerce transactions, and also determine the development status of the entire cross-border e-commerce industry.

3.1.3 Features of Cross-Border E-Commerce Platforms

1. Globality

With the development of modern Internet technology, cross-border e-commerce platforms enable buyers and sellers around the world to conveniently conduct business activities. Compared with traditional international trade, cross-border e-commerce breaks free from spatial restrictions: sellers from one country can post specific information about products and services on the cross-border e-commerce platform and keep the information on the platform for a long time; buyers from one country can search for information posted by sellers from various countries on the cross-border e-commerce platform, thereby selecting more suitable products and services. Cross-border e-commerce platforms maximize the sharing of information resources to sellers and buyers worldwide, and lower the threshold for participating in cross-border trade, allowing more individuals and businesses to participate in cross-border trade. At the same time, as a medium for buyers and sellers to communicate and negotiate, cross-border e-commerce platforms expand the scope of trade, reduce the cost of goods, and consumers no longer have to cross borders or pay high prices to purchase their favorite goods, they only need to use cross-border e-commerce platforms to get reasonably priced products.

2. Paperless

As the carrier of cross-border e-commerce activities, cross-border e-commerce platforms undertake the intermediate links in traditional trade activities and realize paperless trade. The ordering contracts, transportation terms, insurance terms, and goods documents in traditional international trade are all completed through written content. Cross-border e-commerce sends these contracts, terms, and documents in electronic form, transforming cumbersome written documents into concise electronic documents, greatly improving the efficiency of information exchange and goods trading between buyers and sellers. However, although paperless trade brings convenience, it also brings potential risks. Compared with formal written documents, electronic documents are more easily tampered with, and the enterprises or individuals involved in the transaction may suffer huge losses as a result. Most of the existing laws in the international trade industry are established for written document content. The rapid development of paperless cross-border trade has led to a blank area in the relevant regulatory field, and the legislative issues for electronic documents urgently need to be resolved.

3. Timeliness

Cross-border e-commerce platforms use electronic technology to transmit information, accelerating the communication efficiency of consumers, merchants, logistics providers, and other parties, and are time-sensitive. In traditional cross-border trade activities, the main ways for buyers and sellers to exchange information are through mail, fax, etc., which are limited by geographical location and communication technology, resulting in a time difference in the sending and receiving of information. International trade involves the choice of different payment currencies, and currency exchange rates change rapidly. The existence of time difference may cause one party to the transaction to suffer huge losses, or even refuse to perform the contract to avoid losses. The timeliness of cross-border e-commerce platforms perfectly solves the problem of time difference, the sending and receiving of information is almost simultaneous, and through the cross-border e-commerce platform, buyers and sellers can communicate directly, reducing many links in traditional cross-border trade such as agents, retailers, etc., and is more timely.

3.1.4 Functions of Cross-Border E-Commerce Platforms

(1) Product Display Function

Displaying products is a prerequisite for successful sales. Whether facing individual consumers, corporate customers, or government purchasers, cross-border e-commerce platforms must clearly and intuitively display products to consumers to increase their awareness and purchase demand for their products. The product display of cross-border e-commerce is roughly the same as domestic e-commerce, both use computer processing systems to continuously establish subheadings or secondary headings, and try to divide and manage products into different categories as much as possible.

(2) Product Sales Function

Cross-border e-commerce platforms are an innovation in international trade methods and an extension of domestic e-commerce platforms. Their essence is the electronic transformation of traditional cross-border business activities. Therefore, product sales are one of the basic functions of cross-border e-commerce platforms, and all other functions are implemented around product sales. Compared with traditional offline product sales, the product sales function of cross-border e-commerce platforms breaks through the limitations of time and space. Whether it is day or night, any consumer in any place covered by the Internet can place an order for their favorite products with a click of the mouse.

(3) Order Management Function

Most of the order management process of cross-border e-commerce platforms is similar to general business activities, except that these activities are all implemented on cross-border e-commerce platforms. Specifically, it includes: ① Online ordering and receiving electronic orders: allowing consumers to submit orders through websites or electronic methods (such as EDI), and supporting cross-border e-commerce sellers to regularly receive orders submitted by consumers; ② Order preprocessing: including merging multiple orders from the same user, splitting orders due to insufficient inventory, etc.; ③ Order status inquiry: supporting cross-border e-commerce sellers to inquire about order status online, ensuring that consumers can understand the progress of the order in real time; ④ Emergency order processing: when necessary, it can handle urgently inserted orders to meet consumers' special needs; ⑤ Order creation and entry: cross-border e-commerce sellers can create and enter orders, including product, quantity, price, payment method, etc.; ⑥ Order tracking and updating: real-time tracking of order status and progress, providing real-time updates, so that cross-border e-commerce sellers can process and ship in time.

(4) Inventory Management Function

Compared to domestic business activities, cross-border e-commerce transactions involve complex cross-border logistics, long logistics cycles, and complex transportation methods. Therefore, one of the necessary conditions for a cross-border e-commerce platform to stand out from intense competition is an efficient inventory management function. Inventory management includes the quantity, timing, and location of inventory. The change in inventory management of cross-border e-commerce platforms mainly lies in the choice of location. Early cross-border e-commerce platforms directly stocked in their own country, using overseas transit methods, that is, overseas sellers delivered goods to transit companies, and then sent the goods to the customer's country through cross-border logistics, went through customs clearance, and finally mailed to consumers by domestic express delivery. The overseas transit method is inefficient and costly. The current cross-border e-commerce platforms have chosen to reserve inventory in "overseas warehouses". "Overseas warehouses" are generally set up in the host country's bonded area or free trade zone. After consumers place orders on the platform, the cross-border e-commerce platform ships from the "overseas warehouse" set up in that country, and the logistics company of that country directly delivers from the warehouse to the customer. The supply chain management efficiency of cross-border e-commerce platforms has been improved due to the emergence of "overseas warehouses", solving the problem of warehousing logistics.

(5) Information Processing Function

The cross-border e-commerce platform is a platform for communication and exchange between the main bodies of cross-border e-commerce transactions. This platform must filter out information that matches different customer needs from different cross-information. With the continuous development of network technology and the advent of the era of big data, cross-border e-commerce platforms can access more information. Cross-border e-commerce platforms mainly process the following two types of information:

One is customer terminal information, such as customer product preferences, geographical distribution, age distribution, etc. Cross-border e-commerce platforms can mine deeper sales potential by analyzing customer terminal information. Through computer analysis and processing, cross-border e-commerce platforms can analyze the consumption habits of each user, predict consumer behavior, provide personalized web page product pushes, and promote product sales.

The other is channel introduction information, that is, information about which channel customers mainly enter the webpage and shop. Cross-border e-commerce platforms will use marketing methods such as search engines, website alliances, email marketing, and social marketing to expand the market. The overseas market is difficult to expand, but mastering channel introduction information can still make cross-border e-commerce platforms understand which channels are more attractive to customers for advertising.

(6) Customer Service Function

The customer service function mainly refers to product consultation services, return and exchange services, and warranty services, etc. Compared with early overseas shopping and personal shopping agents, a big difference in cross-border e-commerce is reflected in customer service. Early overseas shopping and personal shopping agents often require consumers to have language skills. If consumers fancy a product on a foreign platform, they need to familiarize themselves with the language of the foreign website in advance, adapt to its website layout and product sales methods, etc., and they cannot get any guarantee in terms of return and exchange services and warranty services. From the seller's point of view, most foreign websites do not support after-sales services for consumers in other countries. From the buyer's perspective, returning goods requires a long and complicated international logistics system. The current cross-border e-commerce platforms have greatly improved the quality of customer service. From the perspective of product consultation services, cross-border e-commerce platforms have specialized language talents. Whether it is from the communication language of the website, the layout form of the website, and the sales method of the product, a certain degree of localization has been achieved, which is more friendly to consumers and facilitates consumers to make shopping decisions; from the perspective of return and exchange services and warranty services, cross-border e-commerce platforms generally set up overseas warehouses in the host country, and have dedicated after-sales customer service to handle, the efficiency is greatly improved, and the rights and interests of consumers are better protected.

(7) Other Auxiliary Functions

The first is the online payment function. Cross-border e-commerce platforms often come with online payment functions. Unlike domestic e-commerce platforms, cross-border payments involve complex settlement issues. The second is the marketing promotion function. In addition to the main displayed products, cross-border e-commerce platform pages often have corresponding advertising sections. Companies in need can spend a certain amount of advertising fees to achieve their own promotion. With the increasing maturity of big data analysis technology, cross-border e-commerce platforms can often analyze consumers' browsing and purchasing records to analyze their shopping preferences, and then push advertisements of corresponding industry companies to consumers. The third is the social platform function. With the rise of various social platforms, the integration of social functions into cross-border e-commerce platforms has become a new hotspot. Many cross-border e-commerce platforms foresee the huge potential hidden in it and begin to open their own social functions.

3.2 Classification of Cross-Border E-Commerce Platforms

3.2.1 Common Classification Methods of Cross-Border E-Commerce Platforms

1. Classification by Transaction Subject Attributes

The subjects of e-commerce transactions are enterprises, individuals, and governments. Combined with the attributes of buyers and sellers, the types of e-commerce are mostly referred to as B2B, B2C, C2C, and B2G. Since the current cross-border e-commerce transactions have not yet involved the government as a transaction subject, cross-border e-commerce platforms can be divided into cross-border e-commerce B2B platforms, cross-border e-commerce B2C platforms, and cross-border e-commerce C2C platforms.

(1) Cross-border e-commerce B2B platform.

The final customers faced by the cross-border e-commerce B2B platform are enterprises or group customers, providing information related to enterprises, products, services, etc. Currently, in the transaction scale of China's cross-border e-commerce market, the transaction scale of the cross-border e-commerce B2B platform accounts for more than 80% of the total transaction scale. In the cross-border e-commerce market, the enterprise market has always been in a dominant position.

Representative companies: Made in China, Alibaba International Station, Global Resources Network.

(2) Cross-border e-commerce B2C platform.

The final customers faced by the cross-border e-commerce B2C platform are individual consumers, who sell products to individual consumers in the form of online retail. Cross-border e-commerce B2C platforms also vary in the sale of different vertical category goods, such as FocalPrice mainly deals in 3C digital electronic products, and Lanting Jishi has an advantage in wedding dress sales. The cross-border e-commerce B2C market is gradually developing, and its proportion in the transaction scale of the cross-border e-commerce market is constantly increasing.

Representative companies: AliExpress, Lanting Jishi, Milan Network, Dalong Network.

(3) Cross-border e-commerce C2C Platform

The cross-border e-commerce C2C platform refers to the online sale of products and services by individual sellers to individual buyers from different customs territories. Individual sellers post product and service sales information, prices, etc. through the platform, individual buyers screen, and finally reach a transaction through the platform, make payment settlement, and deliver goods through cross-border logistics to complete an international commercial activity.

Representative company: eBay.

2. Classification by Service Type

(1) Information Service Platform

The information service platform mainly provides a network marketing platform for domestic and foreign member merchants, transmits the goods or service information of suppliers or buyers and other merchants, and facilitates the completion of transactions between the two parties.

Representative companies: Alibaba International Station, Global Resources Network, Made in China.

(2) Online Trading Platforms.

Online trading platforms not only provide information on businesses, products, services, and more, but also allow users to complete the entire shopping chain online, including searching, consulting, comparing, ordering, paying, logistics, and reviewing. The online trading platform model is gradually becoming the mainstream model in cross-border e-commerce.

Representative companies: Amazon, AliExpress, FocalPrice, eBay.

3. Classification by Platform Operator

(1) Platform-based Cross-border E-commerce Platforms

Platform-based cross-border e-commerce platforms attract merchants by building online malls and integrating logistics, payment, and operation services, providing cross-border e-commerce transaction services. The platform's main profit model is to charge merchant commissions and value-added service commissions.

Representative companies: Amazon, AliExpress, Global Sources, Alibaba International Station.

The main features of platform-based cross-border e-commerce platforms are: ① The trading entity provides a cross-border e-commerce platform for commodity transactions and does not engage in corresponding transaction links such as commodity purchase and sale, ② Foreign brand merchants, manufacturers, distributors, online shop owners, etc. settle in this cross-border e-commerce platform to display and sell goods, ③ There are many merchants and a wide variety of goods.

The advantages and disadvantages of platform-based cross-border e-commerce platforms are clear. The advantages are: ① a wide range of goods sources, ② a wide variety of goods, ③ convenient payment methods, ④ large platform scale, large website traffic; the disadvantages are: ① lack of stable channels for cross-border logistics, customs and commodity inspection, low service quality, ② low quality assurance of goods, prone to various quality problems, leading to low consumer trust.

(2) Self-operated Cross-border E-commerce Platforms

Self-operated cross-border e-commerce platforms build platforms online, and the platform integrates supplier resources to purchase goods at a lower price and sell them at a higher price, mainly profiting from the price difference of goods.

Representative companies: Lanting Jishi, Milan Network, Dalong Network, FocalPrice.

The main features of self-operated cross-border e-commerce platforms are: ① Develop and operate cross-border e-commerce platforms, and act as the main body of commodity purchase to purchase and stock goods from overseas; ② Involve the entire supply chain from commodity supply, sales to after-sales.

The advantages of self-operated cross-border e-commerce platforms mainly include: ① The platform and goods are self-operated, with strong control ability; ② High quality assurance of goods, good merchant reputation, high consumer trust; ③ Stable source of goods; ④ Stable resources for cross-border logistics, customs and commodity inspection; ⑤ Convenient cross-border payment.

The disadvantages mainly include: ① High overall operating costs; ② High resource requirements; ③ High operating risks; ④ High financial pressure; ⑤ Significant problems with unsold goods, returns and exchanges.

4. Classification by the Scope of the Industry Involved

(1) Vertical Cross-border E-commerce Platforms

A vertical cross-border e-commerce platform refers to a cross-border e-commerce model that deepens operations in a certain industry or niche market. Vertical cross-border e-commerce platforms not only include category-specific cross-border e-commerce, but also region-specific cross-border e-commerce platforms. Category-specific vertical cross-border e-commerce platforms mainly refer to cross-border e-commerce models that focus on a certain type of product, with representative companies including Xiaohongshu and Mia; region-specific vertical cross-border e-commerce platforms refer to cross-border e-commerce models that focus on a certain region, with representative companies including Lazada and Zhiyu.

(2) Comprehensive Cross-Border E-Commerce Platform

A comprehensive cross-border e-commerce platform is a concept that corresponds to a vertical e-commerce platform. Unlike vertical e-commerce that focuses on certain specific fields or certain specific categories, the types of goods displayed and sold are diverse and involve multiple industries. Representative companies: AliExpress, Amazon, eBay, Wish, Lanting Jishi, etc.

5. Classification by the Direction of Goods Flow

The flow of goods in cross-border e-commerce crosses national geographical spaces. According to the direction of goods flow, cross-border e-commerce platforms are divided into cross-border import e-commerce platforms and cross-border export e-commerce platforms.

(1) Cross-Border Import E-Commerce Platform

A cross-border import e-commerce platform refers to a cross-border e-commerce platform engaged in import business, specifically referring to foreign goods sold to the domestic market through e-commerce channels, completing product display, transaction, payment through the e-commerce platform, and delivering goods and completing transactions through offline cross-border logistics. Representative companies: Tmall International, JD Global Purchase, Yangmatou, Xiaohongshu, etc.

(2) Cross-Border Export E-Commerce Platform

A cross-border export e-commerce platform refers to a cross-border e-commerce platform engaged in export business, referring to domestic goods sold to foreign markets through e-commerce channels, completing product display, transaction, payment through the e-commerce platform, and delivering goods and completing transactions through offline cross-border logistics. Representative companies: Amazon, eBay, AliExpress, Global Sources, Dalong.com, Lanting Jishi, etc.

3.2.2 *Other New Types of Cross-Border E-Commerce Platforms*

With the development of the cross-border e-commerce market, under the continuous development and application of digital technology, many companies have entered the cross-border e-commerce track, bringing some new cross-border e-commerce operation models and cross-border e-commerce platform types, represented by cross-border live broadcast e-commerce platforms, cross-border social e-commerce platforms, and cross-border e-commerce independent stations.

1. Cross-Border Live Broadcast E-Commerce Platform

A cross-border live broadcast e-commerce platform refers to conducting cross-border e-commerce business in the form of live broadcast, which can be regarded as the result of the integration of live broadcast e-commerce and cross-border e-commerce. In 2020, under the impact of the epidemic, the live broadcast e-commerce model exploded, and the new retail format of "live broadcast + e-commerce" accelerated, helping companies expand domestic and foreign markets. From 2020 to 2021, well-known domestic e-commerce platforms and short video platforms have joined the cross-border live broadcast e-commerce industry, pushing cross-border live broadcast e-commerce to a historical height. For example, in March 2020, Amazon began to open live broadcasts (Amazon Live) to Chinese sellers, in May 2020, Alibaba International Station started B2B live broadcasts, and in December 2021, Tik Tok Shop officially announced that it was fully open to Chinese sellers, officially entering the cross-border e-commerce field. With the development of the Internet and technology, online live broadcasts will continue to penetrate people's daily lives.

Representing companies: Tik Tok, Amazon, Alibaba International, etc.

2. Cross-Border Social E-Commerce Platform

Cross-border social e-commerce platforms share products through social websites, SNS, microblogs, social media, and online media, and conduct cross-border transactions of goods through social interaction and other forms. Cross-border social e-commerce is a new derivative model of e-commerce and a new form of innovative development of cross-border e-commerce. It falls under the category of "social + cross-border e-commerce". Common operating models of cross-border social e-commerce platforms mainly include membership systems, group buying models, and community group buying. Cross-border social e-commerce platforms are more about traditional social platform companies expanding their business into the cross-border e-commerce field, such as: In May 2020, Meta (formerly Facebook) officially launched Facebook Shops and Instagram Shops, adding online shopping entrances in the app to layout cross-border e-commerce business; Pinduoduo officially launched its cross-border social e-commerce platform Temu in North America on September 1, 2022, and officially entered the Australian and New Zealand markets on March 13, 2023.

Representing companies: Temu, Meta, etc.

3. Cross-Border E-Commerce Independent Site

The cross-border e-commerce independent site, also known as the independent site, refers to a cross-border e-commerce seller developing an independent cross-border e-commerce website, including the website domain, independent server, and independent website program, to display products, select, pay, and place orders to foreign users through online sales. The cross-border e-commerce website manager operates completely independently, without any platform restrictions, to achieve cross-border transactions. The independent site can be seen as reaching overseas consumers in a DTC (Direct-to-Consumer) manner. The emergence and rise of independent sites are mainly because cross-border e-commerce sellers are increasingly restricted by third-party cross-border e-commerce platforms, so they turn to build their own cross-border e-commerce websites to achieve autonomous control and coordination of various resources.

Representing companies: Shopify, SHEIN, Anke, etc.

3.2.3 Mainstream Cross-Border E-Commerce Platform Model

Among the many classification models of cross-border e-commerce, the hybrid use involving the scope of the industry and the platform operator is more accepted. In addition, the acceptance of classifying cross-border e-commerce according to the direction of goods flow is also high. This section mainly studies the classification model of cross-border e-commerce from the perspective of hybrid use involving the scope of the industry and the platform operator. Cross-border e-commerce platforms can be divided into four types: comprehensive platform type, comprehensive self-operated type, vertical platform type, and vertical self-operated type.

Comprehensive platform-type representative companies include JD Global Purchase, Tmall International, Taobao Global Purchase, Yangmatou, etc.; comprehensive self-operated type representative companies mainly include Amazon Overseas Purchase, Koala Sea Purchase, Little Red Book, Lanting Collection, etc.; vertical platform type participants are relatively few, mainly concentrated in clothing, beauty vertical goods, representative companies include Meilishuo, Haimi Global Purchase, etc.; vertical self-operated type is also rare, representative companies include Mia, Jumei Youpin, Vipshop, etc.

3.3 Interpretation of Platform and Self-Operated Cross-Border E-Commerce Platforms

3.3.1 Platform Cross-Border E-Commerce Platform

1. Interpretation of the Platform Cross-Border E-Commerce Platform

The advantage of platform-based cross-border e-commerce platforms lies in development and operation. Since they do not engage in the procurement and sales of goods, their operational focus is more on the excavation of website traffic, early-stage merchant recruitment, key auxiliary service links, etc. The business content of the platform-based cross-border e-commerce platform is shown in Fig. 3.1.

The key business process of the platform-based cross-border e-commerce platform lies in the early establishment of the platform website, attracting browsing, and developing merchant entry; the daily business focus is on platform management, including the management of merchants, goods, consumers, and the platform itself, ensuring the normal operation of the platform, the quality and image of merchants and goods, holding various market activities to promote product sales, maintaining communication with consumers, and thereby improving the satisfaction of merchants and consumers; in addition, it needs to provide some related services, aiming to make up for the service shortcomings and disadvantages of the merchants on the platform, such as payment, customer service, logistics, supervision and other work links, all of which have become important service content for attracting platform traffic, merchant entry quantity, product sales, and consumer satisfaction.

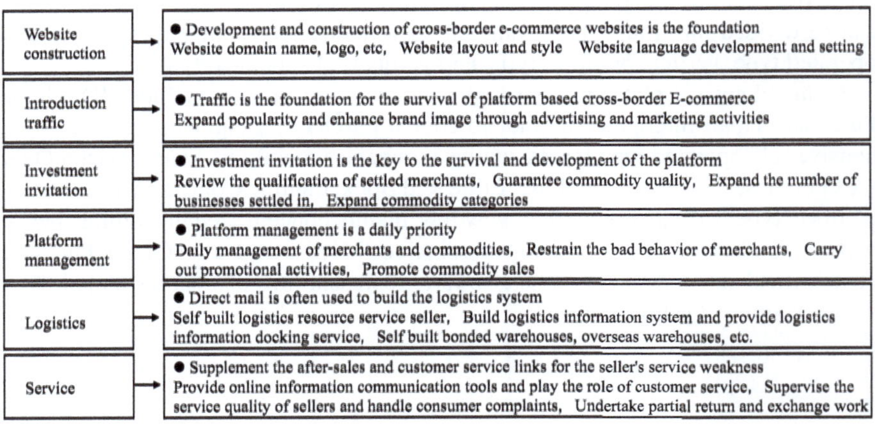

Fig. 3.1 Business content of platform-based cross-border e-commerce platform

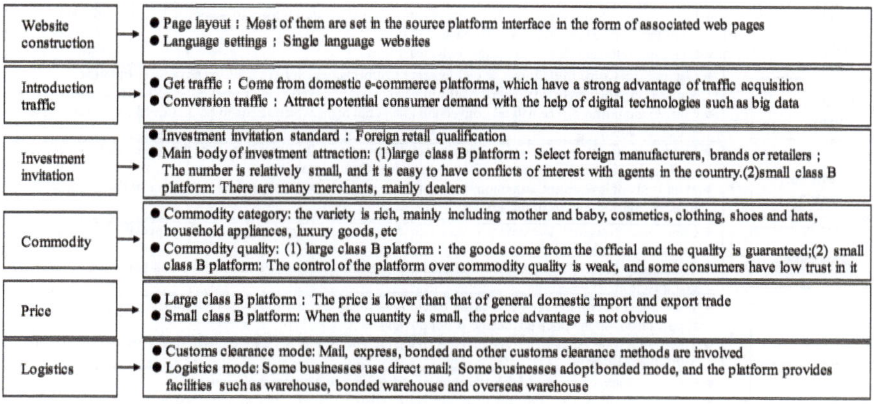

Fig. 3.2 B2C platform-based cross-border e-commerce business content

2. B2C Platform-Based Cross-Border E-Commerce Platform

Combining the types of transaction subjects, we analyze the business process of the platform-based cross-border e-commerce platform. Since the B2B cross-border e-commerce model has a larger single transaction scale but a low usage frequency and is not closely related to people's daily consumption, it will not be further explored here. This book will subdivide the platform-based cross-border e-commerce into B2C platform-based cross-border e-commerce platform and C2C platform-based cross-border e-commerce platform. The business content of the B2C platform-based cross-border e-commerce platform is shown in Fig. 3.2.

The B2C platform-based cross-border e-commerce platform has significant advantages in website traffic and product categories, but there is a certain difficulty in brand merchant recruitment, and it needs to balance between scale and quality. This is mainly because there are fewer large-scale merchants now, coupled with the competition and resource contention between platform-based cross-border e-commerce companies, which makes it difficult to introduce large-scale merchants; although there are more small-scale merchants, the platform also faces the difficulty of controlling the quality of merchants and goods.

3. C2C Platform-Based Cross-Border E-Commerce Platform

The business content of the C2C platform-based cross-border e-commerce platform is shown in Fig. 3.3. The biggest advantage of the C2C platform-based cross-border e-commerce platform lies in the richness of product types, but because the merchants on the platform are individuals and the number is large, the C2C platform-based cross-border e-commerce platform has a weak control ability over sellers and goods,

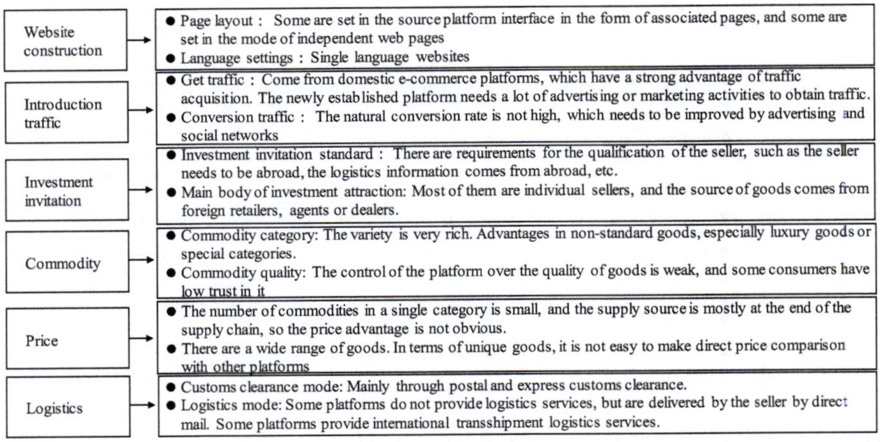

Fig. 3.3 C2C platform-based cross-border e-commerce business content

which can easily lead to risks in product quality, which is also the main reason why consumers have a low trust in C2C e-commerce platforms.

3.3.2 *Self-Operated Cross-Border E-Commerce Platform*

Self-operated cross-border e-commerce platform companies are different from platform-based cross-border e-commerce platform companies, and are more similar to traditional retail companies, just moving the place of goods trading from offline to online. As shown in Fig. 3.4, self-operated cross-border e-commerce platform companies need to fully participate in the entire supply chain of goods, including the selection of goods sold, supplier development and negotiation, operation of e-commerce platforms, etc., and deeply involve in logistics, customer service and after-sales service links.

Since self-operated cross-border e-commerce platforms belong to the B2C model in terms of transaction subject attributes, this section will not further subdivide them based on transaction subject attributes. Instead, they are divided into comprehensive self-operated cross-border e-commerce platforms and vertical self-operated cross-border e-commerce platforms based on the variety of goods.

1. Comprehensive Self-Operated Cross-Border E-commerce Platforms

Comprehensive self-operated cross-border e-commerce platforms have a closer relationship with brand merchants in terms of product sources. As shown in Fig. 3.5, they have a strong ability to guarantee product quality and have a significant price advantage due to the elimination of many costs in the middle. However, the number

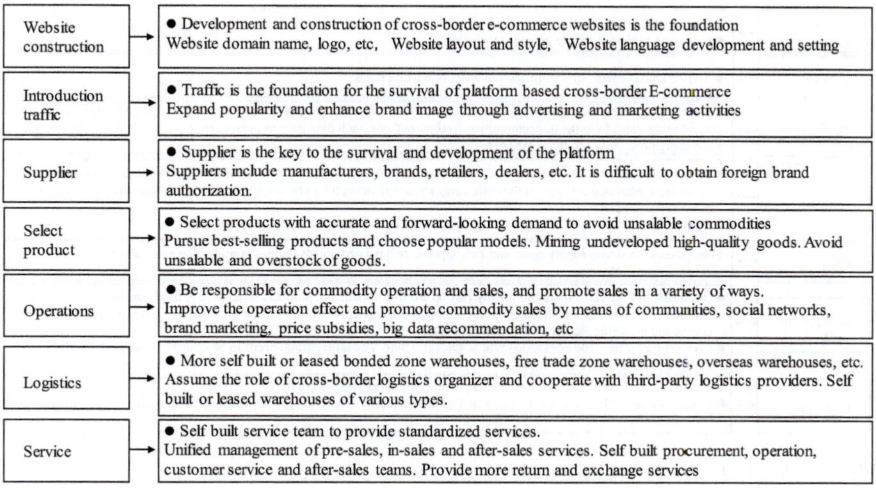

Fig. 3.4 Self-operated cross-border e-commerce platform business content

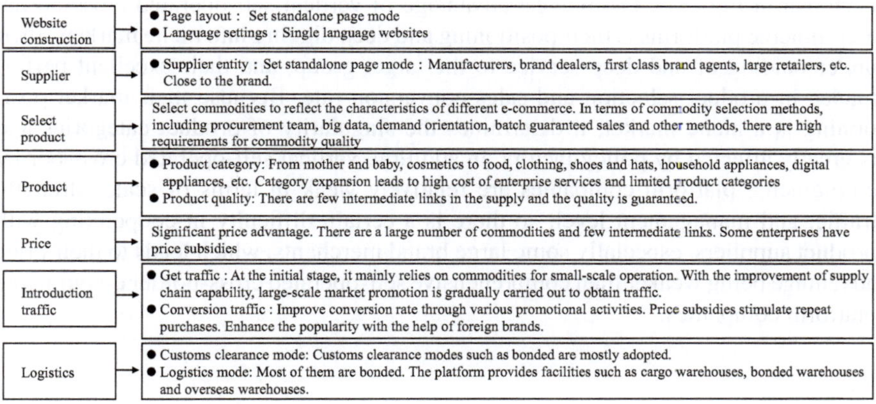

Fig. 3.5 Comprehensive self-operated cross-border e-commerce business content

of their products is far less than that of comprehensive platform-type cross-border e-commerce platforms, and it is difficult to expand product categories, with a significant increase in costs.

2. Vertical Self-Operated Cross-Border E-commerce Platforms

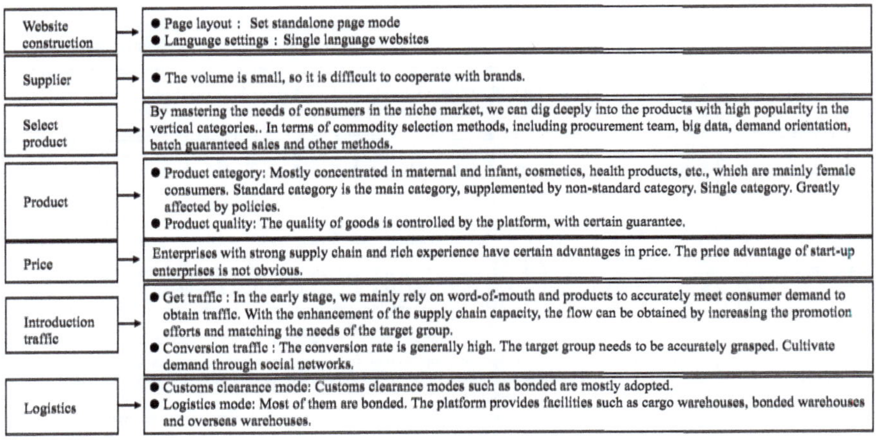

Fig. 3.6 Vertical self-operated cross-border e-commerce business content

The business content of vertical self-operated cross-border e-commerce platforms is shown in Fig. 3.6. The biggest advantage of vertical self-operated cross-border e-commerce platforms is their positioning and deep digging into niche markets, their understanding of and deep service to the target group, and their excellent performance in product selection and sales conversion rate. Because their market positioning is a niche market, it determines the singularity of product categories and is greatly affected by policy factors. In addition, vertical self-operated cross-border e-commerce platform companies are relatively weak in terms of scale, strength, traffic, and management level, so there is a certain difficulty in cooperating with product suppliers, especially some large brand merchants, which leads to their price advantage being weaker than comprehensive self-operated cross-border e-commerce platform companies.

3.4 Interpreting Cross-Border Export E-Commerce Platforms and Cross-Border Import E-Commerce Platforms

Cross-border export e-commerce can be divided into several types. Combined with the type of transaction subject, cross-border export e-commerce platforms can be subdivided into B2B cross-border export mode and B2C cross-border export mode.

3.4.1 B2B Cross-Border Export Mode

1. Information Service Platform

Mode Introduction: The service of completing transaction matching through information release or information search on a third-party cross-border e-commerce platform. Its main profit models include membership service fees and value-added service fees.

Membership service means that the seller enjoys various services provided by the platform after paying a certain membership fee each year. Membership fees are the main source of income for the platform, and this profit model has become saturated in the market.

Value-added services mean that after both buyers and sellers become free members of the platform, the platform provides value-added services for both buyers and sellers, mainly including bidding ranking, pay-per-click, and booth promotion services. Bidding ranking is the most mature profit model for value-added services on information service platforms.

Representative companies: Alibaba International Station, Business Treasure International Station, Global Resources.

2. Transaction Service Platform

Mode Introduction: A business model that can realize online transactions and online electronic payments between buyers and sellers. Its main profit models include commission and display fees.

The commission system is a certain commission charged by the platform after the transaction is completed. The platform can help buyers accurately understand the seller's situation through real transaction data.

The display fee is a charge collected when uploading products, regardless of the size of the booth. As long as the product information is displayed, a fee is charged, which is directly paid online.

Representative companies: Dalong Network, Yitang Network.

3.4.2 B2C Cross-Border Export Model

1. Open Platform

Model Introduction: The content opened by the open platform involves all aspects of export e-commerce, in addition to opening buyer and seller data, it also includes opening goods, shops, transactions, logistics, evaluations, warehousing, marketing promotion and other links and processes of the business, realizing the systematic docking of applications and platform, and building its own developer ecosystem around the platform.

The open platform acts more as a management and operation platform merchant, integrating platform service resources and sharing data to serve both buyers and sellers.

Representative companies: Amazon, AliExpress, eBay, Wish.

2. Self-Operated Platform

Model Introduction: The platform conducts unified production or procurement, product display, online transactions for its operated products, and delivers the products to the final consumer group through logistics.

The self-operated platform introduces, manages, and sells various brands of goods by tailoring procurement standards that meet its own brand demands and consumer needs, highlighting the reliability of its own brand with reliable brands as the support point. The self-operated platform makes efforts in the introduction, classification, display, transaction, logistics distribution, after-sales guarantee and other key links of the entire transaction process, manages through the Internet IT system, builds a large-scale warehousing logistics system, and realizes real-time management of the entire transaction process.

Representative companies: Lanting Jishi, Global Easy Buy, Milan Network.

3.4.3 Cross-Border Import E-Commerce Model

The cross-border e-commerce import model has different types according to different classification standards, and is currently mainly classified from the aspects of business form and customs supervision model.

1. Classified According to Business Form

Before reviewing the models, it is necessary to distinguish between the traditional "overseas shopping" model and the current import e-commerce model. The traditional overseas shopping model is a typical B2C model. Strictly speaking, the original meaning of the term "overseas shopping" refers to: domestic consumers directly shopping on foreign B2C e-commerce websites, and then mailing the goods back to the country through transshipment or direct mail. Apart from direct mail categories, consumers can only receive goods through transshipment logistics. Simply put, it is a transshipment company with a transshipment warehouse overseas that receives goods on behalf of consumers at the transshipment warehouse address abroad, and then sends the goods to the domestic port through third-party or self-operated cross-border logistics.

In addition to the most traditional overseas shopping model, according to different business forms, the existing main operating models of import retail e-commerce are divided into the following five categories: ① Overseas purchasing model; ② Direct delivery/direct shipment platform model; ③ Self-operated B2C model; ④ Shopping guide/rebate platform model; ⑤ Overseas goods flash sale model. Although the operating model adopted by a specific e-commerce platform may be diversified, there is usually a strong model positioning tendency. Therefore, this book will classify it into the corresponding model based on the main positioning of the specific platform at this stage.

(1) Overseas Purchasing Model

The overseas purchasing model is the second cross-border online shopping concept known to consumers after "overseas shopping". Simply put, it is a model in which people/merchants overseas purchase the required goods for Chinese consumers in need and deliver the goods to consumers through cross-border logistics. From a business form, the overseas purchasing model can be roughly divided into the following two categories.

① Overseas purchasing platforms. The operation focus of overseas purchasing platforms is to attract as many qualified third-party sellers as possible, without deeply involving in procurement, sales, and cross-border logistics. The sellers on the platform are generally small businesses or individuals with overseas procurement capabilities or cross-border trade capabilities. They regularly or according to consumer orders, purchase specific goods in bulk, and then send the goods to China through transshipment or direct mail after receiving consumer orders. Overseas purchasing platforms follow the typical cross-border C2C platform route. The purchasing platform profits by charging entry fees, transaction fees, value-added service fees, etc. to the sellers on the platform.

Advantages: It provides consumers with a relatively rich selection of overseas product categories, and has a large user traffic.

Disadvantages: Consumers are skeptical about the real qualifications of the sellers on the platform, and the transaction credit link may be one of the problems that overseas purchasing platforms need to solve most urgently; the involvement in the cross-border supply chain is shallow, or it is difficult to establish sufficient competitive advantages.

Representative companies: Taobao Global Purchase, JD Overseas Purchase, eBay Global Marketplace, US Shopping Network.

Taobao Global Purchase and JD Overseas Purchase have a certain level of traffic, but transaction credit, after-sales service, etc. are always places where consumers have more concerns. Many consumers feel frustrated because they cannot effectively protect their rights after discovering that they have bought fake goods, high imitations, and goods for export to domestic sales. Although the potential development scale of the purchasing platform is huge, if the above problems cannot be effectively controlled, whether the overseas purchasing market can grow to the expected scale is still a big question.

② WeChat Moments overseas purchasing. WeChat Moments purchasing is a primitive business form that naturally grows from mobile social platforms based on acquaintances/half-acquaintances social relationships. Although social relationships play a certain endorsement role in the safety of transactions and the authenticity of goods, there are not a few cases of being deceived. With the tightening of customs policies, the regulatory authorities may change the nature of personal purchasing in the WeChat Moments from gray trade to smuggling. After the overseas purchasing market completes future integration, this primitive mode may be difficult to continue.

Cross-border e-commerce imports can be seen as the compliant mode of overseas purchasing. Many times when we discuss overseas purchasing or cross-border e-commerce imports, we generally blur the two and do not make a strict distinction.

(2) Direct Delivery/Direct Shipment Platform Model

The direct delivery/direct shipment platform model is also known as the dropshipping model. Under this model, the e-commerce platform sends the consumer order information it receives to wholesalers or manufacturers, who then send the goods to consumers in retail form according to the order information. Since the supplier is a brand merchant, wholesaler, or manufacturer, direct delivery/direct shipment is a typical B2C model. We can understand it as a third-party B2C model. Part of the profit of the direct delivery/direct shipment platform comes from the difference between the retail price and the wholesale price of the goods.

Advantages: Deep involvement in the cross-border supply chain, with greater potential for future development. The direct delivery/direct shipment model negotiates directly with reliable overseas suppliers and signs cross-border retail supply agreements when looking for suppliers; in order to solve the problem of cross-border logistics, platforms that choose to build their own international logistics system or reach strategic cooperation with the postal and logistics systems of specific countries.

Disadvantages: Slow merchant recruitment, relatively insufficient traffic in the early stage; a large amount of funds required in the early stage; for the established comprehensive platform, it is difficult to avoid the "fake foreign brands" that falsify procedures.

Representative companies: Tmall International (Comprehensive), Yangmatou (North America), Kuajingtong (Shanghai Free Trade Zone), Dolphin Village (Europe), Yifan Haigou Network (Japan), Xiu.com (Global Fashion Department Store).

(3) Self-operated B2C Model

Under the self-operated B2C model, most goods require the platform to stock up, so it is the most capital-intensive of all models. The self-operated B2C model is divided into comprehensive self-operated and vertical self-operated types.

① Comprehensive self-operated cross-border B2C platform. At present, the only businesses that can be called comprehensive self-operated cross-border B2C platforms are probably Amazon and Walmart's invested Yihaodian. The goods sold by Amazon and Yihaodian in the Shanghai Free Trade Zone's import e-commerce business will be imported through bonded import or overseas direct mail.

Advantages: Strong cross-border supply chain management capabilities, relatively complete cross-border logistics solutions, ample reserve funds.

Disadvantages: Business development will be significantly affected by industry policy changes, and the risk of irreversible fixed asset investment is extremely high.

Representative companies: Amazon, Yihaodian's "Yihaohai Shopping".

② Vertical self-operated cross-border B2C platform. Vertical refers to the platform focusing on a specific category when choosing self-operated categories, such as food, luxury goods, cosmetics, clothing, etc.

Advantages: Supplier management capabilities can be relatively strong.

Disadvantages: Large initial capital support is needed.

Representative companies: COFCO Womai (Food), Mia.com (Maternal and Child), Secoo (Luxury), Sasa.com (Cosmetics), StrawberryNet (Cosmetics).

(4) Guide/Rebate Platform Model

The guide/rebate model is a light asset model, which can be understood in two parts: the traffic generation part + the product transaction part. The traffic generation part refers to attracting user traffic through guide information, product price comparison, overseas shopping community forums, overseas shopping blogs, and user rebates; the product transaction part refers to consumers submitting orders to overseas B2C e-commerce or overseas personal shoppers through site links to realize cross-border shopping. To enhance the richness of product categories and the abundance of goods, these platforms usually pair with overseas C2C personal shopping models.

Therefore, from the perspective of transaction relationships, this model can be understood as a combination of overseas shopping B2C model + personal shopping C2C model. In typical cases, the guide/rebate platform will connect its page with the product sales page of overseas B2C e-commerce. Once a sale is made, the B2C e-commerce will give the guide platform a 5% to 15% rebate. The guide platform gives a part of its rebate as a rebate to consumers.

Advantages: Positioned for the integration of information flow, the model is lighter and easier to operate. The traffic generation part can attract many overseas shopping users to the platform in a short period of time and understand consumer front-end demand well.

Disadvantages: In the long run, there are many uncertainties in scaling up, and other elements need to be configured; control over the cross-border supply chain is weak; the entry threshold is low, there are many participants, and there is a relative lack of competitive advantage. If it cannot reach a certain sustainable traffic scale as soon as possible, its subsequent development may be difficult to maintain.

Representative companies: 55haitao, Geek Haitao Network, Haitao City, Haitao Residence, Haimao Season, Extrabux, Youyou Haitao, What's Worth Buying.

(5) Overseas Flash Sale Model

In addition to the above import retail e-commerce models, the overseas flash sale is a relatively unique operation model. Due to the more complex supply chain environment faced by cross-border flash sales, for a long time, businesses involved in cross-border flash sales have been in a small-scale trial stage. Jumei Youpin's "Jumei Overseas Purchase" and Vipshop's "Global Sale" channels have made high-profile appearances on the homepage of the website, and both companies claim to have strong control over overseas suppliers, guarantee genuine products, offer global free shipping, and all-inclusive prices. The overseas flash sale model is a third-party B2C model.

Advantages: Once the industry position is established, it will form a platform network advantage with concentrated traffic and supply.

Disadvantages: The flash sale model requires high control over supply and logistics; high ability to attract and convert front-end users. Any deficiency in any link may result in failure.

Representative companies: Mitao.com (formerly CN Haitao), Tmall International's Global Flash Sale, Yihaodian's Imported Food Flash Sale, Jumei Youpin Overseas Purchase, Vipshop's Overseas Direct Delivery Special.

2. Classification Based on Customs Supervision Model

The General Administration of Customs of China added codes 9610 and 1210 for customs supervision in 2014, added code 1239 in 2016, and added codes 9710 and 9810 in 2020, forming five basic cross-border e-commerce business models, namely: 9610, 1210, 1239, 9710 and 9810 cross-border e-commerce models. Depending on the direction of goods flow, it can be divided into cross-border imports and exports, among which the cross-border e-commerce import business models include: 1210 online shopping bonded import model, 1239 online shopping bonded import A, 9610 direct mail import model. Cross-border e-commerce export business models include: 1210 export business model, 9610 export business model, 9710 export business model, 9810 export business model.

(1) 9610 Cross-border E-commerce Model

9610, fully named "Cross-border Trade E-commerce", abbreviated as "E-commerce", is applicable to domestic individuals or e-commerce companies that realize transactions through e-commerce trading platforms and adopt the "list verification and release, summary declaration" model for customs clearance procedures of e-commerce retail import and export goods (excluding e-commerce retail import and export goods through customs special supervision areas or bonded supervision places). The list verification and release refers to: import e-commerce companies first push the order information of the imported goods on the trading platform to the cross-border e-commerce public service platform of the business location, and match it with the payment order and waybill to complete the list declaration. After the customs electronically audits and releases the "list", the actual goods are released, solving the problem of fewer orders and more batches for cross-border retail imports, facilitating the actual operation of enterprises and regulatory departments, and greatly improving the efficiency of customs clearance.

(2) 1210 Cross-border E-commerce Model

1210, fully named "Bonded Cross-border Trade E-commerce", abbreviated as "Bonded E-commerce", refers to cross-border e-commerce import companies stocking cross-border e-commerce import goods in customs special supervision areas. After domestic consumers place orders and generate orders, the goods purchased by consumers are cleared through customs in small packages and delivered to domestic buyers. It is applicable to domestic individuals or e-commerce companies that realize cross-border transactions on e-commerce platforms approved by customs and import and export e-commerce retail goods through customs special supervision areas or bonded supervision places (retail import and export goods traded between customs special supervision areas, bonded supervision places and areas outside the territory (places outside) through e-commerce platforms are not applicable to this supervision method). The bonded warehouse refers to a warehouse approved by customs for the storage of imported goods without being subject to customs laws and import control regulations. Imported goods stored in bonded warehouses are exempt from customs duties if re-exported, and must pay customs duties if they enter the domestic market.

(3) 1239 Cross-Border E-commerce Model

1239, fully known as "Bonded Cross-Border Trade E-commerce A", abbreviated as "Bonded E-commerce A", is applicable to cross-border e-commerce retail import goods that enter the country through customs special supervision areas or bonded logistics centers (Type B) by domestic e-commerce companies. Compared with the 1210 supervision method, the 1239 supervision method is applicable to cross-border e-commerce retail import goods that enter the country through customs special supervision areas or bonded logistics centers (Type B) by domestic e-commerce companies. Goods on the list of cross-border e-commerce retail import goods are exempt from submitting permit documents to customs; direct purchase goods are managed according to personal goods supervision requirements, and bonded goods purchased online need to be managed according to goods supervision requirements when entering the "first line" area, and refer to personal goods supervision requirements when leaving the "second line" area.

(4) 9710 Cross-Border E-commerce Model

9710, fully known as "Cross-Border E-commerce Enterprise Direct Export to Enterprise", abbreviated as "Cross-Border E-commerce B2B Direct Export", is applicable to goods directly exported by cross-border e-commerce B2B. 9710 refers to domestic enterprises directly exporting goods to foreign enterprises through cross-border logistics after reaching a transaction with foreign enterprises through a cross-border e-commerce platform. The 9710 supervision model has multiple advantages over traditional foreign trade exports, namely: simplified declaration procedures, priority for inspection, priority for transshipment procedures, reducing enterprise customs clearance costs while greatly improving export enterprise customs clearance efficiency.

(5) 9810 Cross-Border E-commerce Model

9810, fully known as "Cross-Border E-commerce Export Overseas Warehouse", abbreviated as "Cross-Border E-commerce Export Overseas Warehouse", is applicable to goods exported from cross-border e-commerce overseas warehouses. 9810 refers to domestic enterprises first exporting goods to overseas warehouses through cross-border logistics, and delivering to foreign buyers after realizing transactions through a cross-border e-commerce platform. Domestic enterprises deliver exported goods to overseas warehouses through cross-border logistics, including Amazon FBA warehouses/Walmart WFS warehouses, third-party overseas warehouses, or self-built overseas warehouses. After realizing transactions through a cross-border e-commerce platform, they deliver to buyers from overseas warehouses and transmit relevant electronic data according to customs requirements.

3.5 Types of Cross-Border E-commerce Enterprises

Enterprises are the main components of business activities and market activities, and are also one of the most active elements, playing an important role in cross-border e-commerce transactions. Driven by the vigorous development of cross-border e-commerce, more and more enterprises are entering this market. These enterprises come from an increasing number of industries, including not only traditional e-commerce enterprises, but also traditional Internet enterprises, retail enterprises, logistics enterprises, etc.

Based on industry background, the enterprises involved in cross-border e-commerce business mainly include the following categories.

(1) Global e-commerce enterprises radiate their business to cross-border e-commerce business, representative enterprises include Amazon, eBay, etc.
(2) Domestic e-commerce enterprises expand their cross-border e-commerce business. When domestic e-commerce enterprises were established, they mainly focused on or radiated to the domestic market. In order to sustain growth or comply with the development trend of cross-border e-commerce, their business scope expanded from the domestic market to foreign markets, thus developing into cross-border e-commerce enterprises. Representative enterprises include JD.com, Tmall, Pinduoduo, India's Zomato, etc.
(3) Traditional Internet enterprises are involved in cross-border e-commerce business, representative enterprises include Koala Haigou, TikTok, Google, etc.
(4) Traditional industry enterprises entering the cross-border e-commerce market. Under the impetus of e-commerce development, traditional enterprises are no longer satisfied with their original physical channels, and have extended their reach to the e-commerce field, gradually stepping into the cross-border e-commerce market. These enterprises are mainly traditional retail businesses, represented by companies such as Walmart, Carrefour, Metro, Home Depot, Lowe's, etc.
(5) Specializing in cross-border e-commerce business. These enterprises were established to operate cross-border e-commerce business and are professional cross-border e-commerce enterprises. From the beginning, they were positioned in the cross-border e-commerce market, represented by companies such as AliExpress, Yangmatou, Lanting Market, etc.

(6) Logistics companies expanding into cross-border e-commerce business. Some logistics companies, with their logistics resources and advantages in the cross-border business ecosystem, have entered the cross-border e-commerce market to achieve diversification, represented by companies such as SF Express Sea Amoy, Cnova Brasil, etc.
(7) Social networking companies are trying to enter the cross-border e-commerce market. In the cross-border e-commerce market, the value and status of social networks are constantly being elevated, especially as the young consumer group is keen on using social networks, which provides development opportunities for some social networking companies, represented by companies like Facebook, etc.

Chapter 4
Cross-Border E-Commerce Consumer Behavior

4.1 Consumer Behavior Theory

4.1.1 Concept of Consumer Behavior

The definition of consumer behavior has different theoretical bases: "Decision Process Theory" defines consumer behavior as the decision process of consumers buying, consuming, and disposing; "Experience Theory" believes that consumer behavior is the experience process of consumers; "Stimulus–Response Theory" believes that consumer behavior is the consumer's response to consumption; "Balance Coordination Theory" believes that consumer behavior is the exchange interaction behavior between consumers and marketers, and is the result of balance between the two. This book believes that consumer behavior refers to the process and activities people engage in when choosing, buying, using, and disposing of products or services to meet their needs and desires. Consumer behavior includes psychological activities and physical activities related to purchase decisions.
The basic issues of consumer behavior include:

- Analysis of consumer characteristics (Who);
- Consumer psychological behavior (What);
- How to explain consumer behavior (Why);
- How to influence consumers (How);
- Trends in consumer behavior (How).

4.1.2 Factors Affecting Consumer Purchases

The purchasing process and behavior of consumers are influenced by various factors. The factors that have a significant impact on consumer purchasing behavior include cultural factors, social factors, individual factors, and group factors.

X. Zhang, *Introduction to Cross-Border E-Commerce Ecosystem*,
https://doi.org/10.1007/978-981-96-1165-2_4

1. Cultural Factors

Culture is a series of values that can only be obtained in society. Society as a whole accepts these values and conveys them to its members in the form of language or symbols. Therefore, the values of a society will affect the purchasing and consumption patterns of its members. Culture not only influences consumer behavior but also reflects consumer behavior. Therefore, culture is a mirror of the values and possessions of society members. The fixed roles of various goods defined by culture are divided into the following categories.

(1) Routine behavior

Routine behavior refers to a series of symbolic actions that occur frequently and in a certain order. For example, gift-giving includes receiving gifts, exchanging gifts, and estimating the recipient's reaction. The exchange of gifts, the types of gifts exchanged, and the occasions for gift-giving have all been socially standardized. Some industries rely on the custom of gift-giving to sell products, such as Christmas sales often accounting for a large part of a retailer's annual turnover. In addition to gift-giving, holidays include routine behaviors, such as consuming specific foods at Christmas. Holidays also include the routine behavior of vacationing, such as annual vacation spots. As a reflection of dominant cultural values, routine behavior varies in different cultures. For example, in Japan, gift-giving is a manifestation of one's responsibility to others in a social group. Gift-giving is a recognized moral requirement, through which mutual obligations between people can be realized. In the United States, gift-giving is individualized, although there is often a sense of obligation involved in gift-giving, this sense of obligation is individualized rather than collectivized.

(2) Pure consumption

Pure consumption is the consumption of goods that promote cooperation, protect nature, and make things better. Consumers who pursue the pure side of consumption are easily attracted by images related to nature or connections to family ties. They love food with natural ingredients and clothing with simple styles. Another aspect of pure consumption is people's affection or even reverence for certain products. People treat jewelry given for a specific event or suits or dresses associated with career or social success with a sacred attitude. Research on the Harley-Davidson subculture shows the respect that motorcyclists have for Harley motorcycles. It is absolutely taboo to touch someone else's bike without permission. The process of cleaning a Harley motorcycle is very complicated, including careful cleaning and polishing. The garage where the motorcycle is parked is almost considered sacred, and the intimate relationships between people (motorcyclists call each other "brothers") are almost the same as in religion. When they ride a Harley motorcycle, they say the feeling is "magically transcendent of the mundane world".

2. Social Factors

Social class refers to the position of consumers in the social hierarchy, dividing them into different social ranks such as upper, middle, and lower based on their power and prestige. This division depends on three important demographic factors: occupation, income, and education level.

Common methods of dividing consumers into social classes include Warner's Status Characteristic Index and the Coleman-Rainwater Social Status Level Division. Society is generally divided into upper, upper-middle, middle, working, and lower class consumers. These groups have significant differences in behavioral norms, values, family norms, and purchasing behavior patterns, manifested in purchases such as clothing, furniture, entertainment products, and even food. For example, upper-class consumers emphasize style and color when buying appliances, while lower-class consumers value the performance of the appliance. Lower-class consumers are more likely to shop at discount stores and nearby stores because they feel more comfortable there, can establish friendships with the salespeople, and easily obtain information. Upper-class consumers are more likely to buy risky products at regular department stores and almost risk-free products at discount stores.

3. Individual Factors

In the consumer decision-making process, personality plays a certain role, that is, different personalities have different performances in the purchasing decision process. The variables that grasp the differences in the consumer purchasing decision process from the perspective of personality are cognitive desire and self-concept.

(1) Cognitive Desire

Cognitive desire refers to an individual's tendency to think, which is a variable to grasp personality differences. In other words, cognitive desire reflects questions such as "how much does an individual think?" and "how much does one love to think?". Consumers with high cognitive desire (those who love to think) pay more attention to the quality of information than consumers with low cognitive desire (those who are unwilling to think), while consumers with low cognitive desire are more easily influenced by peripheral stimuli like advertising models than consumers with high cognitive desire.

(2) Self-concept

The self-concept is a subjective cognition of "who am I" and "what do I look like". Cognitive psychologist Markus proposed the "self-schema" theory, explaining the formation of self-cognition structure. Everyone has a single, integrated self-concept. The self-concept can be seen as a collection of all special schemas about a person's characteristics.

The consumer's self-concept is their reaction to their own attitudes. Regardless of whether these attitudes are positive or negative, they will guide many of the consumer's purchasing decisions: certain products will enhance the consumer's self-esteem or make them identify with their "identity".

4. Group Influence

The groups around consumers are the biggest environmental factors influencing consumer behavior. Reference groups provide a way to analyze this influence. The so-called reference group refers to a group that serves as a reference for the beliefs, attitudes, and behaviors formed by consumers. For example, marketers often advertise their products in a group context, such as a family enjoying oatmeal breakfast, friends drinking soft drinks after playing rugby, neighbors praising the newly purchased car, etc. This is done to reflect the influence of friends and relatives on consumers. In addition, marketers often use "typical consumers" to prove their products. Typical consumers reflect the standards and values of buyers and play a representative role in the consumer reference group.

4.2 Online Consumer Behavior Analysis

4.2.1 Analysis of Online Consumer Purchase Motivation

The purchase motivation is the most direct reason and driving force for consumers to purchase and consume goods. The purchase motivation of online consumers mainly includes convenience motivation, low-price motivation, and performance motivation.

1. Convenience Motivation

Convenience motivation is a reason for consumption that arises to reduce physical and psychological expenditure. Online shopping only requires consumers to click the mouse, find the products they need on the Internet, and complete the purchase process after confirmation, which can save them the trouble of going back and forth to the mall, the time to find and select goods, the time to queue for payment, and also eliminate the physical energy consumption caused by going to the mall to shop. It can be seen that online shopping can facilitate consumers' purchases, reduce the trouble of the purchasing process (online shopping basically adopts home delivery), reduce the labor intensity of consumers, save physical strength, all of which can satisfy consumers' motivation for convenience.

2. Low-Price Motivation

The low-price motivation is a consumer motivation that pursues low prices for goods. One of the important reasons why online shopping has a strong vitality is that the prices of goods sold online are lower than those in physical stores. Because selling products through the internet can reduce the middle links such as dealers and agents, thereby reducing channel costs, the prices of the same goods online are often lower than those in supermarkets and malls, and many online consumers adopt online shopping for this reason.

3. Performance Motivation

Performance motivation refers to the consumer motivation to promote and boast about oneself through the purchase of goods. At present, most internet users are young and highly educated. These young people are in the transition from adolescence to middle age, with the immature psychology of adolescents coexisting with the mature psychology of middle-aged people. Self-expression is their psychological need in consumption. Therefore, they prefer goods that can reflect their individuality, often associating the goods they buy with their personal character, ideals, identity, profession, interests, etc. Young people like to pursue novelty and emphasize individuality, and are unwilling to fall into "mass production", and their consumption psychology of "being different" is stronger than "pursuing popularity". The products offered online include many novel products, that is, new products or fashion products, and these products are generally not available or not easy to buy in the local traditional market. Therefore, online shopping can easily meet their requirements, that is, it can meet their needs to show their individuality and different tastes.

4.2.2 Analysis of Factors Affecting Online Consumer Purchases

1. Product Characteristics

The online market is different from the traditional market, and the consumption demand characteristics of online consumers are also different from the traditional market, which leads to not all goods are suitable for online sales. The pursuit of fashion and novelty of goods is an important purchasing motivation for many online consumers, especially young consumers. Therefore, the products sold online generally need to consider the novelty of the product. If the product is a new product or a fashion product, it can attract the attention of online consumers.

2. Product Price

From the consumer's point of view, price is not the only factor that determines consumer purchases, but it is a factor that consumers must consider when buying goods, and it is a very important factor. For general goods, the price often shows an inverse relationship with the quantity demanded. The same goods, the lower the price, the greater the consumer's demand, and the greater the company's sales. One of the important reasons why online shopping has vitality is that the prices of goods sold online are generally lower. Words like "free shipping", "clearance", and "seckill" on shopping websites can more easily attract these consumers.

3. Sense of Security

The security of online shopping, including the degree of leakage of personal information and privacy, will affect online shopping. Consumers are also worried that the goods purchased online cannot get effective after-sales service. In addition, many online consumers feel that the current online payment system is either too complicated and not easy to popularize, or lacks security, and needs to disclose real names, addresses, and contact information during registration, worrying about being leaked by the website. For this reason, the goods with a large transaction volume in current online shopping are mainly concentrated in books, daily necessities, audio-visual products, clothing, shoes and hats, etc., and the consumption amount is not high. For high-value goods such as jewelry and cars, many consumers are cautious. All of these have greatly restricted the development of online consumption.

4.2.3 Trend of Change in Online Consumer Behavior

1. More Obvious Consumer Individuality

Online consumers have a wide range of interests and are deeply interested in many emerging things, such as online games, online investments, etc. With the rapid development of e-commerce, the original online consumer group, mainly young people, is gradually changing, with more middle-aged and elderly people joining the ranks of online consumption and becoming an increasingly important force. More online consumers advocate personalized consumption and hope to get goods or services different from other consumers. For example, in mid-July 2013, iQiyi PC client was able to recommend personalized video content. As soon as this move came out, it was highly praised by the majority of netizens, and many people became loyal paid members of iQiyi.

2. Higher Demand for Product Quality

Online consumers can not only meet their actual shopping needs online, but also obtain a lot of additional information and enjoy the fun that traditional stores do not have. At the same time, more consumers hope to have more convenient channels and lower prices to buy better quality goods. This is mainly based on two psychological pursuits: one is that the work pressure is high and the time schedule is very tight, consumers expect to save as much time and labor cost as possible, the purchase channel is more convenient, but the requirements for product quality are not vague. These consumers have a higher income level and are the main purchasing group for high-end products and imported goods. The other is that they have more discretionary time and hope to find lower prices through online shopping to achieve psychological satisfaction. Such consumers will spend a lot of time on the Internet to compare goods and prices, and will stay up all night for a certain e-commerce shopping festival. This kind of consumer seeking low prices is actually the backbone of online consumers.

3. Mobile Shopping is Becoming Mainstream

According to the "53rd China Internet Development Statistics Report" released by the China Internet Network Information Center, in 2023, China's mobile Internet access traffic reached 3015 billion GB, a year-on-year increase of 15.2%; as of December 2023, the scale of Chinese mobile Internet users reached 1.091 billion, an increase of 25.62 million compared to December 2022, and the proportion of Internet users using mobile phones to access the Internet was 99.9%. This all shows that mobile shopping has become a mainstream trend. In the era of mobile Internet, users' acceptance of mobile APPs is obviously faster than expected, for the following reasons: the rapid development of the number of mobile phone users and mobile Internet users in China; the widespread popularity of cheap smartphones and tablets; the increase in Internet speed and the reduction in wireless broadband tariffs; traditional e-commerce has laid the foundation for the development of mobile e-commerce.

4. Wider Application of O2O

O2O, or Online To Offline, simply means "pulling customers online and consuming offline". For the O2O model, its core concept is to guide online users to physical stores, provide high-quality services by the entity, realize online payment through the Internet, provide real-time consumption data to merchants, and then accurately push the merchant's product information to consumers. This model is the best way for service-oriented and especially experiential products, which is quite different from the concept of traditional e-commerce. Traditional e-commerce relies on the network to complete product purchases to final use, lacking the participation of merchants. O2O drives offline transactions through online promotion and transaction engines to increase the participation of merchants and the experience of users. The value generated by this integration is astonishing. And the data analysis based on this provides an inexhaustible driving force for continuous development. E-commerce is mainly composed of information flow, capital flow, logistics, and business flow. The characteristic of O2O is to put information flow and capital flow online, and put logistics and business flow offline. At present, the O2O model has been widely used in online tourism, real estate, ticket booking, mobile Internet, catering, car rental, electronic coupons, luxury goods, and many other fields.

5. Live Shopping is Emerging

According to the "53rd China Internet Development Statistics Report" released by the China Internet Network Information Center, as of December 2023, the scale of China's online live streaming users reached 816 million, an increase of 65.01 million from December 2022, accounting for 74.7% of the total netizens; among them, the scale of e-commerce live streaming users was 597 million, an increase of 82.67 million from December 2022, accounting for 54.7% of the total netizens. Particularly, the 2022 pandemic has promoted the online migration of merchants, and live streaming applications have fully played their roles in marketing and entertainment. Live streaming e-commerce represented by Douyin, Taobao, etc. has emerged. Live streaming platforms have attracted many internet celebrities, brands, and professional institutions to enter their live streaming ecosystem, including Yaowang Network, Oriental Selection, Make a Friend, etc. Overall, the scale of live streaming e-commerce users still has a large growth space, live streaming e-commerce has become the new normal of e-commerce, the "people-goods-field" range of live streaming e-commerce is rapidly expanding, becoming the "standard configuration" of e-commerce. From the perspective of live streaming categories, the advantages of popular consumer goods such as clothing, daily necessities, food and beauty are obvious, and the trend of category richness is obvious.

4.3 Cross-Border E-Commerce Consumer Analysis

4.3.1 Portrait of Chinese Cross-Border E-Commerce Consumers

1. Consumers Show Significant "Three Highs" Characteristics

Compared with the group of online shopping users in China, cross-border e-commerce consumers show "three highs" characteristics, namely high age, high education, and high income, which are significantly different from the overall characteristics of Chinese online shopping consumers and also different from the characteristics of Chinese internet users. The proportion of Chinese cross-border e-commerce consumer groups in the 26–40 age range is 74.7%. Compared with Chinese online shopping consumer groups, cross-border e-commerce consumers are older, especially those aged 31–40. The proportion of users is higher than the overall online shopping users. In addition, the proportion of consumers with a bachelor's degree or above is 74.6%, and those with high school or below are less than 5%, which is also higher than the overall education level of online shopping users. The most consumers have a monthly income of over 10,000 yuan, accounting for more than 25%, which is also significantly higher than the overall online shopping users. The "three highs" characteristics of cross-border e-commerce consumer groups also represent their higher consumption capacity.

2. Consumers Have a High Willingness to Buy

Among the cross-border e-commerce consumer groups, more than half are employees of enterprises and institutions, and there are more general staff, their work and income are relatively stable, the work pressure and intensity are not very high, they have more spare time, and have the energy and time to choose online channels for cross-border purchases. Most consumers are married with children, more than half of the consumers have one child, their life status is relatively stable, initially most of them buy maternal and child products through cross-border e-commerce channels, this part of the consumer group has a strong willingness to buy, and they are also the main consumer group of cross-border e-commerce.

3. The Consumer Group Has Significant Characteristics, with a High Proportion of Women

The characteristics of cross-border e-commerce consumers in China are distinct, such as digital men and beauty women; the young prefer personal care, while the elderly love health care. This is significantly different from the characteristics of online shopping consumers in our country. Male cross-border e-commerce consumers are more willing to buy maternal and infant products and 3C digital products, while females are more willing to buy cosmetics, personal care, and maternal and infant products. The 31–35 age group is the peak of urban population birth, and this age group has a very strong demand for maternal and infant products; the group over 60 years old has a higher demand for food and health products. In terms of income, low-income groups prefer to buy special price products, high-income groups shop more frequently, spend more on average per month, like to buy branded products, have a higher demand for clothing, hats and shoes, and are easily attracted by online advertisements. Not only that, among the cross-border online shopping groups in China, it shows a predominantly female characteristic, which is also significantly different from the overall Chinese online shopping users and the online user group.

4. Consumers Are Mostly Distributed in the Eastern Coastal Areas

The distribution of cross-border e-commerce consumer groups is most dense in the eastern coastal areas, and there are also many cross-border e-commerce consumer groups in Jiangsu, Beijing, and Shandong. This is related to the economic development, income level, consumption concept, and exposure to new things in the eastern coastal provinces. These factors have collectively stimulated the consumer groups in the eastern coastal areas to choose online channels to buy goods across borders. With the development and maturity of the cross-border e-commerce market, some new trends are emerging in the Chinese cross-border e-commerce group; the consumer group is extending from large cities to medium-sized cities, especially the group size of second and third-tier cities is growing significantly, and it is also expanding from the eastern coastal areas to the central and western regions.

5. The Scale of Consumers in Third and Fourth-Tier Markets is Huge

The cross-border e-commerce consumption capacity of consumers in third and fourth-tier cities is significantly higher than that in first and second-tier cities, mainly because the number of physical stores selling foreign goods in these cities is far less than that in first and second-tier cities. A large amount of cross-border e-commerce consumption demand has to be met through cross-border e-commerce, which also reflects that the middle and high-end consumption capacity in these cities cannot be ignored. In addition, the rural cross-border e-commerce consumer group should not be underestimated. According to data from JD Global Purchase, rural consumers are gradually choosing cross-border e-commerce platforms to buy foreign goods, with maternal and infant products, watches, small appliances, and health products being the preferred categories.

4.3.2 *Characteristics of Chinese Cross-Border E-Commerce Consumer Behavior*

1. The Scale of Cross-Border e-commerce Consumers Has Surged, but the Usage Rate is Still not High

By 2023, the scale of cross-border e-commerce users in China will reach 189 million; the scale of online shopping users in China during the same period will be 915 million, and the usage rate of cross-border e-commerce consumers will be 20.66%, which has increased from previous years. The base number of cross-border e-commerce users is becoming larger and shows a trend of annual growth, but whether it is the overall scale or the proportion in the scale of online shopping netizens is still not high. This also shows that the usage rate of the Chinese cross-border e-commerce consumer group is low, and there is still a large market space.

2. Cross-Border e-commerce Consumption is Similar to Daily Internet Usage Time

The time distribution of cross-border online shopping is generally consistent with the daily internet usage trends of online users, but there are also some differences. Overall, the time for cross-border online shopping develops with the internet usage habits of online users, with a higher frequency of use during daytime working hours, from 9 am to 6 pm, the time distribution trend is relatively high. However, the time distribution curve for cross-border online shopping is slightly steeper than the internet usage time of netizens, and there are three peaks at 10:00, 14:00, and 22:00, and the late-night time period is also a frequent occurrence of cross-border online shopping, and it is even more active. These are the significant differences between cross-border online shopping and the daily internet usage habits of netizens.

3. Guidance and Recommendations from Acquaintances Have a Significant Impact on the Choice of Cross-Border e-commerce Platforms

Mr. Fei Xiaotong once proposed the concept of "acquaintance society" in "Rural China" to describe interpersonal communication and relationships in traditional Chinese society. When consuming or shopping, people are deeply influenced by the opinions and behaviors of neighbors, friends, relatives, and acquaintances around them, and they are also more likely to consult or refer to the opinions and views of the acquaintance group around them. In the early stages of cross-border e-commerce and the market for overseas shopping and purchasing agents, Chinese cross-border e-commerce consumers often shop for foreign goods through relatives, friends, classmates, and other groups living or studying abroad. When contacting, understanding, and visiting cross-border e-commerce websites, Chinese cross-border e-commerce consumers need some guidance, which is mainly related to the consumers' lack of understanding of new things and the current situation of the popularity of cross-border e-commerce still needs to be developed. In addition to shopping guide websites and recommendations from friends and relatives, social media is also an important way for Chinese cross-border e-commerce consumers to understand cross-border e-commerce websites. In addition, Chinese cross-border e-commerce consumers also have a certain degree of targeting when visiting cross-border e-commerce websites, and the proportion of visiting cross-border e-commerce websites through independent search, direct input of URLs, personal favorites, etc., is relatively high.

4. The Demand Characteristics of the Cross-Border Shopping Consumer Group Are Distinct and Significant

Cross-border e-commerce consumers have a higher awareness of brands and quality requirements, which is a reflection of this group's pursuit of quality life and a direct demand for enthusiasm for cross-border online shopping. Differentiated, diversified, and personalized demands are also the main reasons for consumers to choose cross-border e-commerce. Especially after segmenting the cross-border e-commerce consumer group, it is found that the demand characteristics of different segmented groups are obvious and the differences are significant. With the gradual popularization of cross-border e-commerce, more and more consumers' purchasing needs are gradually shifting from standard products to personalized, differentiated products. In addition to maternal and infant products, cosmetics, digital goods, and other standard explosive goods, some limited, niche, and even global first-release products that boast personality are also popular with consumers. The age range of 31–35 is the peak of urban population birth, and the demand for maternal and infant products in this age group is very strong. Male consumer groups prefer maternal and infant products and 3C digital products, women are more willing to buy cosmetics and maternal and infant products, young groups have a strong desire to buy cosmetics, and older groups have a significant demand for food and health products.

5. Stimulated by the New Model of Cross-Border E-Commerce, New Consumption Habits Are Gradually Emerging

Starting in 2020, almost all mainstream overseas social media platforms have added live streaming features, including Facebook, Instagram, YouTube, etc. In the first half of 2022, TikTok ranked first in overseas App Store and Google. The download volume on Play is nearly 600 million times, an increase of 88.7% over the same period last year. In the mature development stage of cross-border e-commerce, cross-border live-streaming e-commerce, as one of the innovative models, is receiving more and more attention and love from consumers. Under the stimulation of new models such as cross-border live-streaming e-commerce, some new consumption habits of cross-border online shopping consumers are constantly emerging, such as: consumers prefer the fun and immersion of live-streaming shopping, which helps them to understand product information more comprehensively and find the most cost-effective purchase method in a variety of promotional discounts.

4.3.3 Cross-Border E-Commerce Product Consumption Characteristics

1. Traditional Products Turn from Blue Ocean to Red Ocean

The predecessor of cross-border e-commerce originated from overseas purchasing and acquaintances bringing goods from overseas, mainly for the following reasons: ①There are no related products in China; ②It is difficult to buy related products in China; ③The domestic price of the product is higher than the foreign price; ④The quality of related domestic products is not as good as foreign products. In the global cross-border e-commerce market, traditional products represented by consumer electronics, household appliances, clothing and shoes, media products, food and beverages, cosmetics, etc., are mainstream, and consumers in many regions have a general demand for them. These mainstream products have become the top five best-selling products in cross-border e-commerce in most countries. With the promotion of cross-border e-commerce, it is becoming more and more convenient for consumers to buy products from overseas markets. The Internet has broken the asymmetry of information, and consumers can quickly obtain relevant product information through e-commerce trading platforms. Major cross-border e-commerce companies are stimulating the intensification of market competition, especially using price competition as the main means, trying to quickly seize market share in the early stages of development. The result of vicious price competition has directly led to the rapid transition of traditional products from the blue ocean to the red ocean, with traditional products such as consumer electronics, household appliances, clothing and shoes, cosmetics, food and beverages, and infant products being the most obvious.

2. New Products Emerge, Leading to a New Blue Ocean

With the expansion of cross-border e-commerce globally, the fierce competition of traditional products has led to a sharp reduction in profits, consumers' demand for product types is also increasing, and merchants are also involved in more types of products. Many factors are driving the emergence of new products, which are growing significantly and gradually becoming a new blue ocean in the cross-border e-commerce market. For example, e-cigarette products have become a new growth point, the demand for wig products has surged, and the demand for home products has increased. According to monitoring data from the China E-commerce Research Center, some new products have entered the top five best-seller list, such as jewelry and watches in the US market, entertainment products in the Canadian market, tourism and cultural products in the French market, event tickets in the German market, tourism products in the Singapore market, toys and games in the Indian market, gardening tools and crafts in the Polish market, etc. Not only that, fashion accessories, outdoor products, luggage products, and car accessories have also become faster-growing new products in the cross-border e-commerce market.

3. The Regional Differences of Products Are More Prominent

Traditional products have become best-sellers in most countries, but upon closer analysis, they also show regional differences. Globally, the regional differences in products are more pronounced, mainly manifested in differences between different regions, different levels of economic development, differences between different language regions within the same region, and differences between different countries within the same region. For example, there are different best-selling products in regions such as North America, Europe, Asia–Pacific, and Latin America, differences between developed regions such as North America and Europe and developing regions such as Latin America, and different best-selling products in different language countries in Europe such as the UK, France, and Germany, and the best-selling products in the United States and Canada in North America are also different. For example: consumers in Russia, Poland, Ukraine, Turkey, and Australia purchase more Chinese kitchen and restaurant supplies; buyers in countries such as Russia, Ukraine, Poland, Belarus, and Turkey prefer to buy Chinese mobile phones and electronic accessories; buyers in countries such as Russia, Poland, Ukraine, Turkey, Australia, and Spain purchase more Chinese smart products, including smart bracelets, smart glasses, smart health products, etc.; buyers in countries such as Russia, Ukraine, Poland, Australia, Kazakhstan, etc. love to buy Chinese skirts and clothing.

4.3.4 Cross-Border E-Commerce Consumer Evaluation

1. Quality and Price Are the Main Factors Affecting Consumers' Cross-Border Online Shopping

The main considerations for consumers choosing cross-border online shopping are guaranteed product quality and low product prices. The guarantee of product quality is a demand change that accompanies consumers' development of the online shopping market. The primary factor for consumers to initially choose online shopping or cross-border online shopping is to consider the price of the product, especially if it is lower than the price of the offline physical channel; as the consumption concept becomes more mature and is affected by the shopping experience of low-priced and poor-quality products, the product price is no longer the primary factor considered by consumers, and it has turned into a demand for product quality, focusing on the quality assurance of the purchased goods. This consumer demand also affects cross-border online shopping. This determines that when consumers choose cross-border online shopping, the primary consideration is product quality, and they are unwilling to buy inferior products again, even if they are inferior products purchased at low prices.

Although the product price is no longer the primary factor for consumers to choose cross-border online shopping, it is still a major factor for consumers to choose cross-border online shopping. This phenomenon is significantly related to the substitution effect of online and offline shopping. Consumers are more willing to buy online because the price of goods is lower than offline channels. For cross-border online shopping behavior, consumers also mainly consider that the price of goods purchased through this channel is lower than offline physical channels, such as overseas shopping and purchasing agents. The main reason for the repeated bans is that their prices are cheap. This is mainly because the cost of online channels is lower than offline physical channels, which in turn drives the product prices of cross-border online shopping channels to be lower than offline physical channels.

In addition, there are some factors why consumers are willing to buy goods through cross-border e-commerce platforms, such as not being able to buy on domestic websites, product brand preferences, and product richness. These factors also have a high degree of influence on consumers' cross-border e-commerce shopping preferences.

2. The Impact of Logistics and Payment Links on Consumers' Cross-Border Online Shopping Has Decreased

In the early stages of cross-border e-commerce development, cross-border logistics and cross-border payment links became the main factors affecting consumers' cross-border online shopping. With the development of cross-border e-commerce itself, especially the continuous development and improvement of information technology, digital technology, and network technology, technical bottlenecks including cross-border payments and cross-border logistics have been effectively resolved. Cross-border logistics has emerged with many new models, which are effectively applied to the logistics link of cross-border e-commerce, improving the timeliness of cross-border logistics, reducing the cost of cross-border logistics, and increasing consumer satisfaction with the logistics link. Cross-border payments, with the promotion of electronic payments and mobile payments, are widely used in cross-border e-commerce transactions and are no longer a problem restricting cross-border e-commerce transactions. Therefore, the impact of logistics and payment environment on consumers' choice of cross-border online shopping has decreased, and it is no longer the core factor affecting consumers' choice of cross-border online shopping.

3. The Delivery Speed that Consumers Care Most About Still Needs to Be Improved

Cross-border e-commerce platforms, cross-border logistics, cross-border payments and other links have greatly improved compared to the early stages of cross-border e-commerce development, and consumer satisfaction ratings have also improved. In cross-border e-commerce transactions, consumers value product quality, product price, payment security, website reputation, product variety, payment convenience, website popularity, delivery speed, etc. In terms of cross-border e-commerce platforms, cross-border payments, and cross-border logistics, consumer satisfaction ratings are high. Therefore, consumers rate product quality, product price, payment security, website reputation, product variety, payment convenience, and website popularity highly. However, consumers do not rate the delivery speed of cross-border e-commerce transactions highly, and generally believe that there is still a lot of room for improvement in delivery speed. The final delivery of goods and the last mile of logistics have become the pain points with low ratings from consumers in cross-border e-commerce, which is also one of the main reasons affecting consumers' choice of cross-border e-commerce for cross-border online shopping.

4.4 Differences in Cross-Border E-Commerce Consumer Behavior

4.4.1 Comparison of Consumers Between Overseas Platforms and Domestic Platforms

Cross-border e-commerce platforms are the medium and place for cross-border goods transactions. When consumers make cross-border online purchases, they mostly choose cross-border e-commerce platforms, whether they are overseas or domestic cross-border e-commerce shopping websites, which reflects the behavior differences of cross-border e-commerce consumers. For Chinese consumers, overseas websites include Amazon, eBay, Wish, Lazada, AliExpress, etc.; domestic websites include JD Global, Xiaohongshu, Kaola Haigou, etc. Although different cross-border e-commerce platforms have some differences, such as different types attracting different consumers, overall, the consumer differences shown by overseas and domestic cross-border e-commerce platforms are quite obvious, as shown in Table 4.1. Consumers choose to shop on overseas cross-border e-commerce platforms mainly because they value the guaranteed product quality and affordable prices, which are significantly higher than other factors; consumers also believe that overseas platforms have high website popularity and good reputation. Consumers' positive reviews of domestic cross-border e-commerce platforms are mainly reflected in payment security, affordable prices, and convenient payment; while their evaluations of packaging completeness, delivery personnel attitude, and customer service attitude are generally average.

By comparing consumer reviews on overseas and domestic platforms, we found that overseas platforms are superior to domestic platforms in terms of "guaranteed product quality" and "affordable prices". However, consumer reviews on other aspects of overseas platforms are generally lower than those of domestic platforms, especially in terms of payment, logistics, and customer service. Overall, consumers rate domestic cross-border e-commerce platforms better than overseas platforms, especially in terms of payment, logistics, and customer service, which are the strengths of domestic platforms. However, domestic platforms are significantly weaker than overseas platforms in terms of product quality, which is related to consumers' perception that

Table 4.1 Consumer perception of domestic and foreign cross-border e-commerce platforms

Item	Overseas platform		Domestic platform		Overseas platform-Domestic platform	
	Reason[a]	Main reason[b]	Reason[a]	Main reason[b]	Reason[a]	Main reason[b]
Guaranteed commodity quality	51.30%	38.30%	34.60%	15.30%	16.70%	23.00%
Affordable price	43.80%	16.30%	36.30%	11.60%	7.50%	4.70%
High website popularity	26.30%	4.20%	31.30%	5.00%	–5.00%	–0.80%
Good reputation of the website	24.20%	7.90%	29.40%	3.20%	–5.20%	4.70%
Rich variety of goods	21.30%	4.20%	31.50%	5.30%	–10.20%	–1.10%
More promotional activities	21.30%	2.90%	30.20%	5.60%	–8.90%	–2.70%
Payment security	16.70%	6.70%	40.00%	11.90%	–23.30%	–5.20%
Convenient payment	15.40%	2.10%	35.40%	5.60%	–20.00%	–3.50%
Sufficient inventory of goods	15.00%	1.70%	23%	3.30%	–8.00%	–1.60%
Fast product update	14.20%	1.70%	23.30%	2.20%	–9.10%	–0.50%
Payment diversity	13.30%	1.70%	27.30%	3%	–14.00%	–1.30%
Clear and verifiable order	12.10%	1.30%	29.50%	3.20%	–17.40%	–1.90%
Customer service staff had a good attitude	11.70%	0.80%	19.30%	1.80%	–7.60%	–1.00%
Various ways of customer service communication	11.70%	1.30%	20.70%	2.10%	–9.00%	–0.80%
Fast customer service response	11.30%	1.30%	21.70%	2.10%	–10.40%	–0.80%
Good membership policy	10.00%	1.70%	20.70%	2.20%	–10.70%	–0.50%
Complete and beautiful package	9.20%	0.40%	19.90%	1.70%	–10.70%	–1.30%
The delivery staff had a good attitude	8.80%	2.10%	19.30%	1.60%	–10.50%	0.50%
Fast delivery	8.30%	0.80%	25.00%	3.50%	–16.70%	–2.70%

(continued)

Table 4.1 (continued)

Item	Overseas platform		Domestic platform		Overseas platform-Domestic platform	
	Reason[a]	Main reason[b]	Reason[a]	Main reason[b]	Reason[a]	Main reason[b]
Website page search is convenient	7.50%	1.30%	22.20%	3.20%	−14.70%	−1.90%
Convenient return and exchange	7.50%	1.70%	24.50%	3.40%	−17.00%	−1.70%

[a]"Reason" refers to the fact that consumers choose the "project" as the factor for evaluating the platform
[b]"Main reason" means that consumers choose the "project" as the main factor for evaluating the platform

overseas product quality is better than domestic. Moreover, overseas platforms pay more attention to brand building, resulting in better reputation and word-of-mouth.

4.4.2 Cross-Border E-Commerce Consumer Behavior in Different Countries

1. North America

North America usually refers to regions such as the United States, Canada, and Greenland. It is the most economically developed region in the world, with its GDP ranking first in the world for many years. The United States and Canada are the most important countries in North America, and this book focuses on them.

(1) United States

The United States is currently the world's largest economy. Affected by the pandemic in early 2020, its GDP slightly declined, but the economy gradually recovered from the second half of 2020. The United States has a population of 332 million, making it the third most populous country in the world. Of these, 50.5% are female and 49.5% are male; the median age is 38.3, indicating a relatively young population. The 2020 census results released by the U.S. Census Bureau show that the adult population (18 years and older) grew by 10.1% over the past decade, reaching 258.3 million, accounting for 77.9% of the total population; the population aged 16 to 64 reached 211 million, accounting for 63.6%. The large population base and more than half of the mature population ratio mean strong consumption capacity and market. According to Statista data, the per capita e-commerce consumption in the United States in 2020 was $2,400, ranking second in the world. The country's immigrant nature has resulted in a diverse racial and cultural population structure. The census results also show that the current total population of the United States is 57.8% white, 18.7% Hispanic, 12.4% African American, and 6% Asian. According to a UGA report, the purchasing power of minority ethnic groups is growing faster than that of white consumers. Nielsen's statistics also show that African Americans have made significant contributions to the overall market. In some key product categories, their spending accounts for more than 50% of total spending.

Datareportal's statistics show that as of January 2021, the United States had 298.8 million internet users, an increase of 3.7% year-on-year, resulting in an internet penetration rate of 90.0%. Social media users reached 240 million, accounting for 72.3% of the total population. The developed internet infrastructure and social media provide a solid foundation for the development of the e-commerce market. The habit of heavy use of social media by consumers, coupled with the increasingly mature shopping environment on social media, gives cross-border social e-commerce greater possibilities. Datareportal data shows that Americans spend about 7 h a day on the internet on average, with social media accounting for 2 h of this time. According to a study by Visiture, 75% of people admit that they will make a purchase after seeing something on social media; 90% of people say they will turn to social media to help make purchasing decisions.

According to Jungle According to Scout data, after the outbreak of the pandemic in 2020, up until the second quarter of 2021, 48% of consumers reported that their consumption remained unchanged, 29% reported a decrease in consumption, and 23% reported an increase in consumption. At the same time, financial strain was a major reason for the decrease in consumer spending. During the pandemic, 23% of people obtained loans in various forms, and 27% were heavily reliant on government economic stimulus policies. Financial progress and pandemic prevention requirements prompted Americans to lean towards cheaper, safer online consumption. On one hand, the number of purchases at physical retail stores like Best Buy, Target, Home Depot, Lowe's, etc., significantly decreased, while online platforms of large retailers such as Amazon, Walmart, eBay, etc., remained strong. On the other hand, data shows that when shopping online, 45% of consumers use browser extensions or plugins to search for discounts, and 33% of consumers look for second-hand products. After a reduction in consumer spending, more and more Americans choose to prioritize the purchase of necessities, with 33% of consumers buying more daily necessities and 28% buying more cleaning supplies. However, 21% of consumers increased their spending on beauty and personal care, pet supplies, and 20% of consumers increased their spending on toys and games, home and kitchen supplies, gardening and outdoor, crafts and sewing products, etc. In addition, the pandemic has prompted consumers to buy more health products. Data shows that 23% of consumers will increase their spending on vitamins and dietary supplements, and 18% of consumers will increase their spending on fitness equipment. Overall, the home economy is still hot, health needs are upgraded, and outdoor needs are rebounding. Americans care most about the quality of goods, followed by packaging, and finally the price. Therefore, the quality of the product is key to entering the American market. In the American market, there is a large price difference between high, medium, and low-end goods. For example, a mid-to-high-end suit retails for 40–50 dollars, while a low-end one costs less than 5 dollars. Americans pay great attention to packaging, which is on par with product quality. Therefore, the packaging of export goods must be novel, elegant, beautiful, and generous, capable of producing a comfortable and satisfying effect, in order to attract buyers. Many Chinese crafts have not been able to enter the American supermarket due to packaging issues. For example, the famous Yixing purple clay pot, which is only packaged in yellow straw paper, with 80 pots in a large box, padded with scrap paper or straw, is very simple and is considered low-end goods in the eyes of buyers, and can only be sold in small shops or stalls. This shows how important packaging is. In addition, each season has a sales peak for product turnover. If the sales season is missed, the goods will have to be discounted. The sales seasons for American department stores and supermarkets are: January to May for spring, July to September for early autumn and back-to-school period, mainly selling student supplies; September to October for autumn, November to December for holidays, namely the Christmas period. This is also the tax refund period, and people often take the opportunity to purchase goods and buy Christmas gifts. At this time, stores across the United States are bustling, and popular goods will quickly sell out. Sales during this period account for about 1/3 of the annual total. Americans have a wide range of online times, due to the United States spanning three time zones, so buyers in different time zones have different online shopping times. In order to increase the attention rate of the goods posted, sellers should actively summarize and choose a time period when buyers' online shopping times are concentrated to carry out targeted work. (2) Canada. Canada is vast and sparsely populated, with a high level of wealth. According to World Bank data, Canada's GDP in 2020 was approximately 1.64 trillion US dollars, ranking ninth globally, with a per capita of about 43,000 US dollars, ranking 20th globally. In 2020, affected by the pandemic, data from the International Monetary Fund showed that Canada's economy shrank by 5.4% overall. Among them, household expenditure in 2020 decreased by 6.1% overall. Canadians are very receptive to cross-border shopping, and a report from eTail Canada shows that nearly half of Canadians' online shopping is done on foreign websites. Among them, 56% of Canadian online shoppers turn to the United States, and 35% turn to China. However, to support domestic enterprises, Canadians have begun to turn to domestic e-commerce to buy goods. Data from the 2020 Canadian E-commerce Report shows that the proportion of cross-border shopping dropped from 75% in 2019 to 67%; CIRA's Canadian Internet Profile Report shows that 71% of Canadians say that when they have a choice, they prefer to shop online from Canadian retailers.

Canada's e-commerce infrastructure is highly developed. Data from Datareportal shows that Canada has 45.63 million internet users, accounting for 94% of the total population; social media users are 32.20 million, accounting for 84.9% of the total population. According to PayPal Canada's "Trends and Expenditures: PayPal Canada 2021 Consumer Shopping Research", 47% of Canadian social media users have completed purchases through various social media platforms; according to Canada Post's "2020 Canadian E-commerce Report" data, 55% of e-commerce sellers sell online through social media, of which 95% use Facebook, 69% use Instagram, and only 14% use Twitter. At the same time, according to data from the United States

International Trade Administration, in 2021, Canada had more than 27 million e-commerce users, accounting for 72.5% of the population, and it is expected to grow to 77.6% by 2025. In 2020, Canadians spent 52 billion Canadian dollars on e-commerce, an increase of 20.7% from 2019, and 48% of Canadians use e-commerce platforms more frequently than before the pandemic, and their online shopping expenditure has also increased compared to before the pandemic.

According to data from Statistics Canada, the online shopping rate of all age groups is over 50%, with the 25–44 age group having the highest online shopping rate, at 95%; the 15–24 age group is next, at 90%; the 45–64 age group is at 83%; and even those over 65 have a rate of 55%. According to the "2021 Canadian Online Shopper Research", as the penetration rate of e-commerce continues to increase, Canadian consumers have higher expectations and requirements for the customer experience, focusing on high-quality sales services and after-sales support. Setting up a free customer service hotline or online customer service is very effective in maintaining customer relationships. Canadians value a simple, affordable, and convenient return process. When consumers choose sellers, free returns are the biggest influencing factor considered besides free delivery. The report also shows that the categories that Canadians buy the most are clothing and accessories, followed by computer electronics, with beauty products ranking third. Other hot-selling categories include shoes, home and garden, health products, home decor, sports equipment, toys, office supplies, jewelry, maternity and baby products, pet supplies. At the same time, Canada has a long winter lasting from six to nine months, a vast landscape, and abundant outdoor resources, and the whole nation loves outdoor sports. Therefore, winter ice and snow sports, skiing, snowboarding and their peripheral products, such as ski suits, ski goggles, ski socks, etc., are all hot sellers. In terms of consumer marketing preferences, young Canadian consumers are gradually dominating on social media websites. They respond more quickly to mobile advertising, especially social media advertising. In addition, 38% of respondents said that they were influenced by promotional emails when choosing retailers, and 16% of respondents said they were influenced by advertisements and flyers in the mail.

2. Europe

Europe is traditionally divided into five regions: Northern Europe, Western Europe, Central Europe, Southern Europe, and Eastern Europe. In 2020, Europe's total economic output was $20.82 trillion, ranking third globally and accounting for approximately 24.6% of the world's total GDP. Among them, the country with the highest GDP in Europe is Germany, ranking fourth globally, followed by the UK, France, Italy, and Russia. In terms of total population, as of October 2020, the total population of Europe was approximately 745 million people, with Russia leading with 143 million people and Germany second with 82.29 million people. However, many European countries are currently facing issues of declining birth rates and an aging population. There are many countries in Europe, and they have vastly different habits in terms of home life and online shopping. According to Statcounter data, in terms of shopping preferences, 32% of Swedes love to buy health and beauty products online, and they like to shop at H&M. Dutch people mainly buy travel and event tickets online, and they prefer domestic retailers like Bol.com. French people like to shop online and often use "online experience" services. British people like to buy fashion and sports goods online, Belgians like to buy clothes and appliances, and Poles like to buy furniture. On the purchasing website, Poles, Romanians, Turks, Hungarians, and Swedes tend to buy goods from domestic e-commerce, with this ratio exceeding 90%. In Germany, Amazon occupies a portion of online sales, and the local Otto is also the most popular e-commerce platform. Smaller countries like Cyprus, Malta, Luxembourg, and Iceland prefer to shop abroad. In terms of purchasing habits, Italians and Spaniards are more impulsive, making online purchase decisions in less than an hour, while French people consider more and on average take 8 h to decide to buy a pair of sports shoes. The average order time for Europeans is 2 h and 20 min. For platforms looking to break into the European market, during the gap from adding to the shopping cart to purchasing, they can offer special discounts or discounts to potential customers via email to close the deal.

(1) Germany

Germany is a highly developed industrial country, with the largest economy in Europe. The level of urbanization in Germany is high, with the urban population accounting for 76.3% of the total population and a population density of 240 people per square kilometer. The average age in Germany is currently 45.7 years, making it a relatively middle-aged country. According to a report by Statcounter, in 2020, 95% of Germans were internet users, with over 50 million people using the internet daily, each user spending an average of 182 min online per day, and more than half of the population using mobile networks. In recent years, the number of online shoppers in Germany has been increasing annually, and in 2020, due to the impact of the pandemic, its growth rate reached 5.01%. In terms of e-commerce scale, Germany's e-commerce scale in 2020 was 83.3 billion euros. In terms of social media usage, about 38 million German users are active on social media, spending up to 3 h a day, mostly on Facebook, Pinterest, and Twitter. German consumers buy foreign products mainly for two reasons: one is that foreign products are cheaper, and the other is that they cannot find the products they want within Germany. The main categories of goods that Germans like to buy include clothing and footwear, culture and entertainment, medical supplies, home appliances and digital products, sports and leisure, furniture and decoration, audio and video products, beauty and skincare, etc. Interestingly, the category of food and groceries, which is very popular in the UK, is not very popular in Germany. German online shoppers prefer to visit German websites and websites with.de domains. According to a report by PostNord, Amazon is the largest e-commerce trading platform in Germany, followed by eBay. In terms of logistics preferences, Germans prefer daytime home delivery services, and nighttime home delivery services are also popular, but mailbox delivery services that do not require personal signatures are not widely accepted. Germans are meticulous and have high requirements for product details. If sellers want to enter the German cross-border e-commerce market, they need to pay attention to: setting up clear and detailed product pages, product prices, and a comprehensive return policy. In addition, having a local return address is very important, which can not only increase potential customers but also control return costs.

(2) United Kingdom

The UK's economy is second only to Germany, with a population of 67.2 million and a median age of 40.5 years. The UK is one of the most developed e-commerce markets in the world, with online sales accounting for 23% of the UK's total retail sales, far ahead of the United States. According to Internet World Stats data, as of the end of 2020, the UK's internet penetration rate was as high as 94.9%, of which about 92% of people have tried online shopping. According to Pattern's "2021 UK Consumer Shopping Trends Forecast", the pandemic will continue to drive the growth of online shopping in the UK, with 39% of Britons expected to increase their spending on non-food items online in 2021, while 30% of Britons will increase the number of items they buy on Amazon. In terms of social media usage, by age group, according to Statista data, the most popular platform among 15–25 year olds in the UK is Youtube, with a usage rate of 82%; for the 26–35 age group, Facebook is the most popular, with a usage rate of 82.5%; when the age group reaches 36–45, the usage rate of Facebook drops to less than 30%, and YouTube is only 13.2%. According to the E-commerce in Europe report, the top five categories that UK online shoppers were keen on in 2020 included clothing and footwear, culture and entertainment, food and drink, home appliances and digital products, and beauty and skincare. In terms of delivery methods, Britons prefer daytime home delivery services, accounting for 64%, in contrast, nighttime home delivery services only account for 11%. A free return policy is a major factor attracting Britons to shop. However, since it takes 6 days to receive a refund through online returns, this means that sellers need to solve the last mile delivery and return issues to meet customer expectations.

(3) France

France is a developed holiday destination, with the northeastern region influenced by German culture, and most of the southern region falling within the scope of Southern Europe. In 2020, France's domestic GDP was 2.6 trillion US dollars, the per capita GDP was 40,520.65 US dollars, the total population was 67.29 million, and the median age was 42.3 years. In 2020, France had 4,100 active online shoppers, making it the second-largest e-commerce market in Europe; France opened 17,400 new online stores, and e-commerce's share of the overall retail industry jumped from 9.8% in 2019 to 13.4% in 2020. Many local French retailers have developed and expanded their online businesses to mitigate the impact on their physical businesses, and with the promotion of services such as home delivery and online shopping pick-up, sales have grown by more than 50% year-on-year. As of the end of December 2020, France's internet penetration rate was about 92.3%, with a total of 60.42 million internet users. In France, YouTube is the most popular social media platform, followed by Facebook, and the usage rates of Instagram and WhatsApp are also high. The French are relatively romantic and fashionable, and clothing and footwear are the most popular categories for online shopping in France, followed by home appliances and digital products, sports and leisure, and culture and entertainment. The French online shopping group prefers to pick up at delivery points, accounting for 42%; daytime home delivery is also popular, accounting for about 25%. The French love shopping on e-commerce platforms, with Amazon being the largest e-commerce platform in the French market, followed by eBay. The local French Cdiscount ranks third and is also the largest e-commerce platform in France. The French are not very keen on cross-border online shopping, with about 60% of respondents saying they would only shop on local e-commerce platforms.

(4) Italy

Italy is one of the four major economies in Europe, but its economic growth has been sluggish in recent years. In 2020, Italy's domestic GDP was 1.65 trillion US dollars, the per capita GDP was 32,901 US dollars, the population was 59.64 million, and the median age was 47.3 years. The pandemic has brought growth opportunities to Italy's e-commerce market. According to PostNord's data, 37% of Italian respondents said that they increased their online shopping frequency during the pandemic, and many people who had never participated in online shopping also chose to buy basic necessities online. In 2020, 49.2 million people shopped online, and 32.1 million people made cross-border online purchases. In 2020, Italy's internet penetration rate was 81%. As of January 2021, Italy had 41 million social media users. Facebook is the favorite social media platform for Italians, followed by Instagram, which focuses on photo sharing, and LinkedIn, a professional social networking platform. According to PostNord's report, clothing and footwear are the first choice for Italians' online shopping, which is related to Italy's preference for fashion. Ranked second is home appliances and digital products, and third is culture and entertainment. In terms of logistics preferences, daytime home delivery service is the favorite delivery method for Italian online shopping consumers, with 70% of people choosing it, significantly higher than other logistics methods. Although mailbox delivery that does not require personal signature is ranked second, its proportion is only 9%. The proportions of other delivery methods are even lower. Similar to other European countries, Amazon is the largest e-commerce platform in Italy, with a traffic of 44.78% in 2021; eBay ranks second, with about 12.23% of the traffic. In contrast, the strength of Italy's local e-commerce platforms is relatively weak.

(5) Spain

In 2020, Spain's domestic GDP was 1.28 trillion US dollars, with a per capita GDP of 29,600 US dollars, a population of 47.4 million, and a median age of 44.9 years. Affected by the pandemic, Spain was one of the countries in the Eurozone that suffered the most severe recession in 2020. Spain is the 13th largest e-commerce market in the world and ranks fourth in the European e-commerce market. In 2020, Spain's e-commerce market grew by 35%, making it one of the fastest-growing markets in Europe. In 2021, 93% of people in Spain had access to the internet. According to a survey by the European Commission, 90% of Spaniards have online shopping experience, 71% have experience with cross-border e-commerce, especially with Chinese online stores. As many as 40% of respondents said they had purchased goods from Chinese e-commerce in the past year, 11% higher than the

European average. WhatsApp is the most commonly used social media in Spain, followed by Facebook and YouTube, with Instagram being the fastest-growing social media platform in terms of user numbers. For e-commerce sellers, social media advertising is a topic of great interest. Spaniards often buy clothing, shoes, household electronics, and books online. The largest segment of the market is fashion. In recent years, the prospects for the development of the video game industry in Spain have been very good, and game broadcasters have become the most popular profession among young Spaniards. Therefore, there is a high demand among young Spaniards for live streaming equipment, such as webcams and microphones, and monitors, headphones, and gaming chairs are also selling well. Spaniards prefer home delivery services when shopping online, especially daytime delivery services. Price has always been a key point of concern for Spaniards. When shopping online, Spaniards pay more attention to the cost-effectiveness of products. Spaniards like free gifts, no matter what the gift is, as long as they receive a free gift when shopping online, they will be happy. The phenomenon of online shopping abandonment is quite serious in Spain. On the one hand, it stems from price, and on the other hand, it stems from issues of confidence and trust. Some people may feel uneasy because they cannot see the product in person, and some people may hesitate because they need to enter personal detailed information when making online payments. To increase sales opportunities, sellers need to overcome potential trust issues, provide shoppers with a lot of product information, photos and customer reviews, and cooperate with trustworthy payment merchants. When doing cross-border e-commerce business in Spain, attention should also be paid to language settings. According to a study by OCU, nine out of ten Spaniards feel embarrassed when communicating in English. Therefore, it is necessary to set up Spanish for the website. The top three cross-border e-commerce platforms in Spain are Amazon, AliExpress, and eBay. In addition, Spain's e-commerce platforms include all-category e-commerce platforms, department stores, electronics, classified ads, sports and fashion, and other categories. This shows the diversity of Spaniards' online shopping needs.

(6) Russia

In 2020, Russia's domestic GDP was 1.48 trillion US dollars, the per capita GDP was 11,786 US dollars, the total population was 146 million, and the median age was 39.6 years. Russia is the largest country in the world by area and is a unified multiethnic country composed of 194 ethnic groups. The main ethnic group is Russians, accounting for about 77.7% of the total population. Since the economic crisis in 2014, coupled with Western economic sanctions, Russia's economic growth has been slow. The pandemic has further exacerbated the Russo-Ukrainian conflict, making Russia's economy even worse. At the same time, Western sanctions, inflation, and currency devaluation continue to plague Russia. Online shopping in Russia grew by 59% from 2019 to 2020. As of January 2021, Russia had 116 million Internet users, with an Internet penetration rate of 80.9%. The number of online shopping users exceeds 30 million, and 90% of overseas products shipped to Russia come from China. The penetration rate of local e-commerce in Russia is only 9%, and the sales of the top three local e-commerce platforms account for only 24% of Russia's total e-commerce sales in 2020. According to Euromonitor data, more than half of Russian online shoppers are aged between 25 and 35, and over 50% of online shoppers are women, mainly concentrated in the two major cities of Moscow and St. Petersburg. Most Russian online shoppers have an average order value of no more than 30 US dollars, and only about one-fifth of online shoppers spend up to 60 US dollars per order. In 2020, the top five demands for e-commerce product categories in Russia were electronics, clothing and shoes, food, furniture and household items, and beauty and health. Affected by the pandemic, young people are more inclined to shop online. Sports and outdoor activities are very popular in Russia, and sports and related equipment are booming. Russians prefer to shop on Russian websites, and 62% of consumers prefer to use local e-wallets and debit cards for payment. Over 100 million Russians visit at least one social media site every day. The most visited social media in Russia are, in order: Vkontakte, YouTube, Odnoklassniki, Facebook, Instagram, Twitter. Different social media have very different audiences. 80% of Vkontakte users are under 34 years old. Odnoklassniki targets middle-aged groups, mostly between 34 and 45 years old. Facebook and Twitter are mainly used by users with advanced technology, social skills, or business skills. By promoting through mainstream Russian social media, sellers can fully grasp the consumption habits and preferences of Russian-speaking countries, customize exclusive products for consumers according to market demand, and thus improve corporate competitiveness. In 2021, the e-commerce platform preferred by Russian consumers was avito, Russia's largest classified information website, which covers categories including goods, cars, real estate, employment and services, similar to "58.com in China". The second place is market.yandex.ru, a comparison shopping site under Yandex, a major Russian search engine. It is worth noting that AliExpress jumped to the top of the Russian e-commerce platform popularity list in 2020, becoming the most watched e-commerce platform and the largest cross-border e-commerce platform for Russians. The challenge of entering the Russian cross-border e-commerce market lies in logistics and payment, with the biggest challenge being logistics.

(7) Poland

Poland is the fifth most populous country in the EU and the fastest-growing economy in the EU and Central and Eastern Europe. In 2020, Poland's domestic GDP was 594.16 billion US dollars, the per capita GDP was 16,945 US dollars, the population was 38.02 million, and the median age was 41.7 years. Poland's communication infrastructure is developed, the acceptance of online shopping is high, and the e-commerce market is developing rapidly. According to Internet World According to Stats data, 29.75 million Poles have access to the internet, with an internet penetration rate of 78.2%. According to Eurostat data, in 2020, the number of online shoppers in Poland accounted for 72% of the internet population. According to data from the Polish Data Center, in 2020, 65.9% of Poles used social media in their daily lives. The main users of social media are those aged 25 to 44. YouTube is the most used social media platform in Poland, followed by Facebook. From a consumer perspective, the number of people discovering goods through social media is the highest. Merchants can let users discover their products through social media, generate interest, and make purchases. This is also one of the reasons why more and more merchants are using social media as a main way to attract traffic. Polish online shoppers are sensitive to price and pay great attention to discounts. According to relevant data, 66% of e-commerce consumers aged 18 to 45 have had cross-border shopping experiences, with nearly half of them maintaining a relatively frequent cross-border online shopping frequency. Chinese cross-border e-commerce is the favorite choice of Polish online shoppers. Polish online shoppers generally pursue a "value for money" consumption experience. They are keen to compare prices, quality, and website brands, and have a strong interest in special offers. Clothing and footwear, makeup and skincare, and household electronics are the top three product categories for Polish online shopping. In addition, Polish online shoppers also have a significant preference for medical products, furniture and home furnishings, books, auto parts, and baby products. They will conduct a comprehensive examination of online stores when shopping online, including whether product details can be clearly displayed, whether the price is reasonable, whether shipping is included, and the speed of delivery. Polish online shoppers have high demands for delivery time and prefer to use self-pickup lockers.

(8) Other Countries

Buyers from countries such as Belgium, the Netherlands, and Luxembourg are usually steady and plan-oriented, focusing on appearance, status, etiquette, and proceduralization. They value credibility and have high business ethics. Buyers in Luxembourg are mainly small and medium-sized enterprises, generally with a high return rate, but are unwilling to take any responsibility for logistics, and usually do more business with suppliers from Hong Kong, China. In summary: product quality and logistics transportation must be strong. Portuguese buyers are generally easy-going, self-centered, but have poor coordination and are not punctual. They are mostly engaged in agriculture and handicrafts, with fewer manufacturers. They speak directly and are unwilling to beat around the bush, with a phenomenon of "male superiority and female inferiority". Topics can start from bullfighting and carnations, but remember not to mention "thirteen" and "Friday". They like cooking, pay attention to culinary skills, are keen on picnics, enjoy life, and appreciate the scenery. In summary: the price is straightforward, if you can do it, you can do it, if you can't do it, you can't do it, or you can only reduce it so much. Choose scenes like picnics, parties, etc., and choose colors like purple, rose red, rose gold, etc. The product detail description should be objective and accurate, or what kind of experience the product can bring to the buyer. Greek buyers are honest but inefficient, do not pursue fashion, and like to waste time. They are cheerful, easily excited, but also easily calmed down, also taboo "thirteen" and "Friday". They have a sense of humor, like to drink alcohol and strong coffee, and enjoy the slight drunkenness. They don't like black, don't like cats, and are generous to guests. In summary: do not sell them black, cat-shaped goods; use more life scenes, express more coffee shop, bar leisure time, etc. They also like to bargain, the direct response is to tell them that this thing is worth it. Nordic countries mainly include Denmark, Finland, Iceland, Norway, and Sweden. These countries are politically stable, and the people have a high standard of living.

Kindness and amiability are the symbols of the Nordic people. The common characteristic of Nordic buyers is that they value the environmental friendliness of products. They do not like and are not good at bargaining. If the product quality is excellent, environmentally friendly, and the certificates are complete, they will choose to place an order directly, rarely using internal mail or Dunhuang to communicate with the seller about the price issue. In addition, Nordic people are very interested in novel consumer goods.

3. Latin America

Latin America consists of Mexico, most of Central America, South America, and the West Indies. It is rich in natural resources but has a low economic level. The residents of this area mainly rely on agricultural production. The industry is mainly primary processing, except for Barbados, all other countries are developing countries. Latin America is a highly price-sensitive market, and the cost-effectiveness of Chinese goods is just in the most acceptable price range for most consumers, which is very conducive to opening up the market.

The languages used in Latin American countries are mainly Spanish, Portuguese, English, French, and Dutch. Among them, Spanish is the most widely used and is the official language of most countries, while Brazil mainly uses Portuguese. The network environment in Latin American countries is gradually improving, and the infrastructure level of mobile internet is relatively high. The e-commerce market in Latin America is still in the early stages of development, and the coverage of mobile payments and digital payments needs to be improved. Many users still prefer cash on delivery. The political stability index in Latin America is not high, the corruption index is high, and inflation fluctuates dramatically. For cross-border e-commerce sellers, it is necessary to anticipate fluctuations in the local political, currency, and other economic environments.

In Latin America, more and more people are shopping overseas through the internet. Clothing, accessories, electronics, and travel products are the most popular cross-border online shopping products among Latin American people. Latin American internet users account for 10% of the total global users. Brazil occupies half of the e-commerce market in South America; Argentina's e-commerce market is growing the fastest. Foreign e-commerce websites offer a wider range of choices and often cheaper prices. According to a survey on cross-border shopping motivations by Nielsen Market Research, the first reason is "online shopping saves money," and another major reason is "you can find more products online that are not available locally."

(1) Brazil

Brazil is the largest country in Latin America in terms of area and population, and its economic strength also ranks first in Latin America. Brazil's internet infrastructure is gradually improving, and the internet penetration rate has increased. According to Datareportal data, as of January 2021, Brazil has 160 million internet users, with an internet penetration rate of 75.0%; Brazil has 150 million social media users, accounting for about 70.3% of the total population; the number of e-commerce consumers reached 105 million, accounting for about 50% of the total population. 79.4% of netizens use shopping apps, and 50.8% of e-commerce transactions are completed through mobile devices. Therefore, Brazilian online shoppers prefer mobile devices. The average order value of online shopping in Brazil is relatively low, with an annual shopping expenditure of about 345 US dollars. Mobile platform shopping prefers lower-value products. How to increase the average order value and profit is a key focus for sellers entering the Brazilian market. As Brazil has gathered a large number of immigrants from Europe, Africa, and Asia, local festivals also incorporate features from various places, in addition to traditional Western holidays such as Christmas and Easter, there are also Afro-religious holidays such as "Yemanja". The Brazilian Carnival is one of the biggest local festivals. The six major local holidays in Brazil are Mother's Day, Valentine's Day, Father's Day, Children's Day, Black Friday, and Christmas, and their online shopping expenditure accounts for a quarter of the total annual e-commerce sales. In Brazil, the most popular categories are electronic products and accessories, including headphones, sound bars, TV sticks, graphics cards, etc.; clothing and shoes rank second, and beauty products rank third. Brazilian consumers also have three major characteristics, namely: most of the online shopping group are heavy users of social media, they are accustomed to searching for product reviews on different platforms before shopping online, and they have a high acceptance of social media advertising; they like free delivery; they have a high acceptance of cross-border e-commerce shopping and Chinese goods. Mercadolibre, OLX, Americanas are the top three local e-commerce platforms in Brazil. AliExpress and Shopee, which have Chinese e-commerce genes, are also favored by Brazilians.

(2) Mexico

Mexico is a populous country in Latin America, and its economic development level is leading in Latin America. Because Mexico is adjacent to the United States and is a member of the "USMCA Agreement", it has become one of the most open economies in the world. In 2020, the total population of Mexico reached 129 million, with a median age of 29.2, and a majority of young people. According to data from the Mexican Online Consumption Association (AMVO) in June 2021, over 80% of Mexican online shoppers are under the age of 44, with 51.4% being male and 48.6% being female. Mexican online consumers prefer categories such as fashion and electronics, mobile phones, travel and transportation, game consoles and electronic games, etc. Mexican consumers prefer to buy branded products and prefer personalized customization services; they start to pay attention to the convenience and experience of online shopping, and free delivery has become a major factor in promoting transactions. A 2021 survey of Mexican consumers showed that about the motivations for people's purchases, 35% of people enjoy the convenience of shopping anytime, anywhere, 27% of people said they can find discounts and promotions, and 23% of people said the internet can provide them with a variety of products. Mercado Libre, Amazon, and Copple are the top three e-commerce platforms in Mexico.

(3) Argentina

Argentina is the third-largest economy in Latin America, only behind Brazil and Mexico. In 2020, the total GDP was 383.07 billion US dollars, the per capita GDP was 8555 US dollars, the population was 45.37 million, and the median age was 31.5 years. Argentina has a high rate of urbanization, with 92.2% of the population living in cities. The population of Argentina is mainly composed of European immigrants, most of whom are from Italy (over 55%), with the rest being from Spain, France, and Germany. Therefore, their consumption habits are more like Europe compared to other Latin American neighbors. Argentina has the highest internet penetration rate in Latin America, with an internet penetration rate of 91.2% and a smartphone penetration rate of over 70%. According to Statistic's data, as of September 2021, Argentina had 35.75 million social media users, with Facebook being the most visited social platform. Argentina's e-commerce market is large, only behind Brazil, Mexico, and Colombia. Looking at the income level of the consumer group in Argentina, over 68% of the population has a higher income level. When shopping, 81% of consumers choose to search online, and nearly 55% of people choose to shop online. Argentinians prefer to buy international brands, and a diverse range of categories and competitive prices are important factors influencing their shopping. According to Statistic's data, the top three categories of interest for online shopping in Argentina in 2020 were clothing, electronics, and footwear. However, the actual categories of goods purchased were food and beverages, home and garden, tools and building materials, fashion clothing, and sportswear. In addition, luxury goods are an important segment of the Argentine market. Luxury fashion clothing is the most popular category, followed by watches and jewelry. This indicates that there is a great opportunity for luxury clothing and watch brands to enter the Argentine market. Mercado Libre is the most popular e-commerce platform in Argentina.

(4) Colombia

Colombia is located in the northwest of South America and is the third-largest country in Latin America. In 2020, the total GDP was 271.3 billion US dollars, the per capita GDP was 5389 US dollars, the population was 51 million, and the median age was 31.3 years. Colombia is the largest manufacturing center in Latin America. Colombia also has a high rate of urbanization, with 81.6% of the population living in cities. Colombia has a high internet penetration rate and is strongly influenced by digital trends and technologies. Colombia has 39 million social media users, 60.6% of whom shop through social media, with YouTube being the most frequently used social media. According to Statistic's data, in 2020, over 71% of online shoppers were from middle and high-income families. Affected by the pandemic, in 2020, Colombia saw a significant increase in online sales of fashion clothing, electronic media, toys and handicrafts, home decorations, and food personal care categories. Influenced by American culture, since 2014, Black Friday has become the biggest e-commerce holiday in Colombia. 2021 data shows that the most popular e-commerce platform in Colombia is Mercado Libre, with a total visit of about 170 million times, far exceeding the second-place Amazon (61.3 million times); however, in terms of traffic growth, Amazon has the highest growth rate. Therefore, Amazon is still Mercado Libre's strongest competitor in Colombia.

4. East Asia

(1) Japan

Japan is one of the main markets for cross-border e-commerce sellers, characterized by high average order value and high requirements for product quality. At the same time, cross-border e-commerce sellers face issues such as Japan's stagnant economy, declining consumer power, and falling yen exchange rate. Japan has a severe aging problem, with its per capita purchasing power ranking 29th globally. Japan's internet penetration rate is as high as 94%, and compared to physical channels, online shopping is the main procurement method for Japanese people. In addition to shopping on e-commerce platforms, Japanese people also like to shop on independent sites. Therefore, independent sites in Japan have ample room for development. In addition, home appliance malls, online auction sites, flea market websites, and apps are also channels where Japanese people often shop. The most important categories of e-commerce sales in Japan are food and personal care, followed by clothing and fashion accessories, with toys ranking third. YouTube is the social media most used by Japanese internet users, with a usage rate of 72.5%; followed by Line, with a usage rate of 71.5%. In addition, Twitter has a usage rate of 47.4%; Instagram has a usage rate of 34.5%; Facebook has a usage rate of 31.5%. Japanese people have a high demand for live broadcasts and videos. The main characteristics of Japanese consumer behavior are: (1) Decreasing birth rate, solo living. The proportion of unmarried people in Japan is increasing, and even among those who are married, their social desire to have children is clearly declining. The decrease in birth rate means that young people or young families in Japan do not have the pressure of child-rearing, and consume more for themselves; the phenomenon of "solo living" is becoming popular, and products and sizes for one person are more popular. (2) Middle-aged and elderly people occupy half of the consumer market. Mobile phones have become a new battlefield for online shopping for the elderly in Japan, and they are very active in online shopping. (3) Japan values loyalty and prefers branded products. Japanese consumers dislike risk and are unwilling to buy unknown products without absolute quality assurance. (4) The point system is popular. The culture of consumer points in Japan permeates all industries. Japanese consumers prefer to use points to purchase goods or exchange for electronic coupons. (5) Adherence to aesthetic standards. Japanese consumers insist on high aesthetic standards, requiring simplicity and aesthetic value. Japan is Amazon's second-largest market. According to a survey by NTTCom Research, the prevalence of Amazon Prime members in Japan is low, with only 16.6% of online shoppers being members, compared to 65% in the United States. Looking at the best-selling categories on e-commerce platforms, small appliances, consumer electronics, clothing, groceries, food and beverages, and furniture and home furnishings are popular. Rakuten and Yahoo are two other large e-commerce platforms in Japan.

(2) South Korea

With a shared East Asian culture, cross-border e-commerce sellers in the Japanese market will also pay attention to the South Korean market. South Korea is the world's fifth-largest e-commerce market and Asia's third-largest. The internet penetration rate is as high as 96.3%, and the scale of mobile consumption is also very large. Young people aged 20–29 are the largest shopping group in South Korea, and more and more South Korean young people like online shopping mainly because of its convenience. The trend of mobile shopping is significant, with about 37% of mobile shoppers surveyed saying they have installed about 4–6 mobile shopping apps on their phones. According to Statistic survey data, the hot categories for online shopping in South Korea in 2020 were food and beverages, household appliances, electronic products, communication equipment, and catering services. In addition, clothing, furniture and pet categories are also popular. The use of social media in South Korea is as high as 89.3%, almost twice the global average of 53.6%. South Korea's social media usage rate is second only to the United Arab Emirates, ranking second in the world. As of April 2021, YouTube attracted 32 million unique visitors in South Korea, making it the most used social media in South Korea, while Instagram is most widely used among teenagers and young people. Gmarket is the largest shopping platform in South Korea, followed by Coupang.

5. Southeast Asia and India

Southeast Asia is composed of 11 countries, with Indonesia, Thailand, Malaysia, Singapore, the Philippines, and Vietnam having the most prominent markets. Southeast Asia has a large young population, which is the core target group for cross-border e-commerce. The cross-border trade environment with China is good, and ASEAN has surpassed the EU to become China's largest trading partner. The internet penetration rate in Southeast Asia is accelerating. According to Statistic's data, in 2020, Malaysia, Singapore, and Thailand all had high internet penetration rates. Southeast Asian consumers prefer social media.

(1) Indonesia

In 2020, Indonesia's domestic GDP was 1.06 trillion US dollars, ranking first in Southeast Asia, with a per capita GDP of 3922 US dollars and a population of 274 million. Indonesia requires people to have a religion, about 87% of the population is Muslim, making it the country with the most Muslims in the world. Religious culture is prevalent in Indonesia, and its consumers' consumption preferences and habits are very different from those in China and the West. There is a high demand for religious clothing and religious festival supplies, and brands that align with Islamic spirit are preferred. Indonesia has a large young population, and millennials and Generation Z are the main force in the Indonesian e-commerce market. These young people pursue fashion and novelty, like to follow trends, and electronic products, trendy brands, and fashion products are the main purchase categories; on the other hand, they are conservative and fashionable due to Islamic beliefs. Products that can satisfy their religious beliefs and sense of fashion are very popular. According to Deloitte survey data, 31% of respondents said that practicality and convenience are the main drivers of online shopping; 26% of respondents said that online shopping allows them to buy the products they want at lower prices. Indonesian online shopping consumers like to view product reviews and evaluations through search engines and social platforms before shopping online. The categories that Indonesians like to shop online include fashion, electronics and media, toys, furniture and appliances, food and personal care, etc. The Indonesian e-commerce market is dominated by Shopee and Tokopedia, accounting for about two-thirds of the market size.

(2) Malaysia

In 2020, Malaysia's domestic GDP was 0.34 trillion US dollars, with a per capita GDP of 10,270 US dollars and a population of 32.75 million. In terms of population, Malaysia's population structure has two main characteristics, the first is a large young population, and the second is the coexistence of multiple ethnicities, languages, and religions, among which about 66% of Malaysians are Muslims. Chinese people account for 23% of the population in Malaysia. English, Malay, and Chinese are all common languages in Malaysia. Malaysia's internet infrastructure is becoming more and more perfect. As of January 2021, the internet penetration rate in Malaysia was 84.2%. During the same period, there were 28 million social media users. Social media influences the shopping decisions and channels of Malaysians. YouTube is the most commonly used social media by Malaysians, followed by WhatsApp and Facebook. Malaysians pay attention to cost-effectiveness when shopping online, and social media has a greater influence. The products that Malaysians prefer to shop online mainly include clothing and shoes, electronic products, gifts, kitchenware, furniture and decorations, fashion accessories, jewelry, etc. According to iPrice's data, in the third quarter of 2021, the Malaysian e-commerce market was almost dominated by Shopee and Lazada, but Shopee is gradually widening the gap with Lazada and firmly ranks first. Malaysia's local TV platform PG Mall is also on a rapid rise.

(3) Thailand

Thailand's domestic GDP in 2020 was 0.5 trillion US dollars, with a per capita GDP of 7,190 US dollars, a population of 69.8 million people, and Buddhism as the main religion. Thailand is the second largest economy in ASEAN, with a developed agriculture and tourism industry, and is also the automotive manufacturing center of Southeast Asia. The proportion of the population over 65 years old in Thailand is 13%, which has entered an aging society. Thailand faces two major population issues: a gradually flattening population growth rate and an intensifying aging population. According to Datareportal, as of January 2021, Thailand had 48.59 million internet users, with an internet penetration rate of 69.5%; according to PwC, Thailand is the largest social e-commerce market in Southeast Asia, with 51% of online shoppers shopping directly through social platforms. The most commonly used social platforms in Thailand are YouTube, Facebook, and Line. Generation X and Generation Y consumers are the largest consumer groups in Thailand. Online advertising is one of the main reasons influencing Thai consumers' shopping. Thai people's consumption habits are similar to other Southeast Asian countries, with online spending mainly focused on electronics, fashion beauty, furniture, and home goods. In terms of Thai e-commerce platforms, Shopee and Lazada dominate.

(4) India

India's domestic GDP in 2020 was 2.6229 trillion US dollars. The per capita GDP was 1797.76 US dollars, and the population was 1.38 billion people. The common languages are Hindi and English. The prevalence of mobile internet in India has surged from 320 million users in 2015 to 600 million users in 2019. Young people in India are increasingly favoring digital content and social media. India's towns have become an important driving force for its e-commerce development, with small-town consumers accounting for four-fifths of new online shoppers. In addition to small towns, women and the elderly are also increasing their frequency of online shopping. Beauty, health and personal care, electronics, fashion, food, and home goods are all popular online shopping categories for Indians. The use of social media in India is increasing, with Facebook being the first choice for social e-commerce. Instagram's potential in India is not to be underestimated, with Indian and American users tied for first place. India is a market with unstable trade and e-commerce policies. 2020 was painful for Chinese cross-border e-commerce platforms and sellers who have deeply cultivated the Indian market. In June 2020, the Indian government announced a ban on 59 Chinese apps including Club Factory, SHEIN, and TikTok.

6. Africa

Africa has 54 countries, a young population, rapidly developing cities, and disposable income that is increasing rapidly each year. The population of Africa is growing rapidly, and the population structure in the next few decades will tend towards youth, with a high acceptance of online shopping. It is estimated that by 2025, the scale of e-commerce in all countries on the African continent will reach 75 billion US dollars. According to data from the United Nations Conference on Trade and Development, from 2014 to 2018, the annual growth rate of e-commerce users in Africa was 18%, higher than the global average of 12%. According to predictions by McKinsey, by 2025, the number of mobile phone users in Africa will reach 634 million, with a penetration rate of 52%. Currently, Nigeria, South Africa, Kenya, Rwanda, Ghana, and Egypt are the core economies in Africa. According to research by KPMG, in South Africa, 60% of people shop online every few months, 70% of Kenyans and Nigerians and 60% of South Africans have tried online shopping, but most Ghanaians (55%) and Ugandans (51%) have never shopped online. Although Africa's e-commerce market is still in its infancy, Africa has a dense, young population with a strong acceptance of the internet and online shopping. Africa lacks material resources and has a weak industrial base, but locals love China's high-quality and affordable products, especially hair care (wigs, hair care oils, etc.), beauty products (lipstick, foundation, etc.), home textiles (mosquito nets, bedding, lamps, etc.), market categories (clothing accessories, shoes and bags, etc.), and building materials. The mainstream popular e-commerce platforms in Africa include Jumia, Takealot, Souq, etc.

(1) South Africa

In 2020, South Africa's GDP was 301.9 billion US dollars, the per capita GDP was 5067 US dollars, and the population was 59.83 million. The common language is English, and the main religion is Christianity. The level of economic development in South Africa is uneven, with 67% of the population being urban residents. The youthful population structure, rapid urban development, and rapid growth in disposable income of residents have promoted the development of e-commerce in South Africa. South African consumers love clothing products. Women like to buy colorful clothing and accessories with ethnic elements, while men prefer blue and gray suits. South Africans are price-sensitive and like to buy promotional products and products with coupons, so international promotion days like Black Friday and Cyber Monday are popular. To buy their desired products, South Africans are willing to spend more time on social media looking for product recommendations.

(2) Nigeria

In 2020, Nigeria's GDP was 432.294 billion US dollars, the per capita GDP was 2273 US dollars, and the population was 206 million. Nigeria's manufacturing industry is developing slowly and has to rely on imports to meet consumption. Nigeria's demand for Chinese-made products is growing. According to Internet World Stats data, as of March 2021, the internet penetration rate in Nigeria was 73%. The population of Nigeria is showing a trend towards youth. Nigerians prefer fashion categories, 3C electronics, and food categories, pay more attention to the price and freshness of goods, and like to follow more innovative products. Similar to South Africa, Nigerian consumers are accustomed to shopping on social media and pay attention to product reviews when shopping. Nigeria has many ethnic groups and rich languages. When cross-border e-commerce sellers enter this market, they should pay more attention to the preference differences of consumers in this market.

7. Middle East

The Middle East region, linking Asia, Europe, and Africa, is an important transportation hub between the East and West. The people in the Middle East mainly believe in Islam, Judaism, and Christianity. Each ethnic group still retains its own religious beliefs and customs, with significant cultural differences. The Middle East region has a clear trend of a young population. The internet penetration rate in the Middle East is higher than the global average. The per capita GDP of several wealthy countries such as Qatar, the UAE, and Saudi Arabia is very high. The average order value of online shopping in the Middle East is high, about 150 US dollars, but the shopping frequency is low. Consumer characteristics in the Middle East have a significant religious and cultural color. Although women wear black veils, they have a strong demand for fashion and beauty. Consumers in the Middle East are mainly Muslims, with unique consumption needs. Vertical fields facing such groups, such as Muslim clothing and beauty makeup, have good development prospects. Another feature of the e-commerce market in the Middle East is a preference for own-brand goods. Due to religious and cultural restrictions, residents in the Middle East live conservatively offline, but this also stimulates their strong demand for new forms of entertainment and social interaction, such as the Middle East is one of the fastest-growing emerging regions in the digital game market. Pan-entertainment products, such as game consoles, handles, e-sports game sets, and novel electronic products have a good market. Gardening supplies are also one of the unique needs of consumers in the Middle East, because Middle Eastern countries yearn for green plants. The e-commerce in the Middle East presents a tripartite pattern, including international e-commerce platforms, local e-commerce platforms, and Chinese e-commerce platforms. More and more independent sites are also beginning to develop the Middle East market.

8. Oceania

(1) Australia

Australia's domestic GDP in 2020 was 1.36 trillion US dollars, per capita GDP was 52,825 US dollars, and the population was 25.7 million. Australia is a mature developed economy. For cross-border e-commerce sellers, Australia seems not the best choice, located in remote areas with sparse population. But in recent years, the rise of many online platforms and the emergence of logistics centers all over Australia, more Australians are beginning to participate in online shopping, and Australia is becoming another cross-border e-commerce blue ocean market. According to Statistic data, Australia's internet penetration rate exceeded 80% in 2020, and the smartphone penetration rate was 79.4%. The social media penetration rate was 79.9%, with the most users on YouTube and Facebook. 40% of cross-border online shopping consumers like goods from China, mainly because of price advantages and domestic scarcity. Australians' preferred product categories include health and beauty, home goods, home gardening, entertainment goods, books, and specialty foods and wines. Comprehensive e-commerce platforms and fashion platforms occupy 62% of the online shopping market. eBay Australia is the most popular platform in Australia, with 32% of the top sellers coming from China.

(2) New Zealand

New Zealand's domestic GDP in 2020 was 209 billion US dollars, per capita GDP was 41,127 US dollars, and the population was 4.8 million. At present, China is the main import and export country of New Zealand. As of January 2021, nearly 2 million New Zealanders shop online. New Zealanders are passionate about sports, especially rugby. Rugby kits and cheering goods are popular items among New Zealanders. In addition, many New Zealanders also enjoy a self-sufficient lifestyle and purchase agricultural equipment to achieve this lifestyle.

Chapter 5
Cross-Border E-commerce Supply Chain Management

5.1 Content of E-Commerce Supply Chain Management

5.1.1 The Impact of E-Commerce on Supply Chain Management

The emergence and development of e-commerce is the result of economic globalization and innovative network technology. E-commerce has completely changed the original ways and means of interaction for logistics, information flow, and capital flow, enabling full utilization of resources, improving efficiency, reducing costs, and enhancing service quality.

1. E-commerce Enables the Realization of Supply Chain Management Thinking

E-commerce is a human–computer interactive management information system centered on managers. It applies advanced management ideas to all levels within and outside the enterprise, implements business process reengineering, and realizes the whole process of supply chain management with the help of computers. Through the use of e-commerce, it effectively connects the relationships between suppliers, manufacturers, distributors, and users in the supply chain.

2. E-commerce Promotes the Development of the Supply Chain

The application of e-commerce promotes the development of the supply chain and also compensates for the shortcomings of the traditional supply chain. From the perspective of infrastructure, traditional supply chain management is generally established on private dedicated networks, requiring a large amount of capital, and only some large enterprises have the ability to build their own supply chains, but these supply chains lack flexibility. E-commerce allows the supply chain to share a global network, enabling small and medium-sized enterprises to join the global supply chain at a lower cost.

X. Zhang, *Introduction to Cross-Border E-Commerce Ecosystem*,
https://doi.org/10.1007/978-981-96-1165-2_5

3. Supply Chain Management is an Indispensable Part of Executing E-Commerce

Supply chain management is not only an important part of and link in e-commerce, but also an important means for enterprises to improve their business management level. By utilizing the advantages of e-commerce, timely collecting information and conducting statistical analysis based on this, valuable data is generated for application in the optimization and integration of vertical integration of enterprises' daily operations and upstream and downstream supply chain enterprises. Supply chain management provides a supply–demand connection channel between manufacturers and other enterprise systems, quickly reflects customer needs through e-commerce, and provides customers with the products or services they need at the right time, place, and quantity and at a favorable price, creating value for customers, suppliers, and enterprises.

5.1.2 Principles of E-Commerce Supply Chain Management

The e-commerce supply chain refers to conducting business activities between enterprises and their suppliers, customers, and other trading partners using the network and electronic information technology. It is a new channel to reduce costs, improve service quality, and open up added value. E-commerce supply chain management spans the entire process from raw material supply, production manufacturing, product distribution, transportation and delivery, warehousing and inventory to product sales, involving many independent companies and customers, such as manufacturers, suppliers, transporters, and retailers. The content of e-commerce supply chain management includes production planning and control, inventory control, procurement, sales, logistics, demand forecasting, customer management, and partner management. Its essence is the management of information flow, logistics, and capital flow. Therefore, the basic principles of e-commerce supply chain management are explained from these "three flows".

1. Information Flow

Users place orders online in the distributor's e-commerce transaction system, the distributor's order processing is completed in real time, and immediately places an order online to the product manufacturer for procurement. The product manufacturer completes the distributor's procurement order in real time and purchases parts or raw materials from the upstream supplier. Because it is an online order, the distributor, product manufacturer, and supplier get the demand information almost simultaneously.

2. Logistics

Like traditional supply chain management, the direction of logistics in e-commerce is from the supplier to the product manufacturer, then to the distributor, and finally to the user. The difference is that the information flow directs the logistics. The high degree of information sharing and instant communication based on e-commerce brings high speed and real-time logistics, enabling materials or products to arrive at the designated place at the designated time, thereby reducing or even eliminating the inventory held by enterprises at each node.

3. Capital Flow

Just like traditional supply chain management, the flow of funds in e-commerce goes from the user to the distributor, then to the product manufacturer, and finally to the supplier. The difference is that the payment method is mainly online, which greatly improves the execution speed of orders and the speed of delivery.

5.1.3 *Main Content of E-Commerce Supply Chain*

1. Order Processing

When a customer order is received, the core enterprise promptly analyzes the performance requirements of the required product, determines whether it can meet the technical indicators in the order, and further analyzes the product cost, quantity, and profit in the order under the condition that the requirements can be met. If a profit can be made from the order, a purchase contract can be signed with the customer. Then, check the existing inventory, if the product the customer needs is in stock, it is shipped immediately; otherwise, production is organized in a timely manner. By shortening the order cycle, operational efficiency is greatly improved.

2. Production Organization

Enterprises use e-commerce systems to coordinate just-in-time supply programs with suppliers and coordinate production plans with multiple suppliers. In addition, because order processing can provide real-time information about the company's related products, sales, and services, to some extent, sales forecasts will become more accurate, which in turn greatly improves production organization management.

3. Procurement Management

Through the e-commerce system, effective information sharing and rapid transmission of information with suppliers can be achieved. On the one hand, demand information and return information are provided to suppliers through the Internet, and at the same time, supplier quotations, product catalogs, and query execution are obtained, forming a stable and efficient procurement and supply system; on the other hand, through online procurement bidding and other means, integrating procurement bidding and Internet advantages, expanding the range of procurement resource choices, rationalizing procurement work, greatly reducing procurement personnel, and effectively reducing costs.

4. Distribution and Transportation Management

The e-commerce system can supervise the shipment of distribution centers, track the transportation of goods to warehousing, and manage the operations of distribution, replenishment, picking, and circulation processing, realizing integrated logistics management throughout the distribution process. In addition, through the management and optimization of transportation resources, transportation methods, and transportation routes, effective organization and scheduling of transportation tasks can be achieved, transportation costs can be reduced, and effective tracking management of transportation matters and goods can be achieved, ensuring that designated goods can be delivered to designated places at designated times.

5. Inventory Management

Through the e-commerce system, the enterprise notifies the supplier about order delivery delays or inventory emergencies, enabling inventory managers and suppliers to track the existing inventory of goods, obtain real-time information to be prepared, and achieve effective warehouse management. Inventory management under e-commerce can timely reflect sales and inventory dynamics, and achieve cross-regional, multi-inventory management, improve the utilization of warehousing resources, and thereby promote the reduction of inventory levels and reduce the total inventory maintenance costs.

6. E-Commerce Payment Management

The e-commerce payment system refers to the exchange of goods or services between consumers, merchants, and financial institutions using secure electronic means, that is, sending payment information of new payment methods (including electronic cash, credit cards, debit cards, smart cards, etc.) through the network securely to banks or corresponding processing institutions to achieve electronic payment. It is a comprehensive system that integrates shopping, payment tools, security technology, authentication systems, credit systems, and modern financial systems. By connecting the e-commerce system with banks, replacing the original check payment mode with e-commerce, and replacing the original cash payment method with credit cards, it can greatly reduce settlement costs and accelerate the return of goods, improving the use of funds. At the same time, using secure electronic transaction protocols ensures the security of the transaction process and eliminates concerns about online transactions.

7. E-commerce Supply Chain Finance

Supply chain finance refers to banks revolving around core enterprises, managing the cash flow and logistics of upstream and downstream small and medium-sized enterprises, and transforming the uncontrollable risks of individual enterprises into the controllable risks of the entire supply chain enterprises. Through supply chain information technology, various types of information are obtained, and risks are controlled to the lowest financial services. Supply chain finance realizes the integration of logistics, business flow, cash flow, information flow, etc. Supply chain financing and general loan financing have significant differences and need to be realized through dynamic management of goods rights in logistics.

5.2 Cross-Border E-Commerce Supply Chain Management System

5.2.1 Cross-Border E-Commerce Supply Chain Process

In cross-border e-commerce transactions, whether it is physical goods, virtual goods or services, they all belong to the category of goods, are manufactured by manufacturers, provided by suppliers to display and sell on the cross-border e-commerce platform, and finally purchased and consumed by consumers. This constitutes the flow of goods from the source of production to the final consumer, which is actually a supply chain activity. In the cross-border e-commerce supply chain, there are also links such as goods flow, information flow, cash flow, and logistics; at the same time, manufacturers, suppliers, cross-border e-commerce platforms, and consumers all have more or less direct or indirect connections and intersections with goods flow, information flow, cash flow, and logistics, thereby forming a cross-border e-commerce supply chain network structure, as shown in Fig. 5.1. In addition to manufacturers, suppliers, cross-border e-commerce platforms, and consumers, there will be suppliers of suppliers, consumers of consumers, etc., depending on the number of goods circulation links, which further increases the complexity of the cross-border e-commerce supply chain. Not only that, there will also be other related or supporting organizations and individuals that generate various activities and intersections with the node organizations of the cross-border e-commerce supply chain. In the cross-border e-commerce supply chain, the important chain nodes are manufacturers, suppliers, cross-border e-commerce platforms, consumers, as well as payment, logistics, customs, and commercial inspection related nodes.

5.2.2 Cross-Border E-Commerce Supply Chain Design Principles

Based on the characteristics of the supply chain in the cross-border e-commerce environment, it is necessary to redesign and transform the traditional supply chain and build a new model of the supply chain. In the process of redesigning the supply chain, this book proposes the following methods and principles.

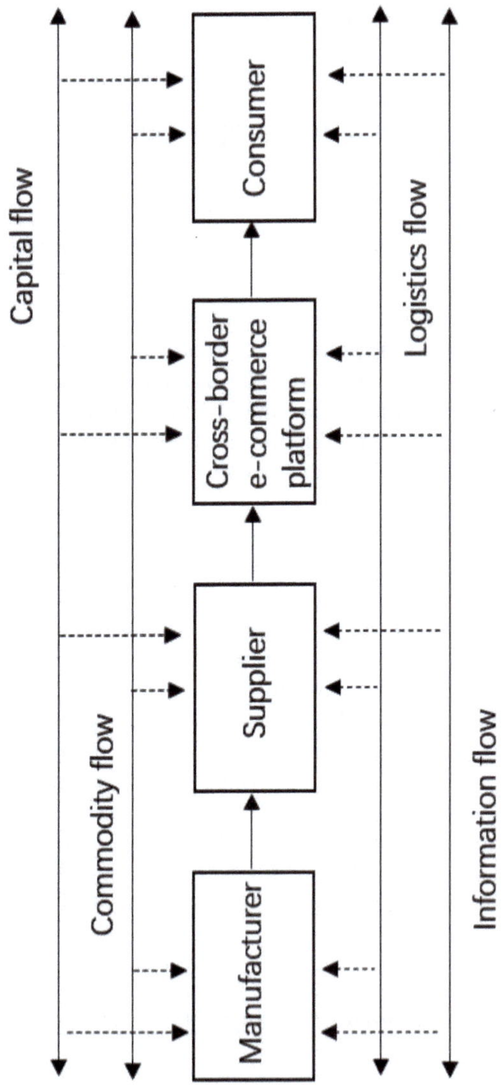

Fig. 5.1 Cross-border e-commerce supply chain flow chart

1. Establish a Dynamic Alliance Based on the Supply Chain

In the cross-border e-commerce environment where demand uncertainty is increasing, the supply chain must have sufficient flexibility to support the acquisition of raw materials and the production of products in new platforms and ways at any time, meet customer needs and complete the final delivery work. Establishing a dynamic alliance can greatly enhance the flexibility of the supply chain. The transformation of the supply chain from function-oriented to process-oriented makes enterprises abandon traditional management thinking and regard various businesses within the enterprise and between node enterprises as a whole functional process, forming an integrated supply chain management system. Through effective management of the integrated supply chain, the entire supply chain will achieve the global dynamic optimal goal. The highest level of supply chain integration is the issue of strategic cooperation between enterprises. When enterprises join the supply chain in the form of dynamic alliances, they start the process of cooperative countermeasures. Enterprises seek win–win or multi-win goals through a negotiation mechanism.

2. Build a Unified Information Platform

In the cross-border e-commerce environment, the uncertainty of customer demand greatly increases, which will increase the risk of building a supply chain. Building a unified information platform, increasing communication between various supply chain nodes, will effectively prevent information delay, reduce the "bullwhip effect" of the supply chain, increase the response speed of the supply chain, and thus reduce the risk of building a supply chain.

3. Unified Management of "Virtual Trade Community"

Although information sharing in the supply chain can be achieved through information technology, supply chain partners still have some sensitive information they are unwilling to share with others, and the problem of information asymmetry still exists. Establishing an integrated management information system, unifying the management of the "virtual trade community", strengthening coordination between enterprises, and ensuring the security of supply chain partner information can effectively realize the full sharing of key information in the supply chain, thereby improving the management efficiency of the entire supply chain and maximizing supply chain efficiency.

4. Pay Close Attention to Customer Needs and Value Customer Service

The supply chain shifts from product management to customer management, and the characteristic of customer demand-driven makes enterprises pay more attention to customer needs, and through technologies such as data warehousing and data mining, increase the accuracy of understanding customer needs. Based on understanding customer needs, the supply chain can provide personalized services to customers through technologies such as mass customization.

5. Transforming Internal Business Processes of Enterprises

In the traditional enterprise "hierarchical" organizational structure, the efficiency of information transmission is not high, making it difficult to improve the efficiency of internal business. Only by transforming the internal organizational structure of the enterprise, breaking the original functional organizational structure, striving to achieve a flat organizational structure, reducing the transmission links of information flow, redesigning the business process of the enterprise, and reducing the links of the entire business process, can the business efficiency of the organization be improved.

5.2.3 Basic Requirements for Cross-Border E-Commerce Supply Chain Design

1. Customer First

Customers are very important to any supply chain. Therefore, the design of cross-border e-commerce supply chains should consider the principle of customer first. Customer service starts and ends with the customer, and the customer is the one who can feel all the complex interrelated effects in the supply chain. The design of cross-border e-commerce supply chains must have high flexibility and quick response capabilities in order to meet the actual and potential needs of customers.

2. Clear Positioning

The cross-border e-commerce supply chain consists of raw material suppliers, manufacturers, distributors, retailers, logistics and distribution providers, and consumers. The cross-border e-commerce supply chain requires that all members of the supply chain have strong competitiveness. No matter what each member does for the entire supply chain, it should be specialized, and specialization is an advantage. Whether the enterprise is in a dominant or subordinate position in the supply chain, it must clearly understand its positioning advantage in the supply chain. Determine your position based on your own advantages, and formulate related development strategies accordingly, make appropriate adjustments and choices to your business activities, focus on cultivating your business advantages, and ensure that you participate in the supply chain with your advantageous business. Only in this way can the enterprise be recognized in the cross-border e-commerce supply chain, cooperate with other enterprises, and ultimately achieve a win–win situation.

3. Risk Prevention

Affected by natural and non-natural factors, the operation of the cross-border e-commerce supply chain actually has uncertainty, thus facing certain risks. For example, due to the influence of uncertain factors, market demand is always changing and unstable, so each node enterprise must maintain a certain inventory. In order to achieve the goal of serving customers, sufficient inventory (i.e., safety stock) must be maintained, so that even if problems occur upstream, it will not affect customer service. Therefore, in the design of cross-border e-commerce supply chains, various risk factors should be measured and explained, understand the impact of various uncertainties on the system range, and formulate corresponding preventive measures.

4. Act According to One's Ability

The establishment and operation of cross-border e-commerce supply chains is a highly complex project, requiring participating entities to possess strong economic strength, high decision-making levels, and advanced supply chain operation skills. Therefore, companies should make rational judgments and act according to their capabilities based on their actual situation, such as what kind of supply chain to establish, their position and role in it, and the expected operation of the supply chain, so that the operation of the supply chain can be under their control.

5.2.4 Basic Content of Cross-Border E-commerce Supply Chain Design

1. Selection of Supply Chain Partners

Every supply chain includes multiple suppliers, manufacturers, and retailers from various links such as procurement, supply, production, warehousing, transportation, sales, as well as many companies specializing in logistics services. The members of the supply chain encompass all companies and organizations that interact directly or indirectly from the place of origin to the place of consumption to meet customer needs. Therefore, the selection of members of the cross-border e-commerce supply chain is the foundation of supply chain design. The selection of supply chain members is bidirectional. Generally speaking, members participating in the supply chain form relatively stable trading partnerships based on market transactions for common interests. However, the main company of the supply chain, especially the core company, leads the existence and management of the entire cross-border e-commerce supply chain, and therefore has a certain initiative in the selection of other members of the supply chain; other non-main companies, with relatively small scale and economic strength, are in a subordinate position in the cross-border e-commerce supply chain and often cannot dominate whether they can become members of the supply chain. In this sense, the selection of members of the cross-border e-commerce supply chain and their partners is unidirectional.

2. Network Structure Design

The entire cross-border e-commerce supply chain network structure is composed of supply chain members, the connections between members, and the way supply chain processes are connected. The network itself reflects the distribution of supply chain members and their relationships with each other. The center of the design of the cross-border e-commerce supply chain network structure is to ensure that the network can reasonably use and allocate resources, improve logistics efficiency, and thus achieve the goal of improving the overall value of the cross-border e-commerce supply chain.

3. Organizational Mechanisms and Management Procedures

The organizational mechanisms and management procedures of the supply chain are key to ensuring the effective operation of the cross-border e-commerce supply chain. Since the supply chain involves multiple business links of multiple companies, and these companies are independent market economic entities with their own management systems, to achieve seamless connection of the supply chain, all independent companies must reach consensus on related links to ensure overall coordination. The organizational mechanisms and management procedures of the cross-border e-commerce supply chain are actually a collection of the organizational mechanisms and management procedures of the member companies. Each member company must design related organizational mechanisms and management procedures from the perspective of the overall supply chain. Especially for core companies, their organizational mechanisms and management procedures are key to the efficiency of the entire supply chain.

4. Basic Rules of Supply Chain Operation

The cooperation between node companies on the cross-border e-commerce supply chain is based on trust. The establishment and maintenance of trust relationships, in addition to the sincerity and actions of each node company, also requires a common platform, that is, the basic rules of supply chain operation, which mainly include coordination mechanisms, information openness and interaction methods, planning and control systems for production logistics, overall inventory layout, fund settlement methods, dispute resolution mechanisms, etc. Computer systems, corresponding software, and information systems are the necessary basis for the implementation of the rules of operation of the cross-border e-commerce supply chain.

5.2.5 *Evaluation Indicators of Cross-Border E-Commerce Supply Chain Design*

The rationality and effective operation of cross-border e-commerce supply chains can be examined from the following aspects.

1. Sensitivity

Sensitivity is the degree to which a company understands market changes through supply chain operations. It is the speed at which a cross-border e-commerce supply chain system deftly uses and reorganizes internal and external resources. Faced with increasingly short product lifecycles and increasingly stringent and unpredictable demands, companies must have the ability to keenly perceive market changes and the ability to change.

2. Responsiveness

Merely anticipating customer needs is not enough for future successful companies, they must respond faster than their competitors. Companies should have the ability to take action in advance for real and potential customers. Once there are signs in the market, they should be able to immediately perceive changes in customer needs and try to meet their unexpected needs. An excellent cross-border e-commerce supply chain can adapt not only to predictable environments but also to unpredictable ones.

3. Coordination

The cross-border e-commerce supply chain is an integrated network of multiple companies, each of which is an independent interest entity, so the coordination of the supply chain is more complex and more difficult than the coordination between departments within the company. The coordination of the cross-border e-commerce supply chain includes interest coordination and management coordination. Among them, interest coordination must make the distribution of interests between companies in the chain more clear when building the supply chain organizational structure; management coordination is to coordinate the effective flow of logistics and information flow with the support of information technology according to the requirements of the supply chain organizational structure, in order to reduce the operating cost of the entire supply chain and improve the response speed of the supply chain to the market.

4. Intelligence

With the continuous iteration and application of digital technology, cross-border e-commerce supply chains need to continuously introduce and update relevant digital technologies. Especially when facing various situations in the enterprise and the supply chain, through digital technology, it can quickly and timely grasp and make correct decisions, effectively integrate various resources to solve, which is the manifestation of the intelligence of the cross-border e-commerce supply chain.

5.2.6 Cross-Border E-Commerce Supply Chain Optimization

1. Cross-Border E-Commerce Platform Alliance, Unified Bargaining with Foreign Brand Merchants

Domestic small and medium-sized cross-border e-commerce companies have low bargaining power, and the main reason they cannot directly contract with foreign suppliers is scattered demand and insufficient demand scale. At present, most cross-border e-commerce imports are purchased by individuals or professional teams from overseas retailers and then sold to domestic consumers, without opening up the supply chain to get the real source of goods. If several cross-border e-commerce platforms can form an alliance, negotiate collectively, and obtain the authorization of some famous foreign brands, they can reduce the cost and expenses of the supply link.

2. Break Through Traditional Thinking and Exchange Ideas with Foreign Sellers

At present, 90% of the self-operated models on the cross-border e-commerce import platform are purchased through intermediaries. Small and medium-sized cross-border e-commerce companies have low bargaining power and find it difficult to directly sign supply contracts with foreign brand merchants. Large cross-border e-commerce import platforms have large purchase volumes and strong bargaining power, but they also find it difficult to sign contracts with foreign brand merchants. There are many reasons for this, such as cultural differences, account period issues, etc. Therefore, if cross-border e-commerce import companies want to achieve coordination and docking of sources with foreign brand merchants, they need to adapt to different business styles, different racial cultures, and thinking methods under different political systems, and there is indeed a long way to go.

3. Cooperate with Cross-Border Logistics Supply Chain Service Providers

The main logistics models for cross-border e-commerce include postal parcels, international express, dedicated logistics, overseas warehouses, etc. The postal network is comprehensive, but the timeliness is poor; international express is timely, but the cost is also high; dedicated logistics reduces costs through scale effects. Cross-border e-commerce import companies choose suitable logistics service providers based on product characteristics, and sometimes even need to adopt a composite logistics supply model to meet consumer needs, such as Tmall International's overseas direct mail products using segmented carriage and express joint transport, etc., to integrate various logistics service channels to reduce cross-border logistics costs, while also facilitating logistics monitoring and ensuring traceability of goods.

4. Carry Out Big Data Analysis and Implement Precise Marketing

Optimizing the supply chain needs to cooperate with big data platforms, grasp consumers' personal information and transaction information in time, understand the needs and focus of the target audience, understand consumers' consumption psychology and habits, carry out targeted precise marketing, just like Taobao's "Daily Recommendations" and "Personal Customization", build their own ecosystem around consumers, and layout offline services and own stores or brands.

5.3 Cross-Border E-Commerce Procurement Management

5.3.1 Concept and Characteristics of Cross-Border E-commerce Procurement

1. Concept of Cross-Border E-commerce Procurement

(1) Cross-Border E-commerce Procurement

Cross-border e-commerce procurement refers to the process of establishing an e-commerce trading platform, publishing procurement information, or actively searching for suppliers and products online, realizing online ordering, online payment of goods, and delivery of goods through logistics, completing the entire transaction process. The whole process of cross-border e-commerce requires the coordination of procurement supply, logistics distribution, electronic payment, after-sales service, etc. Any problem in any link may affect the development of cross-border e-commerce.

(2) Product Code

Also known as product code or product number, it refers to a sequence of symbols assigned to a certain product for manual or computer recognition and processing of goods. The product code is extremely important in cross-border e-commerce procurement, and the scientific nature of the product code will directly affect the cross-border e-commerce procurement process.

(3) Procurement Plan

The cross-border e-commerce procurement personnel make predictive arrangements and deployments for the procurement activities of materials during the planning period based on understanding the market supply and demand, mastering the characteristics of e-commerce operations, and the consumption rules of materials.

(4) Procurement Order

The formal, final confirmation document about procurement business proposed by cross-border e-commerce procurement personnel to suppliers according to the procurement plan.

(5) Procurement Tracking

Cross-border e-commerce procurement personnel track the materials and products purchased according to the procurement order, deal with various problems encountered from the time of placing the order to receiving the purchased materials, such as quality, quantity, deadline, etc. Cross-border e-commerce procurement tracking is a business work that runs through the entire process of cross-border e-commerce procurement, which refers to the process of monitoring the procurement of raw materials, production, quality inspection, delivery by suppliers, and the transportation, warehousing, and distribution of goods by logistics providers after the order is issued.

(6) Procurement Arrival Handling

Cross-border e-commerce procurement personnel handle various dispositions of the received procurement materials, including arrival preparation, arrival counting, arrival inspection, arrival shelving, etc.

2. Characteristics of Cross-Border E-commerce Procurement

(1) Fast Inventory Turnover

In the process of cross-border e-commerce procurement, it responds to user needs in real time, reduces inventory, improves logistics speed and inventory turnover rate, transforming cross-border e-commerce companies from "purchasing for inventory" to "purchasing for orders".

(2) Multiple Batches, Small Quantities, Quick Response

To improve the inventory turnover speed of cross-border e-commerce procurement, it is necessary to achieve multiple batches, small quantities, and quick responses. This puts higher demands on suppliers and increases the production costs of suppliers.

(3) The Extensiveness of Procurement

All suppliers can bid to the purchaser, and the purchaser can also investigate all suppliers. This can expand the range of cross-border e-commerce suppliers and generate economies of scale.

(4) The Interactivity of Procurement

In the process of cross-border e-commerce procurement, the purchaser and the supplier can exchange real-time information through emails, social software, etc., which is convenient, fast, and low-cost.

(5) High Procurement Efficiency

In the process of cross-border e-commerce procurement, it can break through the constraints of time and space, and collect, process, and apply procurement information at a speed close to real-time.

(6) Transparency of Procurement

Cross-border e-commerce procurement can make the procurement process open, fair, and just, eliminating corruption in the procurement process. By making procurement information public on the website, the computer can automatically complete the selection of suppliers according to the set standards, which is conducive to real-time monitoring, avoiding black holes in procurement, and making procurement more transparent and standardized.

(7) Standardization of Procurement Processes

Cross-border e-commerce procurement is based on the optimization of business processes, and is carried out according to the prescribed standard processes, which can standardize procurement behavior and the procurement market, and reduce the arbitrariness of the procurement process.

(8) The Transformation of Procurement Management to Supply Chain Management

The purchaser can timely send information such as quantity, quality, service, and delivery period to the supplier through the business website or EDI, and adjust the procurement plan in time according to the demand, so that the supplier can strictly provide products according to the requirements, achieving timely procurement and production.

5.3.2 Cross-Border E-Commerce Procurement Process

1. The Operation Process of Cross-Border E-Commerce Procurement

The procurement operation process refers to the entire process of a company selecting and purchasing various raw materials, parts, and other items needed for production. According to the phased division of the procurement process, the procurement operation process mainly includes three aspects: one is sourcing, as a buyer needs to find corresponding suppliers, investigate their product quality, quantity, price, etc., to see if they meet the purchase conditions; the second is ordering, after the buyer selects the supplier, they need to convey detailed purchase plans and demand information to the supplier in the form of orders and negotiate settlement methods, so that the supplier can accurately carry out production and supply; the third is procurement, which requires regular tracking and evaluation of the management of procurement materials, seeking a more efficient procurement operation process.

Based on the logic of the procurement operation process, the operation process of cross-border e-commerce procurement is similar, specifically referring to the entire process of cross-border e-commerce companies selecting and purchasing various goods they need. The process of cross-border e-commerce procurement can also be divided into the above three aspects, namely sourcing, ordering, and procurement.

2. Key Tasks in Cross-Border E-Commerce Procurement

(1) Formulate Procurement Plans

The procurement plan is the basic basis for cross-border e-commerce companies to carry out procurement and is an effective measure to do a good job in corporate cash use forecasting. Therefore, companies should formulate reasonable procurement plans based on procurement needs, financial conditions, procurement timing, etc., and strictly implement them.

(2) Selecting Suppliers

For suppliers in the supply chain, cross-border e-commerce purchasers can transmit procurement plan information to them via the internet and require them to execute it. For suppliers not in the supply chain, the procurement department can compile a list of suppliers for the required items, and select the best from suppliers who offer good quality, low prices, timely delivery, and attentive service.

(3) Business Negotiations

In the process of negotiating with the selected suppliers, cross-border e-commerce companies need to understand both themselves and the other party, and clarify the following issues:

- What do they hope to achieve?
- What does the other party require?
- What concessions need to be made for the negotiation to be successful?
- Signing the Procurement Contract

After successful negotiations, the next step is to sign the procurement contract, clarifying the rights and obligations of both parties and the handling of any violations.

(5) Customs Clearance of Goods

After placing an order online, a goods list is made according to the customer's order, and customs clearance activities are completed. The main modes of customs clearance for cross-border e-commerce imports in China are as follows:

The first is express clearance. After confirming the order, the foreign supplier delivers the goods directly to the consumer via international express, without any customs documents. Its advantage is flexibility, shipping only when there is business, without the need for advance stocking. The disadvantage is that it is mixed with other express shipments, resulting in lower logistics clearance efficiency, and costs will rise rapidly when the volume is large. This model is suitable for stages with fewer business volumes and occasional sporadic orders.

The second is consolidated clearance. The merchant packs multiple sold items together and transports them to a domestic bonded warehouse via international logistics. The cross-border e-commerce company handles customs clearance procedures for each item. After customs inspection and release, it entrusts domestic express delivery to deliver to the consumer. Each order comes with customs documents. The advantage is flexibility, no need for advance stocking, and compared to express clearance, the clearance efficiency is higher, and the overall logistics cost is reduced. The disadvantage is that packing operations must be completed overseas, resulting in high operation costs and slightly longer overseas shipping times. This model is suitable for stages when business volume is rapidly growing, with multiple orders each week.

The third is stockpiling clearance. The merchant bulk stocks foreign goods in a bonded warehouse under customs supervision. After the consumer places an order, the cross-border e-commerce company handles customs clearance procedures for each item based on the order. After customs inspection and release, it entrusts domestic express delivery to deliver to the consumer. Each order comes with customs documents. The advantage is that goods are bulk stocked in advance in the bonded warehouse, resulting in the lowest international logistics cost. Orders can be shipped immediately from the bonded warehouse, with the highest clearance efficiency, and can respond promptly to after-sales service requests, providing the best user experience. The disadvantage is that using a bonded warehouse incurs storage costs, and

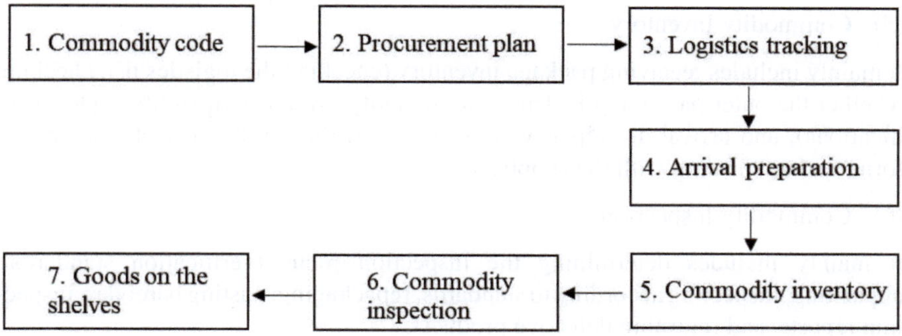

Fig. 5.2 Management process of cross-border e-commerce procurement

stocking will tie up funds. This model is suitable for stages with larger business scales and stable business volumes.

(6) Goods are Stored in the Bonded Warehouse and Registered and Shelved

After the consumer pays online, it involves domestic distribution and other services. After the consumer receives the goods and conducts acceptance, and confirms the online transaction, it means the transaction is successful.

3. Management Process of Cross-Border e-commerce Procurement

The management process of cross-border e-commerce procurement is shown in Fig. 5.2.

(1) Product Coding

There are two types of product codes: one is the product code, and the other is the specification code. Product codes are unchangeable and must be decided by the highest management level of the cross-border e-commerce company.

(2) Procurement Plan

The procurement plan is generally formulated in the form of a "procurement plan table". The content includes supplier codes, product codes, procurement prices, logistics information, logistics costs, payment methods, shipping dates, arrival dates, procurement quantities, etc.

(3) Logistics Tracking

The content of logistics tracking includes when the supplier ships, when the supplier hands over the goods to the logistics company, the status of the goods in transit, the arrival time of the goods, and the preparation for receiving the goods at any time.

(4) Arrival Preparation

Based on the results of logistics tracking, be prepared for the arrival at any time. The preparation content mainly includes yard preparation, personnel preparation, equipment preparation, and shelf preparation.

(5) Commodity Inventory

It mainly includes receiving package inventory (checking the logistics list, checking whether the outer packaging is damaged), quantity inventory (quantity, style, specifications), and arrival discrepancy confirmation (filling in the arrival discrepancy form, and confirming with the supplier).

(6) Commodity Inspection

It mainly includes determining the inspection focus (verification standards), unpacking, inspecting according to standards, repackaging, pasting barcodes, inspection reports, and returning defective products.

(7) Commodity Shelving

It mainly includes product coding, product introduction, product promotion information, etc.

4. Optimization of Cross-Border e-commerce Procurement Process

(1) Product Coding is Done Right the First Time

Once the product code is determined, it cannot be changed at will. Changing the product code requires a high cost.

(2) Transition from Supplier Management to Supply Chain Management

Treat cross-border e-commerce companies and suppliers as a virtual enterprise alliance, and treat suppliers as a department in this virtual enterprise alliance, to achieve profit sharing and risk sharing.

(3) Accurate and Reasonable Procurement Plan

The procurement time, procurement quantity, arrival time, etc., should be as accurate as possible, truly "procure for orders", and strive to achieve "zero inventory".

(4) Visualization of Logistics Tracking

Use GPS technology, sensor technology, and information and communication technology to track the procurement goods in real time and visualize the entire process, achieving seamless docking between suppliers, logistics providers, and cross-border e-commerce companies.

(5) Automation of Receiving Processing

Use barcode technology, microcontroller technology, automatic control technology, and sensor technology to automate the counting, verification, and shelving of arrivals, improving warehousing efficiency.

(6) Informationization of Procurement Management

In the process of cross-border e-commerce procurement, develop a "procurement management information system" to realize the informationization of procurement management.

5.3.3 Cross-Border E-Commerce Procurement Tracking

1. Content of Cross-Border e-commerce Procurement Tracking

(1) Shipping date, neither late nor early;
(2) Product quality, prevent defective products;
(3) Product quantity;
(4) Logistics information;
(5) Arrival date, neither early nor late;
(6) Invoice.

2. Types of Cross-Border e-commerce Procurement Tracking

(1) Production Tracking

Tracking is completed by issuing instructions to the manufacturer. Four key factors need to be grasped: the first is the date of the product's shelving; the second is the quantity of goods in transit and in stock; the third is the supplier's production capacity; the fourth is the calculation of tracking time and tracking volume.

(2) Stall Pickup Type Reorder

Stall pickup type reorder refers to a product that has a mature stock supplier, where the stock can be directly purchased from the supplier. The characteristics of the stall pickup type reorder are: first, the purchase time can be ignored, the supplier has stock inventory available, and the production cycle of the product is not calculated during the purchase process. Second, there is generally no minimum order restriction for stall pickup type reorders. Two key factors need to be grasped for stall pickup type reorders: one is supply capacity management; the other is red line inventory management of the product.

(3) Custom Development Type Reorder

Custom development type reorder is for custom products, suitable for industries with customized production needs. Custom development type reorder needs to grasp two key factors: one is that the purchase order and sales order have a strong correlation, and the corresponding purchase order needs to be generated according to the detailed content of the sales order, and the purchase orders of the same product cannot be merged for purchase; the second is that the sales staff must track the operation process of the sales order. The tracking process of the production status of the custom development type reorder is not only operated by the purchaser, but the sales staff also need to track the entire purchase or production process to meet the customer's attention to the purchase process.

Chapter 6
Cross-Border E-Commerce Payment Management

6.1 Basic Knowledge of Cross-Border Payment

6.1.1 Concept of Cross-Border Payment

1. Background of Cross-Border Payment

With the development of cross-border e-commerce, the number of users on cross-border e-commerce platforms is continuously increasing, and the total transaction volume of cross-border e-commerce is showing a rapid upward trend. Therefore, the demand for fund settlement services is constantly expanding, bringing huge opportunities for financial institutions providing cross-border payments. At present, with frequent economic exchanges between countries, the role of cross-border electronic payments is becoming more and more important, occupying an increasingly important position in the entire payment system, playing an important role in both cross-border e-commerce transactions and daily personal consumption.

The settlement methods in traditional international trade cannot meet the needs of cross-border e-commerce transactions. This is mainly because the transaction amount of each ticket in cross-border e-commerce is small and the batches are many, resulting in a small amount of each settlement. In the traditional settlement process, the main settlement methods are letters of credit, telegraphic transfers, remittances, and collections. These settlement methods are mainly based on commercial credit, but in cross-border transactions, exporters often bear a large risk, on the one hand, a large amount of funds are occupied, on the other hand, it is difficult to obtain trade financing. Among the settlement methods, letters of credit rely on bank credit, have low risk, and can provide financing services for exporters, but there are complicated procedures and high fees. The transaction amount of each cross-border e-commerce transaction is very limited and cannot bear the high fees in traditional trade settlement. Therefore, third-party payment for small international trade has emerged. With the development of cross-border e-commerce, both traditional commercial banks and

X. Zhang, *Introduction to Cross-Border E-Commerce Ecosystem*,
https://doi.org/10.1007/978-981-96-1165-2_6

Internet financial institutions have turned their development focus to cross-border third-party payment services.

2. Definition of Cross-Border Payment

Cross-border payment refers to the behavior of transferring funds across countries or regions using certain settlement tools and payment systems due to international debts and credits generated from international trade, international investment, or other aspects between two or more countries or regions. For example, when Chinese consumers purchase goods from foreign merchants on cross-border e-commerce platforms, or when foreign consumers purchase goods from Chinese merchants, due to different legal currencies, it is necessary to use certain settlement tools and payment systems to realize the conversion of funds between two countries or two regions, and the flow of funds from the buyer to the seller, to ultimately complete the transaction. Cross-border payments are used in traditional international trade, where the payment method is mainly offline payment, the amount is large, and the involved entities are mostly organizational forms, generally using telegraphic transfer (T/T), collection (D/P, D/A), letter of credit (L/C), Western Union remittance, etc. With the promotion of internet technology, information technology, payment technology, etc., cross-border e-commerce has developed rapidly, promoting the innovation of cross-border payment methods. A new type of cross-border payment method has emerged, namely cross-border electronic payment, or also known as cross-border internet payment, specifically providing online payment services for trading parties in different countries or regions through the internet. Cross-border electronic payment is a category of cross-border payment. Whether it is cross-border payment or cross-border electronic payment, the payment serving cross-border e-commerce transactions under the rapid development of cross-border e-commerce is all cross-border payment under cross-border e-commerce, unless otherwise specified in this article, the cross-border payment involved refers to the cross-border payment serving cross-border e-commerce transactions.

Common cross-border payment methods include commercial banks, third-party payment platforms, and professional remittance companies. Among them, third-party payment platforms are used more frequently. Third-party payment platforms are favored by more and more cross-border payment users due to their convenience and low rates. Common third-party payment tools include PayPal, Alipay, etc.

In cross-border e-commerce, cross-border payment is no longer limited to traditional offline payment, and the use of electronic payment is becoming more and more widespread. Electronic payment can reduce costs and manage risks for users, and its efficiency has become one of the important factors affecting cross-border e-commerce. Cross-border electronic payment is the core link of cross-border e-commerce, involving multiple entities such as enterprises, individuals, banks, and third-party payment platforms. Common cross-border electronic payment methods mainly include mobile payment, virtual currency, online banking payment, third-party payment, etc.

3. Participants in Cross-Border Payments

The main participants in cross-border payments include domestic and foreign banks, remittance companies, international credit card organizations, cross-border collection companies, and third-party cross-border payment companies, etc.

Domestic and foreign banks refer to financial institutions that operate currency credit business, such as: Bank of America, Citibank, HSBC, Standard Chartered Bank, Bank of China, etc.

Remittance companies refer to companies that carry out international remittance business, such as: Global Speed Remittance, MoneyGram, etc.

International credit card organizations refer to credit cards of non-UnionPay organizations, such as: VISA, MasterCard, etc.

Cross-border collection companies refer to companies that carry out international collection business, such as: Pingpong, PayPal, etc.

Third-party cross-border payment companies refer to payment institutions that provide limited services to domestic and foreign consumers, such as: Lakala, etc.

4. Cross-Border Payment Business

Cross-border payment business includes cross-border acquiring, cross-border remittance, and cross-border foreign exchange settlement and sales.

Cross-border acquiring refers to the process of handling payments from domestic and foreign consumers or merchants' bank cards/accounts on behalf of merchants. When conducting cross-border acquiring business, it is necessary to understand foreign card acquiring, overseas acquiring, and international acquiring. Among them, foreign card acquiring appears in export business, mainly serving domestic merchants to collect payment from foreign consumers; overseas acquiring mainly involves domestic consumers purchasing goods from foreign merchants; international acquiring is when the merchant, consumer, and payment institution belong to different countries, such as when domestic consumers purchase products or services from overseas merchants, they use domestic payment, first pay to the domestic payment institution, and then the domestic payment institution settles funds to the overseas payment institution through a cooperative bank.

Cross-border remittance refers to the business of personal online banking customers remitting foreign exchange to recipients who have opened accounts in foreign banks within a specified limit. Cross-border remittance methods include: cash, telegraphic transfer, foreign currency drafts, traveler's checks, credit cards, etc. Taking telegraphic transfer as an example, the remitter first purchases foreign exchange, and then the remitting bank, according to the remitter's request, instructs the receiving bank to pay the funds to the recipient through an encrypted telegram.

Cross-border foreign exchange settlement and sale is the general term for domestic and foreign foreign exchange settlement and sale, which is the exchange between foreign currency and RMB through banks. Among them, cross-border foreign exchange settlement refers to the behavior of the owner of foreign exchange income selling his foreign exchange income to a designated foreign exchange bank, and the designated foreign exchange bank pays the equivalent domestic currency at a certain exchange rate; cross-border foreign exchange sale refers to the behavior of the designated foreign exchange bank selling foreign exchange to the foreign exchange user, and collecting the equivalent RMB according to the RMB exchange rate on the day of the transaction.

6.1.2 Third-Party Payment Related Knowledge

1. Definition of Third-Party Payment

Third-party payment refers to a network payment mode in which an institution with certain strength and credit guarantee establishes an effective connection between merchants and banks through internet technology to facilitate transactions between the two parties. Institutions providing third-party payment services must meet certain conditions. The institution has sufficient strength and good reputation as an important guarantee for the business, and needs to sign contracts with major domestic and foreign banks to enhance the credit of both parties. This is equivalent to adding an intermediary in the bank settlement link. In the cross-border transaction process, the buyer pays the payment to this intermediary, then the intermediary notifies the seller to deliver the goods, and after the buyer receives the goods, the intermediary pays the payment to the seller. This way, there is a safe intermediary in both parties, and both parties are constrained by the intermediary. In order to ensure the safety of online transactions, both parties are willing to find a trustworthy third-party intermediary to provide them with fair transaction service guarantees. In fact, the intermediary becomes a transitional account for the payment of funds between the two parties. Although the intermediary plays a supervisory role and assumes custody responsibilities, it does not need to bear the corresponding risks and only provides payment custody services.

Third-party payment has many characteristics, as follows:

(1) Function integration and transaction convenience. There are multiple application programming interfaces in the third-party payment platform, and there are multiple payment methods on the same interface. In the settlement, the third-party payment platform will dock with the bank, not only ensuring the safety of online transactions, but also providing convenience for both parties.
(2) Easy authentication and lower cost. In the transaction process, the e-commerce certification authorization agency no longer needs to authenticate both parties, and the negotiations between the two parties in the transaction process can be reached through the third party, which not only simplifies the transaction process, but also greatly reduces the transaction cost.
(3) Reduce transaction credit risk. Behind the third-party payment platform is a powerful portal website, and it has established a cooperative relationship with the bank, and has enough credit as a reliance. Therefore, the third-party payment platform has a good credit guarantee, and both parties have enough trust in it.

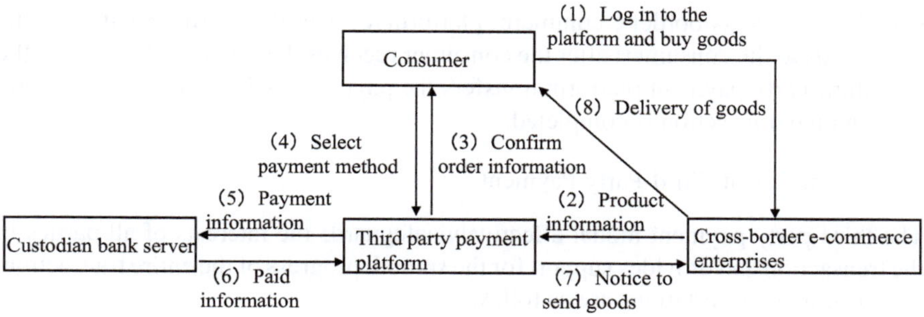

Fig. 6.1 Third-party payment business process

2. Principle of Third-Party Payment

The implementation principle of the third-party payment system is: the third-party institution signs relevant agreements with each major bank, enabling the third-party institution and the bank to exchange data and confirm related information in some form. In this way, the third-party institution can establish a payment process between the cardholder or consumer and various banks, as well as the final payee or merchant.

When the third party is an institution other than a bank with good reputation and technical support capabilities, payment is made through the third party between the cardholder or customer and the bank. The cardholder first passes account information to the third party in some form of electronic data (such as email) as a substitute for the bank account, avoiding the cardholder from directly revealing bank information to the merchant, and also avoiding the need to log in to different online banking interfaces. Instead, each time you log in, you can see the relatively familiar and simple interface of the third-party institution. The third-party payment mode prevents the merchant from seeing the customer's credit card information, and at the same time avoids the theft of credit card information caused by multiple public transmissions on the network. The third-party payment business process is shown in Fig. 6.1.

(1) The consumer logs into the cross-border e-commerce website to select goods, and places an order after reaching a transaction intention online.
(2) The consumer chooses to use the third party as the transaction intermediary, and uses the credit card to transfer the payment to the third party account.
(3) The third-party payment platform sends the order information to the consumer, waiting for the consumer to confirm.
(4) The consumer needs to pay after receiving the order information, and chooses the payment method.
(5) The third-party payment platform sends the consumer's payment information to the custodian bank server.
(6) The custodian bank sends the consumer's paid information to the third-party payment platform.
(7) The third-party payment platform notifies the cross-border e-commerce platform to ship.

(8) After the cross-border e-commerce platform receives the instruction, it sends the goods to the consumer; after the consumer receives the goods and confirms, the third-party payment platform transfers the payment to the merchant's account, and the transaction is completed.

3. Advantages of Third-Party Payment

The third-party payment model effectively safeguards the interests of all parties in the transaction and provides support for the smooth progress of the entire transaction. The specific manifestations are as follows:

(1) The third-party payment platform provides a series of application interface programs, integrates various payment methods into one interface, is responsible for docking with the bank in the transaction settlement, making online shopping more convenient and faster.
(2) Using the third-party payment platform for payment operations is simpler and more acceptable. Through the third-party payment platform, the transaction parties do not need to authenticate each other's identity through the e-commerce certification center (CA), and the negotiations between the merchant and the customer are completed by the third party, making online transactions simpler, faster, and lower cost.
(3) The third-party payment platform itself is attached to a large portal site, and relies on the credit of the cooperating bank as a credit reliance, so the third-party payment platform can better break through the credit problem in online transactions, which is conducive to promoting the rapid development of e-commerce.
(4) For merchants, through the third-party payment platform, they can avoid the risk of not receiving consumer payments, and at the same time provide consumers with diversified payment tools, without the need to open different accounts in different banks, helping merchants reduce operating costs, especially for small and medium-sized enterprises that cannot establish an interface with the bank gateway, providing a convenient payment platform.
(5) For consumers, not only can they avoid the risk of not receiving goods, but the quality of the goods is also guaranteed to a certain extent, enhancing consumers' confidence in online transactions, and without the need to open different accounts in different banks, it can reduce the cost of online shopping.
(6) For banks, through third-party platforms, they can expand their business scope while saving the development and maintenance costs of providing gateway interfaces for a large number of small and medium-sized enterprises.

4. Disadvantages of Third-Party Payments

(1) Risk Issues

In the electronic payment process, funds will stay in the third-party payment organization as sedimentary funds. If there is a lack of effective liquidity management, there may be risks to the safety of funds and payments. At the same time, third-party payment institutions open payment settlement accounts, first collect funds from consumers, and then pay merchants, which may facilitate illegal fund transfers and cashing out, thus forming potential financial risks.

(2) Issues of Certification, Protection, and Development of Electronic Payment Operating Qualifications.

Third-party payment settlement belongs to the non-bank financial services provided by payment clearing organizations, and banks will raise the threshold in the form of licenses. Therefore, for third-party payment companies engaged in financial business, the challenge is not only how to make a profit, but more importantly, whether they can obtain a third-party payment business license.

(3) Malicious Competition Issues

There are issues of malicious competition in the electronic payment industry that harm payment services and even bring negative impacts to the development of the e-commerce industry. Taking China as an example, there are already more than 40 professional electronic payment companies, most of which use pure technical gateway access services with banks. This payment gateway model can easily lead to serious market homogenization and intensify price wars among payment companies.

6.2 Cross-Border E-Commerce Payment Methods

6.2.1 Cross-Border E-Commerce Payment Channels

Cross-border e-commerce payment refers to the situation where consumers buy products from foreign merchants online or foreign consumers buy products from Chinese merchants. Due to the difference in currency, it is necessary to use certain settlement tools and payment systems to realize the fund conversion between two countries or regions, and finally complete the transaction.

Cross-border e-commerce payment services involve multiple entities such as enterprises, individuals, banks, remittance companies, and third-party payment platforms. Typical cross-border e-commerce payment service providers include online banking payment service systems and electronic payment services involving third-party payment platforms.

Different business models of cross-border e-commerce have different payment settlement methods. The cross-border e-commerce payment industry has formed a multi-channel coexistence pattern, including bank telegraphic transfer, express remittance companies, international card organizations, third-party payments, and Hong Kong offshore accounts. Each channel has its own advantages and disadvantages, as shown in Table 6.1.

B2B information service platform model, mainly serving B2B e-commerce enterprises, such as providing online marketing platforms for domestic and foreign

Table 6.1 Overview of common cross-border payment modes

Cross-border payment mode	Main payment instruments	Characteristic
Bank	Bank telegraphic transfer	Traditional payment methods for foreign trade, generally transfer data through swift
Express remittance company	Western Union remittance 、MoneyGram 、etc	Fast arrival, relatively high handling fees, and insufficient outlets
International card organization	Mastercard 、Visa 、etc	Large number of users, linked to the credit system, and high fees
Third party payment	PayPal 、ClickandBuy 、Qiwi wallet 、etc	Easy to use, wide variety
Hong Kong offshore account	Hong Kong account, offshore account (domestic), offshore account (foreign)	Domestic control, overseas operation and free fund allocation

member merchants, conveying the goods or service information of suppliers or buyers and other partners, and ultimately helping both parties complete the transaction. Traditional cross-border large transaction platforms are typically represented by Global Sources, Made in China, Directindustry, etc. Bulk transaction platforms only provide buyer and buyer information, provide channels for merchants to know each other, do not support in-site transactions. Foreign trade transactions are mainly offline payments, with large amounts, generally using T/T, L/C, Western Union remittance, etc.

B2B transaction service platform model, mainly providing transaction, online logistics, dispute handling, after-sales and other services. This type of cross-border platform mainly includes Alibaba International Station, etc. The market concentration of B2B transaction service platforms is high, this platform model mostly uses online payment, payment methods mainly include PayPal, etc.

The B2C open platform model mainly provides services such as transactions, online payments, logistics, dispute resolution, and after-sales, focusing on small-scale wholesale and retail. Representative platforms include Lanting Jishi, Milan Network, Chinavasion, Tomtop, etc. This model generally adopts online payment methods, such as PayPal, credit cards, debit cards, etc.

The B2C self-operated platform model is established through self-built platforms like JD Global Purchase, Global Easy Buy, etc. This model, like the B2C open platform, generally adopts online payment methods, such as PayPal, credit cards, debit cards, etc.

The C2C cross-border e-commerce retail model mainly provides services such as transactions, online payments, logistics, dispute resolution, and after-sales. Representative platforms include AliExpress, Yitang Network, etc. These C2C platforms do not participate in cross-border e-commerce transactions, but charge a certain percentage of commission based on the transactions between the seller and the buyer.

They generally adopt online payment methods, such as PayPal, credit cards, debit cards, etc.

The independent site model, through self-built websites and precise positioning, sells goods overseas. Its main business includes transactions, logistics, payments, customer service, etc. Typical representatives are SHEIN, Anke, etc. Payment methods can vary according to customer needs.

6.2.2 Cross-Border E-Commerce Offline Payment Methods

Cross-border payment tools fall into two categories: one is offline payment, which is more suitable for larger amount cross-border B2B transactions; offline payment refers to methods other than online payment, including letters of credit, collection, telegraphic transfer, Western Union, MoneyGram, Hong Kong offshore accounts, etc. The other is online payment, including various electronic account payment methods and international credit cards, etc. Due to the transaction limit of online payment methods, they are more suitable for small cross-border retail transactions.

1. Letter of Credit

A Letter of Credit (L/C) is a written document issued by a bank (issuing bank) at the request and instruction of the applicant or on its own initiative, to make payment to a third party (beneficiary) or its designated party upon presentation of specified documents under the terms of the letter of credit. In other words, a letter of credit is a written document of a bank's conditional commitment to pay.

In traditional international trade activities, the buyer and seller may not trust each other. The buyer worries that after prepayment, the seller will not deliver the goods as required by the contract; the seller worries that after delivery or submission of shipping documents, the buyer will not pay. In the letter of credit settlement method, the bank replaces commercial credit with bank credit, providing credit guarantees for both parties to the transaction, thereby promoting the smooth completion of the transaction and the safe payment of funds. The letter of credit is a certificate of the bank's conditional guarantee of payment and has become a common settlement method in traditional international trade activities. The buyer first submits a letter of credit application, pays a deposit and bank fees, the bank issues a letter of credit, notifies the seller in a different location, the seller delivers goods according to the contract and the terms of the letter of credit, and the issuing bank pays on behalf of the buyer under the condition of no errors in the review of documents.

(1) Costs: The bank charges for the letter of credit mainly include: ① issuance. Issuance fee, amendment fee, cancellation fee; ② letter of credit transmission. Pre-advice fee, notification fee, transfer fee; ③ letter of credit presentation. Postage, telegram fee, examination fee; ④ letter of credit collection. Negotiation fee, acceptance fee, confirmation fee, reimbursement fee, payment handling fee, transfer fee, no exchange handling fee, discrepancy fee, discrepancy document storage fee; ⑤ and possible fines involved in the letter of credit.

Different banks charge differently for different items. Some are charged at a fixed rate, such as notification fees, discrepancy fees, etc., charged per transaction; some are charged proportionally, such as negotiation fees, exchange fees, etc.; and some are charged cyclically, such as acceptance fees, confirmation fees, etc. In addition, the charging standards between different banks also vary.

(2) Advantages: With the credibility of banks involved, international trade is relatively safer and the risk is relatively lower; the superiority of letters of credit is more prominent when the transaction amount is large, the trading parties do not know each other, and the importing country imposes foreign exchange controls; compared to wire transfers and collection methods, the financial burden of the trading parties in the letter of credit method is more balanced; the buyer needs to pay a certain proportion of margin to open a letter of credit, the proportion of the margin depends on the buyer's credit and strength, the higher the credit, the lower the proportion, the seller can roughly understand the buyer's credit situation from it; even if the buyer refuses to pay, the seller can still control the right to the goods, and the loss is relatively less.
(3) Disadvantages: The letter of credit is an independent, self-sufficient document, and the bank only checks the documents and does not care about the goods, so it is easy to generate fraudulent behavior and there is a risk of false documents; the letter of credit method is complicated and has many links; the letter of credit has high requirements for documents and is easy to be rejected due to discrepancies; the cost is relatively high, affecting the profits of exporters, if the amount of the letter of credit is small, the total bank charges will exceed 1%; encountering soft clause traps, the process of checking certificates and documents requires strong technicality.
(4) Applicable scope: Suitable for offline transactions with a larger transaction amount (generally more than 50,000 US dollars).

2. Collection

Collection is a method of settlement where the exporter, after shipping the goods, issues a draft with the importer as the payer, and entrusts the bank in the exporting place to collect the payment for the goods on behalf of the exporter through its branch or agent in the importing place. It is a form of commercial credit. Depending on whether shipping documents are submitted to the bank at the time of collection, it is divided into clean collection and documentary collection. Documentary collection, depending on the conditions of document submission, can be divided into documents against payment (D/P) and documents against acceptance (D/A).

Collection is a form of commercial credit. When a bank handles collection business, it has neither the obligation to check whether the shipping documents are correct or complete, nor the responsibility to ensure that the payer must pay. Although collection is handled through a bank, the bank only acts as the trustee of the exporter and does not assume the responsibility of payment. The importer's non-payment has nothing to do with the bank. The exporter's collection of payment from the importer still relies on the importer's commercial credit. If the importer refuses to pay, unless otherwise stipulated, the bank has no obligation to manage the goods, and the exporter should still be concerned about the safety of the goods until the other party pays for the goods.

Collection poses a greater risk to exporters, and D/A poses a greater risk than D/P. The documentary collection method is that the exporter ships the goods first and then collects the payment, so it poses a greater risk to the exporter. The importer's payment depends on its commercial reputation. If the importer goes bankrupt and loses the ability to pay, or if the price of goods in the importing place falls after the goods are shipped, and the importer refuses to pay on the pretext, or if the importer has not received the import license in advance, or has not applied for foreign exchange, is prohibited from importing or unable to pay foreign exchange, etc., the exporter will not only be unable to recover the payment on time, but may also lose both the goods and the payment. Although the exporter has the right to claim for various losses suffered, in practice, when the importer goes bankrupt or loses contact, the exporter, even if it can recover some compensation, will find it difficult to make up for all the losses. In today's increasingly fierce international market export competition, exporters sometimes use the collection method to expand sales and capture the market. If the importer has a good reputation and the exporter has its own offices abroad, the risk can be relatively smaller.

Collection is more advantageous for importers, as it eliminates the need for letter of credit procedures and prepayment of deposits, and also allows for the convenience of pre-borrowing goods. Of course, collection is not without some risk to the importer. If the importer pays before obtaining the shipping documents and collecting the goods, and finds that the goods do not comply with the contract or are fake, they may suffer losses. But overall, collection is more advantageous for importers.

(1) Costs. The normal bank charges incurred by collection mainly include collection fees and mailing fees.
(2) Advantages: Compared to letters of credit, the operation of collection is much simpler, the document requirements are relatively simple, and the costs are relatively low; goods are shipped before payment, which is beneficial to importers and facilitates transactions.
(3) Disadvantages. Collection is a settlement method based on commercial credit, and the seller assumes a greater risk; it is disadvantageous for exporters, as whether the exporter can recover the payment on time depends entirely on the importer's creditworthiness; compared to methods such as telegraphic transfer, collection procedures are more complicated and costs are higher.
(4) Applicable scope. For exporters, the risk is greater, and it is only suitable for customers with large amounts, many years of dealings, mutual understanding, and good reputation.

3. Telegraphic Transfer

Telegraphic Transfer is a method of remittance where the remitter deposits a certain amount of money with the remitting bank, and the remitting bank instructs the branch or agent bank at the destination (the receiving bank) to pay a certain amount to the payee via telegram or telex. Compared to letters of credit and collection, telegraphic transfer has a wide range of applications, is easy to handle, has fewer intermediate procedures, is flexible and convenient, and is currently a widely used settlement method.

(1) Costs. The cost of telegraphic transfer is divided into two parts, one part is related to the amount of telegraphic transfer, that is, a 1‰ handling fee, and the other part is unrelated to the amount of remittance, but related to the number of transactions, that is, a telegraphic transfer fee is charged for each remittance. The specific cost is calculated based on the bank's actual rate, and the charging standards of different banks vary greatly. When choosing a remittance bank, it is advisable to make a comparison. Since the remittance handling fee generally has a maximum limit, any amount exceeding the maximum limit is limited to the maximum limit.
(2) Advantages. Telegraphic transfer has no minimum amount limit, and can be used regardless of the amount of money; the remittance settlement procedure is simple and easy to handle, and can be handled by both units and individuals; the receipt of money is fast, and the account is quickly credited; payment can be made before shipment, ensuring that the merchant's interests are not damaged.
(3) Disadvantages. It is necessary to go to the bank counter to handle business, which is limited by the distribution of bank outlets; payment is made before shipment, which can easily lead to distrust by the buyer; both the buyer and seller have to pay handling fees, which are relatively high compared to some online payment tools, and compared to third-party online payment methods, telegraphic transfer procedures are more complicated; in actual business, the risk borne by the buyer is greater.
(4) Applicable scope. It is suitable for all types of international trade transactions, whether it is commodity trade, service trade, technology transfer, etc., and can also be used for cross-border remittances between individuals.

4. Western Union

Western Union is the abbreviation for Western Union International Remittance Company, which is the world's leading express remittance company. It has the world's largest and most advanced electronic remittance financial network, with agent outlets spread across nearly 200 countries and regions.

(1) Costs. The recipient does not need to pay any fees, the remitter needs to pay a handling fee based on a certain proportion of the remittance amount, and if there are other additional requirements, an additional service fee will be charged.
(2) Advantages. The amount of money sent equals the amount received, with no intermediary bank charges; Western Union's global secure electronic system ensures the safety of each remittance, and there are operation passwords and self-selected passwords for verification, ensuring that the remittance is safely delivered to the designated recipient's account; Western Union remittance procedures are simple, using the world's most advanced electronic technology and unique global electronic financial network, the recipient can receive the remittance in full within a few minutes; the handling fee is borne by the buyer, and

the seller does not need to pay any handling fee; Western Union International Remittance Company's overseas agent outlets are located all over the world, including banks, post offices, foreign currency exchange points, train stations and airports, making it convenient for both parties to remit and receive money.

(3) Disadvantages. The remittance handling fee is charged per transaction, and the fee for small amount receipts is high; it is difficult for the buyer to trust the seller during the first transaction, and it is easy to give up the transaction due to the risk of making a payment before delivery; both the buyer and seller need to go to Western Union's offline counter for operation; it is a traditional transaction mode and cannot adapt well to the trend of cross-border e-commerce.

(4) Applicable scope. Payments of less than 10,000 US dollars.

5. MoneyGram

MoneyGram International Remittance is an international remittance method launched by MoneyGram International, a kind of overseas fast remittance business handled through its global network, providing individual customers with this fast, simple, safe and reliable, convenient international remittance service. MoneyGram has agent outlets in nearly 200 countries and regions around the world, and is a remittance institution similar to Western Union.

(1) Fees. There is no charge for MoneyGram's incoming business, and the seller does not need to pay a handling fee. The fees for MoneyGram's outgoing business include handling fees and commissions, and the commission fee standard is deducted according to the amount automatically generated by the MoneyGram system when handling the remittance business.

(2) Advantages. The remittance speed is fast, under normal business conditions of MoneyGram agent outlets (including remittance outlets and payment outlets), MoneyGram remittance can reach the recipient's account within a few minutes after remittance; MoneyGram's charging method is overcharge standard, when the remittance amount is not high, the fee is relatively low; there are no other additional fees and unknown fees, no intermediary bank fees, no telegram fees; the procedures are simple, no need to fill in complex remittance paths, the recipient does not need to open a bank account in advance, can realize fund transfer.

(3) Disadvantages. MoneyGram only provides services on working days, does not provide corresponding services on holidays, and the processing speed is slow; both the remitter and the recipient must be individuals; it must be for overseas remittance, does not provide domestic remittance business; if the customer remits money with a cash account, a certain cash exchange fee needs to be paid; both the buyer and seller need to go to the offline counter for operation, and cannot adapt well to the trend of cross-border e-commerce development.

(4) Applicable scope. It is suitable for overseas students, tourists, inspectors, and workers, and also suitable for medium-sized transactions with an annual remittance amount not exceeding 50,000 US dollars.

6. Hong Kong Offshore Account

An offshore account refers to a bank account opened by a depositor outside their country of residence. Conversely, banks located within the depositor's country of residence are referred to as onshore bank accounts or domestic bank accounts. Accounts opened by foreign institutions in accordance with regulations at domestic banks that have legally obtained offshore banking business qualifications are considered overseas accounts, such as accounts opened by companies in mainland China in Hong Kong, which are Hong Kong offshore accounts. The seller receives remittances from overseas buyers by opening an offshore bank account in Hong Kong, and then remits the money from the Hong Kong account to the mainland account. Offshore accounts are only for corporate account opening and do not support individual account opening. Compared to domestic accounts, offshore accounts are subject to less foreign exchange control, and from the perspective of fund security, offshore accounts are safer and are not as strictly regulated by the State Administration of Foreign Exchange.

(1) Costs. These mainly include the cost of opening a Hong Kong offshore account and subsequent maintenance costs. The cost of opening an account varies slightly from bank to bank, with the cost of handling it in person in Hong Kong being about 1150 Hong Kong dollars; the cost of opening an account via video in mainland China is 1750 to 3150 Hong Kong dollars; if it is inconvenient, you can choose to entrust an agent. Subsequent maintenance costs include: annual review costs (450 + 105) excluding employee declaration costs, tax payment costs for Hong Kong companies after 18 months, remittance costs, and account management fees when the amount of funds does not meet the minimum standard each month.
(2) Advantages. Funds can be freely allocated from offshore accounts, which are equivalent to bank accounts opened overseas, and are not subject to domestic foreign exchange control; deposit interest rates and types are not subject to domestic regulatory restrictions, especially for large deposits, which can be customized according to customer needs in terms of interest rates, terms, etc., flexible and convenient; the Chinese government exempts interest on deposits and withdrawals from offshore accounts from deposit interest tax; accelerates the turnover of domestic and foreign funds, reduces the comprehensive cost of funds, and improves the efficiency of fund use; using an offshore account to receive payments can make a reasonable arrangement for the company in terms of taxation, which is of great benefit to the company's future development; there is no limit to the amount of wire transfers received, and different currencies can be freely exchanged at will.
(3) Disadvantages. The starting savings amount for opening an offshore account is generally higher, with at least 10,000 Hong Kong dollars in activation funds; if the amount of funds is lower than the specified amount each month, a certain account management fee needs to be paid; the money in the Hong Kong bank account still needs to be transferred to the mainland account, which is more troublesome; offshore accounts are often used by criminals to launder money,

have a bad reputation, and the tax situation of offshore companies is subject to stricter supervision; some customers choose the method of underground banks, which carries financial and legal risks.

(4) Applicable scope. Both traditional foreign trade and cross-border e-commerce are applicable, suitable for sellers who already have a certain scale of transactions.

6.3 Cross-Border E-Commerce Online Payment Tools

6.3.1 Mainstream Online Payment Tools

1. PayPal

PayPal, originally a wholly-owned subsidiary of the American company eBay, is headquartered in California, USA. On April 10, 2015, PayPal was spun off from eBay and listed independently on the NASDAQ in the United States. PayPal has partnered with many e-commerce websites and has become one of the online payment methods for cross-border e-commerce platforms. PayPal operates on an account model, requiring both parties to the transaction to have a registered PayPal account. The buyer must bind a credit card account to their PayPal account and then recharge their PayPal account using the credit card before they can make a payment. PayPal transactions do not go through a bank gateway, and if the buyer refuses to pay, they can operate online without any impact on their credit.

PayPal is currently the most widely used online transaction tool in the world, capable of facilitating convenient foreign trade receipts, withdrawals, and transaction tracking; engaging in secure international procurement and consumption; and quickly paying and receiving 25 major international currencies including US dollars, Canadian dollars, Euros, British pounds, Australian dollars, and Japanese yen. When transferring money using PayPal, a certain amount of handling fee is required.

(1) Payment process

When paying an amount to a merchant or recipient through PayPal, the following steps are involved.

① The payer first needs to have an email address, log in to the email address to open a PayPal account, become its user through verification, and provide credit card or related bank information to increase the account balance, transferring a certain amount of funds from the account registered at the time of opening (such as a credit card) to the PayPal account.

② When making a payment, the payer first enters the PayPal account, specifies the remittance amount, and provides the recipient's email account to PayPal.

③ Next, PayPal sends an email to the recipient, notifying them of funds waiting to be claimed or transferred.

④ If the recipient is also a PayPal user, after deciding to accept the funds, the amount specified by the payer is transferred into the recipient's PayPal account.

⑤ If the recipient does not have a PayPal account, the recipient needs to follow the instructions in the PayPal email to connect to the website and register for a PayPal account. The recipient can choose to convert the received funds into a check sent to a specified location, transfer it to their personal credit card account, or transfer it to another bank account.

(2) PayPal restrictions

The most common problem with using a PayPal account is account restrictions, the main types and countermeasures are as follows.

① 21-day limit for new accounts. Restrictions on new accounts are frequent, this is PayPal's review of new accounts, no need to submit any documents, PayPal will automatically lift the restriction after the review, in this case, just be patient and wait.

② Temporary review restrictions. Suddenly being restricted after multiple receipts is because PayPal needs to understand the seller's business model and product information. The seller needs to respond positively and provide relevant information to let PayPal understand the products the seller operates. Common documents for lifting restrictions include credit card proof, address proof, supplier information, invoices, etc.

③ Risk review type restrictions. This type of restriction is triggered by an account risk review. Account risks include two aspects: one is the risk from the buyer, if the buyer's account risk is too high, PayPal will automatically refund, and the transaction cannot proceed; the second is the risk from the seller, then you need to find the reason from several aspects, whether the complaint rate is too high, whether the receipt is too high in a short period, etc.

④ High limit. This type of restriction also comes from high risk, high limit accounts cannot receive or make payments. Product violations and complaint rates can lead to high limits. In addition, if the account is restricted and there is no timely response, the restriction will automatically upgrade to a high limit until it is blocked. So once the account is restricted, you need to respond positively in the account as soon as possible and submit the required documents.

(3) PayPal freezing

PayPal account freezing refers to a transaction in the account being temporarily frozen, and the account user cannot perform operations such as refunding and withdrawing on this transaction. From the registration of an account to receiving payments and then to withdrawal, PayPal has never received any information from the user, so every account is definitely going to be frozen once from opening to withdrawal, and then the account user is asked to submit identity proof, address information, etc. to prove that the user is a real and law-abiding citizen. The following situations can also lead to freezing.

① Immediate withdrawal after receiving payment. For example, if an account receives 1000 US dollars, and immediately withdraws 900 US dollars after receiving the payment, there is a situation where the seller has received the payment and withdraws before the goods are shipped, which inevitably raises suspicion and leads to being frozen.

② The withdrawal amount is too high. For example, if you receive 1000 US dollars and ship the goods, the seller needs to turn over the funds and withdraw all 1000 US dollars, which is quite dangerous. PayPal generally considers a withdrawal amount of 80% to be relatively safe, leaving 20% to prevent the buyer from returning the order and to reassure PayPal.

③ Too many customer complaints and returns. Generally, if the complaint rate exceeds 3%, and the return rate exceeds 1%, PayPal will terminate the cooperation.

④ The products sold have intellectual property issues. Foreign countries pay great attention to the protection of intellectual property rights. If counterfeit or fake goods appear, PayPal will prohibit its transactions. Once international brand merchants complain to PayPal, the consequences are very serious and it will be difficult to use PayPal for payment again.

(4) Fees

The recipient's fee is a bank system occupancy fee of 0.3 US dollars per transaction; a handling fee of 2.9% to 3.9% is charged during the transaction; a cross-border fee of 0.5% is charged for each cross-border transaction; a withdrawal fee of 35 US dollars is charged for each withdrawal.

(5) Advantages

No account opening fee; PayPal is in line with the transaction methods of most countries, has a high reputation internationally, and has a large user base.

(6) Disadvantages.

Does not support counterfeit payment. It tends to protect the interests of buyers, and there is relatively no guarantee for sellers. Transaction fees are mainly provided by sellers. There are many restrictions and fees for withdrawals and other follow-ups, and the account is easily frozen. If there is a dispute in a transaction, and the buyer and seller cannot reach a consensus, PayPal will freeze the entire account of the seller to protect the interests of the buyer from loss (other situations will also freeze the account).

(7) Applicable scope.

Suitable for cross-border e-commerce retail industry, small transactions of tens to hundreds of US dollars.

1. International Credit Card Payment

International credit card payment usually refers to international credit card online payment. International credit card payment is a payment gateway mode for payment gateways. Credit card consumption is a popular consumption method in the world today, especially in Europe and America, where the credit system is very mature, and people are accustomed to using credit cards for advance consumption. Shopping with a credit card online has become mainstream. Online credit card payment can be refused, can protect the interests of consumers, and is convenient and fast to operate, but buyers cannot easily refuse payment, refusal will affect the buyer's credit card credit limit.

(1) Payment process

The credit card payment process is as follows:

① The buyer issues a payment instruction to the issuing bank from his credit card.

② The bank advances the payment to the seller's bank.

③ The bank notifies the cardholder of the due date and amount of the interest-free period.

Although the seller has completed the transaction, only when the buyer takes the following actions can the payment for the goods be 100% guaranteed: the buyer repays before the due date, the transaction is successfully completed, and the seller successfully receives the payment; the buyer first repays part of the debt, generally greater than The minimum repayment amount stipulated by the bank, the rest is treated as a loan from the bank, and agrees to pay interest, and then gradually repay the principal and interest, and finally the buyer gets financing convenience, the bank gets interest income, and the seller gets the payment in time.

(2) Advantages

① Huge customer base: Visa and MasterCard have over 2 billion users, especially in Europe and America, where the usage rate is very high. It caters to the advanced consumption habits of foreign buyers, making payment more convenient.

② Expand potential customers: Credit card payment can be completed as long as the buyer has a credit card. The number of credit card holders is much larger than the number of registrants in payment companies, and it is a consumption mode that many consumers accept and are willing to use.

③ Reduce chargebacks: Since it is a bank-to-bank model, the buyer needs to go to the issuing bank for a chargeback, and the issuing bank will also check the chargeback to see if it is a malicious chargeback (if it is a malicious chargeback, the bank will record it on the cardholder's credit record), which will bring great inconvenience to the buyer's future life, study and work, so the cardholder will generally not refuse payment at will. The chargeback of the account-to-account model has no impact on the cardholder's credit record, so the chargeback rate of credit card payment is smaller than the rate of the account-to-account model. According to statistics from international card organizations, the probability of chargebacks for credit card consumption does not exceed 0.5%.

④ No account freezing: For credit card payments, if there is a dispute in a transaction, the amount of the transaction will be frozen, without affecting the entire account.

The credit card channel pays attention to the interests of both buyers and sellers, and will handle it according to the delivery status of the goods and the attitude of the buyer, and will not close the channel to cause the merchant's funds to be frozen, so the handling of chargebacks is undoubtedly more fair.

⑤ The buyer's payment process is simple and convenient: After selecting the corresponding items on the buyer's page, directly enter the credit card verification page, thereby reducing the payment steps, making it convenient for the buyer to pay, and the payment is fast, only taking 3 to 5 s.

(3) Disadvantages

① There is a need for account opening fees and annual service fees, the threshold is a bit high.

② Chargebacks are still possible. International credit cards themselves have a 180-day chargeback period (some credit cards can even chargeback after 180 days). The so-called chargeback is the behavior of the credit card holder himself actively asking for the money back. Reasons for chargebacks: the customer did not receive the goods; the goods are not as promised; there are quality issues with the goods; transactions with black cards, stolen cards, and business cards.

(4) Scope of application

Credit card payments are generally used for small payments of less than 1000 US dollars in foreign trade, and are more suitable for online retail stores.

6.3.2 Other Online Payment Tools

1. Payoneer

Payoneer was established in 2005, headquartered in New York, USA. It is an institution authorized by MasterCard to issue cards. Its main business is to help its partners distribute funds globally and provide global customers with US bank/European bank receiving accounts for receiving trade payments from European and American e-commerce platforms and enterprises, providing simple, safe and fast remittance services for alliances with a wide and diverse range of payers.

Payoneer's partners cover many fields and services are available in more than 200 countries or regions worldwide. No matter who needs to be paid, whether they are employees, freelancers, alliances scattered in remote areas around the world, or other groups, the payee can apply for a Payoneer prepaid MasterCard and provide a safe, convenient and flexible way of receiving payments. The Payoneer prepaid MasterCard can be used at any MasterCard accepting POS machine worldwide, for online shopping or to withdraw local currency from ATMs.

(1) Fee standard

① A 2% fee is charged for transfers to local bank accounts in more than 200 countries or regions worldwide.

② For funds in the Payoneer MasterCard, each ATM withdrawal costs $3.15. When withdrawing RMB directly from an ATM in China, there may be a currency exchange loss of up to 3%. The maximum daily withdrawal is $2500; there is no charge for POS machine consumption.

③ Supermarket shopping (maximum of $2500 per day, no fees charged by Payoneer).

④ Depending on the different partnership alliances, the above fees may vary.

⑤ The annual fee for the Payoneer MasterCard prepaid card is $29.95, charged once a year.

⑥ 1% of the amount transferred from a US bank account is charged for each deposit.

(2) Advantages

① Convenience. After completing the online registration of a Payoneer account, it automatically links to a US bank account and a European bank account, which can be immediately added to the European and American platforms for ACH/ SEPA deposits or sending European and American bank accounts to European and American customers.

② Compliance. Like European and American companies, it receives payments from European and American companies. Through the cooperation between Payoneer and Chinese payment companies, online foreign exchange declaration and settlement are completed, which can avoid the annual limit of $50,000 for personal foreign exchange settlement.

③ Security. For deposits from European and American customers, full guarantee services are provided for sellers after providing certain documents for review.

(3) Disadvantages

① Funds cannot be transferred between Payoneer accounts, cannot be recharged via bank card or credit card, and cannot receive payments from PayPal.

② High transaction fees.

(4) Applicable audience

Payoneer is suitable for cross-border e-commerce websites or sellers with small single transaction amounts but a wide customer base.

2. ClickandBuy

ClickandBuy is an independent third-party payment company that allows payments and fund transfers over the Internet. Established in Cologne, Germany in 1999, it later set up a business point in the UK. On March 25, 2010, Deutsche Telekom acquired ClickandBuy International Limited. It currently has over 130,000 customers, including the Apple iTunes Store, America Online, MSN, Napster, etc., and can be used in many online stores.

ClickandBuy is a version developed by Deutsche Telekom in response to PayPal. Its online payment system works the same way. Users only need to register an account and shop online through their own payment account without submitting their account information to the online store. ClickandBuy customers can inject funds into their transaction accounts through ClickandBuy and can freely choose any remittance method that suits them. After the remittance to ClickandBuy is confirmed, the funds will be credited to the customer's account within 3 to 4 working days. The minimum transaction amount each time is $100, and the maximum daily transaction amount is $10,000.

(1) Advantages

① Most of the time, the service is free.

② Many online stores accept it, and it can be used internationally.

③ The rights and interests of shoppers can be protected.

④ Interest is earned on account funds overnight.

⑤ Account funds have a price difference with exchange rate fluctuations.

(2) Disadvantages.

① Registration is troublesome and requires special verification.

② Must have a Visa or MasterCard and enable international payment function.

③ Long withdrawal time cycle.

④ May be subject to virus email attacks.

⑤ Every purchase leaves an information trace.

3. WebMoney

WebMoney is by WebMoney Transfer The online e-commerce payment system developed by Techology Company is the most mainstream electronic payment method in Russia. All major Russian banks can independently deposit and withdraw money, and its payment system can be used in 70 countries around the world, including China.

Before using WebMoney, you need to open a WMID first. This ID can be used to chat with others instantly. The ID can have wallets of various currencies, such as the currency in the Z wallet calculated in US dollars is WMZ. It has various uses, the most common one is the Mini version, which only requires registration and account setup to transfer money, but the Mini version has daily and monthly transfer limits. Then there is the Keeper Classic version, which requires software download and installation. The latest version of Keeper Classic requires a second registration through Mini account conversion.

More and more companies and online stores around the world are beginning to accept WebMoney as a payment method. It has become a powerful tool for people to conduct e-commerce. It only takes 3 min to apply for a WebMoney account for free. Transfers between accounts only take 10 s, and the income in the account can be transferred to anyone's account worldwide.

(1) Fees

① A 0.8% handling fee is charged for transfers between different wallets under WMID, paid by the payer.

② WMZ (US Dollar), 0.8% transfer fee, minimum 0.01WMZ, maximum 50WMZ.

③ WME (Euro), 0.8% transfer fee, minimum 0.01WME, maximum 50WME.

④ WMR (Russian Ruble), 0.8% transfer fee, minimum 0.01WMR, maximum 1500WMR.

⑤ WMG (Gold), 0.8% transfer fee, minimum 0.01 g, maximum 2 g.

(2) Advantages.

① Security. Transfers require mobile phone SMS verification, with multiple protection functions such as remote login IP protection.

② Speed. Instant arrival.

③ Stability. The most mainstream electronic payment method in Russia, and all major Russian banks can independently deposit and withdraw money.

④ International. Everyone can open an account online anonymously for free and can operate with zero funds.

⑤ Convenience. Knowing the other party's wallet number can transfer money, no need to go to the bank to handle cumbersome procedures.

⑥ Anonymous application. Protect both parties' privacy.

⑦ Universal. Many foreign exchange, investment sites, shopping websites around the world accept webmoney payments.

(3) Disadvantages.

WebMoney has high fees and a complex process.

4. Paysafecard (Europe)

Paysafecard is a popular prepaid card payment method in Europe. It can be used not only in 37 European countries, but also in Australia and North and South America. Paysafecard has 450,000 sales outlets worldwide, and users can use Paysafecard to pay at more than 4,000 online stores. The process of purchasing PaysafeCard is very simple, and its payment process is also quite fast and safe. Paysafecard is mainly used to purchase virtual products, such as game top-ups, skype top-ups, etc.

When users pay for online shopping, they choose the PaysafeCard payment method, and then just enter a 16-digit PIN Code to complete the transaction. No bank account is needed and no personal information is required. The payment will be deducted from the Paysafecard account, and end customers can check the account balance at any time. Paysafecard can also provide vouchers with a face value of 10/25/50/100 euros. For large transactions, users can use multiple cards in combination, up to 1000 euros.

(1) Advantages

① The payment process is simple, fast, and secure. Consumers do not need to fill in any bank account or personal information, effectively improving the payment experience and ensuring transaction security.

② Real-time transactions, just like PayPal or credit cards.

③ No chargebacks.

④ No deposit or revolving deposit, greatly relieving the merchant's capital turnover pressure. PayPal or credit cards usually require a certain transaction deposit and a 10% revolving deposit.

⑤ No transaction limit, supports British Pound (GBP), Euro (EUR), US Dollar (USD), Swiss Franc (CHF).

(2) Disadvantages

① Transaction fees are expensive. For merchants, the transaction fee is generally around 15%. High fees can be considered a norm for prepaid card payments, and domestic game card payments are generally this fee.

② Companies need to have a business license to activate Paysafecard payments.

(3) Applicable scope

The application range of Paysafecard is very wide, such as games, software, music, movies, communications, entertainment industry.

5. CashU (Middle East)

CashU is a very popular prepaid payment method in the Middle East and North Africa. It is popular in Egypt, Saudi Arabia, Kuwait, Libya, and the UAE. Users buy recharge cards offline and use them to pay online. As many people in this region do not have credit cards or bank accounts, locals prefer to use cash or complete payments.

CashU is affiliated with the Arab portal site Maktoob, mainly used for paying for online games, telecommunications and IT services, and for carrying out foreign exchange transactions. CashU allows payments in any currency, but the account will always display funds in US dollars. CashU is now used by a large number of netizens in the Middle East and the former CIS countries. In the Middle East and North Africa, compared to other payment methods, the biggest advantage of Cashu is that it cannot be maliciously refunded.

CashU is a secure payment method and customized service. The existing services and support in all Arabic and surrounding countries promote online shopping safety, provide convenient and easy-to-use payment solutions, and achieve non-discriminatory online purchases. Over the years, CashU has become a large, trustworthy, and approachable top supplier, creating its availability and user dissemination points in various countries and cities in MENA.

(1) Fees

① Annual fee of 1 US dollar.

② Exchange fees of 5% to 7% for different countries and regions.

(2) Advantages.

① Real-time transactions, just like PayPal or credit cards.

② No chargebacks.

③ No deposit or revolving deposit, reducing the merchant's capital turnover pressure.

(3) Disadvantages.

Transaction fees are relatively high. CashU's fees for merchants are roughly around 6% to 7%.

(4) Applicable scope

E-commerce and gaming companies with Middle Eastern customers.

6. Yandex.Money (Russia)

Yandex.Money is an electronic payment tool under Russia's Yandex. After registration, buyers can recharge their wallets through payment terminals, electronic currency, prepaid cards, and bank transfers (bank cards) in all regions of Russia. Yandex.Money allows users to easily and safely complete internet goods payments, transfer money to others, or receive payments. To strengthen transaction protection, Yandex.Money allows the use of one-time passwords, protection codes, Pin codes, and other security measures, and sends related operation information via email or mobile text messages.

(1) Features

① Convenient recharge, real-time arrival.

② Recharge to the wallet through payment terminals, electronic currency, prepaid cards, and bank transfers (bank cards), real-time arrival.

③ Cannot refuse payment.

(2) Scope of application.

All former Soviet Union countries can use it, including Russia, Ukraine, Armenia, Azerbaijan, Belarus, Kazakhstan, Kyrgyzstan, Moldova, Turkmenistan, Uzbekistan, Tajikistan.

7. Boleto (Brazil)

Brazil is one of the BRICS countries and is a well-developed country in Latin America. In addition to credit cards, locals are accustomed to using Boleto for payment. Boleto, officially known as Boleto Bancário, is a Brazilian official payment method regulated by the Central Bank of Brazil, with about 2 billion transactions per year, 30% of which come from online transactions. As many Brazilians prefer to use cash transactions, and because it is difficult to apply for a credit card that can be used for cross-border transactions, Boleto is often the only supported payment method for companies and government departments. Boleto is the best choice for cross-border e-commerce to break through Brazilian payments, such as AliExpress supports Boleto payments.

Boleto is a cash payment, the seller needs to print an invoice online, the invoice contains the payee, payer information, and payment amount, etc. The payer can print the invoice and go to the bank or post office outlets, as well as some pharmacies, supermarkets, etc. to complete the payment, or can complete the payment through online banking.

Features:

① Non-real-time transactions, buyers can generally complete payment within 3–5 days, depending on the date on the invoice.

② Cannot refuse payment.

③ There is a transaction limit, each Brazilian can pay no more than 3000 US dollars per month.

④ Transaction costs are cheap. Boleto's transaction cost is generally less than 4%.

⑤ No margin or revolving margin, relieving the pressure on the merchant's capital turnover.

8. MOLPay (Southeast Asia)

MOLPay was established in Malaysia at the end of 2005 and is the first third-party payment service company in Malaysia. MOLPay payments cover most of Southeast Asia. The following payment channels can be accessed through MOLPay:

Malaysia: Credit cards (Visa & MasterCard) and Malaysian online bank payments;
Singapore: eNETS, SingPost SAM;
Indonesia: Credit cards, ATM Transfer (VA);
Philippines: Dragonpay;
Vietnam: Nganluong;
Australia: POLi Payments;
China: Alipay, UnionPay, Tenpay.

(1) Payment process

The entire payment process is very similar to the process of using Alipay for payment.

① After creating an order, the user selects MOLPay as the payment method.

② The page redirects to the MOLPay payment page, where the user selects a specific payment method, such as a credit card or bank transfer.

③ Complete the payment.

(2) Features.

① Real-time transactions, just like PayPal or credit cards.

② Non-credit card transactions cannot be refused.

③ Transaction fees are cheap.

④ No margin or revolving margin, relieving the financial pressure on merchants.

6.4 Cross-Border Payment Mode of China's Third-Party Payment Platform

6.4.1 Cross-Border Payment License of China's Third-Party Payment

The cross-border payment license is a certificate issued by the State Administration of Foreign Exchange of China to payment institutions, which allows payment institutions to conduct cross-border e-commerce foreign exchange payment business. In 2013, the State Administration of Foreign Exchange of China issued a pilot guidance on cross-border e-commerce foreign exchange payment business for payment institutions, deciding to carry out pilot work in first-tier cities in China, allowing some payment institutions participating in the pilot to handle cross-border receipt and payment of foreign exchange and foreign exchange settlement business. If the amount of a single transaction in goods trade does not exceed the equivalent of 10,000 US dollars, it can handle centralized receipt and payment of foreign exchange and settlement of foreign exchange business for customers.

The third-party payment institutions applying for a cross-border payment license need to meet the following conditions to be eligible to apply.

(1) A limited liability company or a joint-stock company legally established within the People's Republic of China, and a non-financial institution legal person.
(2) Having the minimum registered capital as stipulated. Contributors who meet the requirements of the method.
(3) Having more than five senior managers familiar with payment business.
(4) Having payment business facilities that meet the requirements.
(5) Having anti-money laundering measures that meet the relevant requirements.
(6) Having a sound organizational structure and internal control system as well as corresponding risk management measures.
(7) Having business premises and security measures that meet the requirements.

(8) The applicant and senior managers have not been punished in the past three years for using payment business to commit illegal and criminal activities, or for handling payment business for illegal and criminal activities.

Third-party payment institutions that meet the above conditions will be approved by the People's Bank of China after being reviewed by the local branch of the People's Bank of China. As of the end of 2022, a total of 35 domestic cross-border payment licenses have been issued in our country, including 30 cross-border foreign exchange payment licenses and 5 cross-border RMB payment licenses.

6.4.2 China's Third-Party Payment Business Process

The cross-border payment services provided by China's third-party payment institutions for cross-border e-commerce mainly include "purchase and payment of foreign exchange" and "receipt and settlement of foreign exchange" businesses. Among them, the purchase and payment of foreign exchange is mainly the foreign exchange purchase and cross-border payment service provided by the third-party payment institution for consumers when they purchase goods through the e-commerce platform, mainly for the business of the import cross-border e-commerce platform, as shown in Fig. 6.2; The receipt and settlement of foreign exchange is the third-party payment institution helping domestic sellers to receive foreign exchange and exchange RMB, and settle RMB, mainly for the business of the export cross-border e-commerce platform, as shown in Fig. 6.3.

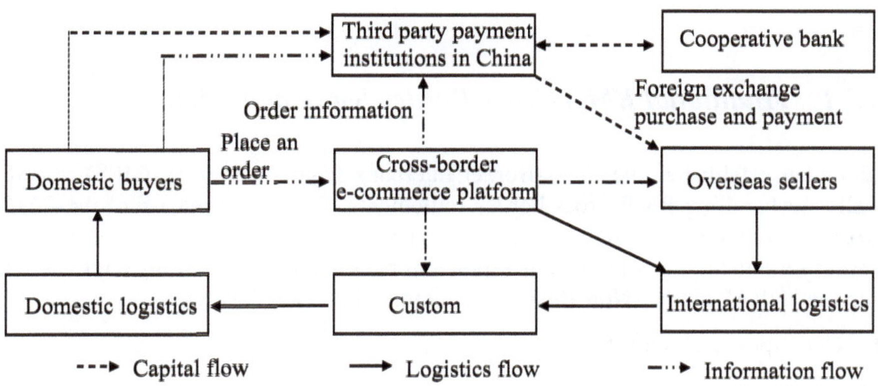

Fig. 6.2 Process of foreign exchange purchase and payment by third-party payment institutions on import cross-border e-commerce platforms

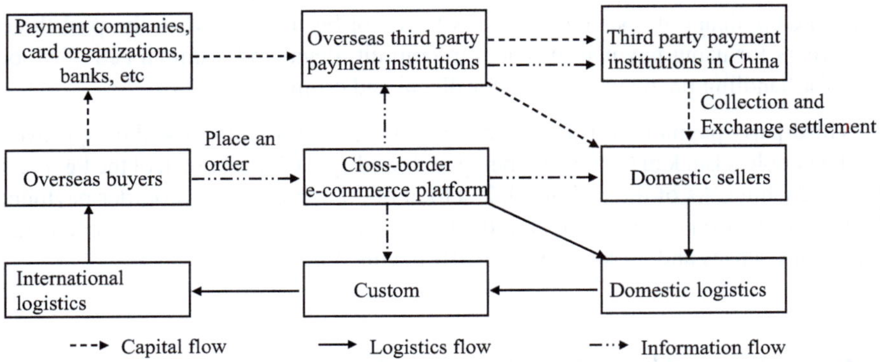

Fig. 6.3 Process of foreign exchange collection and settlement by third-party payment institutions on export cross-border e-commerce platforms

6.5 RMB Cross-Border Payment and Digital RMB

Looking at the global cross-border payment system, the mainstream ones currently include the Society for Worldwide Interbank Financial Telecommunication (SWIFT), the Cross-Border Interbank Payment System (CIPS), the Trans-European Automated Real-time Gross Settlement Express Transfer system (TARGET), the Clearing House Interbank Payments System (CHIPS), the Clearing House Automated Payment System (CHAPS), the Bank of Japan Financial Network System (BOJ-NET), etc. Among them, SWIFT is the world's largest private payment clearing system, mainly for clearing cross-border US dollar transactions.

6.5.1 Traditional RMB Cross-Border Settlement Method

China has established the Cross-Border Interbank Payment System (CIPS), specifically for handling RMB cross-border settlements. Before the release of the RMB cross-border payment system, there were mainly three ways to achieve RMB cross-border settlement, namely: the correspondent bank model, the clearing bank model, and the "NRA" model (Non-Resident Account, abbreviated as NRA).

1. Correspondent Bank Model

The correspondent bank model requires domestic banks with international settlement capabilities to sign an RMB correspondent settlement agreement with foreign banks, open an RMB interbank account for them, and then act as agents for foreign banks to carry out cross-border RMB receipt, payment, settlement, and other services. Example as follows:

Business scenario: Overseas company A and domestic company B do business, A needs to pay a sum of money to B, and it is agreed that this transaction will be settled in RMB.

Preliminary work: A opens a settlement account at Citibank overseas, B opens a settlement account at Agricultural Bank of China domestically; Citibank signs an "RMB Correspondent Settlement Agreement" with Bank of China, and Bank of China opens an "RMB Interbank Account" for Citibank; Citibank and Bank of China use SWIFT connection. Bank of China and Agricultural Bank of China connect through CNAPS.

Business steps: ① A initiates a payment instruction to Citibank, Citibank deducts the money after checking the balance; ② Citibank sends instructions to Bank of China through SWIFT, Bank of China deducts the money after checking the balance of its RMB interbank account; ③ Bank of China transfers money to Agricultural Bank of China through CNAPS; ④ Agricultural Bank of China settles with merchant B.

In the entire process, SWIFT and CNAPS mainly serve to realize payment clearing between banks. Among them, SWIFT is the Society for Worldwide Interbank Financial Telecommunication, an international cooperative organization among international banks; CNAPS is China's modern payment system, providing the final fund clearing system for payment business between commercial banks and between commercial banks and the People's Bank of China.

2. Clearing Bank Model

The clearing bank model requires the central bank to designate a foreign bank (usually an overseas branch) as the RMB offshore clearing bank. The offshore clearing bank signs an RMB correspondent settlement agreement with the offshore commercial bank and opens an RMB interbank account for it, acting as an agent for the offshore bank to carry out cross-border RMB receipt and payment services. Example as follows:

Business scenario: Overseas company A needs to pay funds to domestic company B.

Preliminary work: A opens a settlement account at Citibank overseas, and B opens a settlement account at the Agricultural Bank of China domestically; The People's Bank of China (Central Bank) designates a certain overseas branch of the Bank of China (commercial bank) as the RMB clearing bank for that region; Citibank opens an RMB interbank account at the overseas branch of the Bank of China and deposits funds; Citibank and the overseas branch of the Bank of China connect using SWIFT or the local settlement system; The overseas branch of the Bank of China has an internal connection system with the Bank of China domestically, and the head office connects with the Agricultural Bank of China domestically through CNAPS.

The clearing bank model and the agent bank model do not differ much in terms of the experience for the payer and payee, the core difference lies in the location of the fund settlement. Specifically:

The premise of the agent bank model is that domestic banks have the capability to handle international settlement business. It mainly connects with overseas banks through SWIFT, and when an overseas bank and a domestic agent bank settle, this fund is an international settlement (overseas settlement);

The premise of the clearing bank model is that the domestic bank's overseas branch is designated by the People's Bank of China (Central Bank) as the overseas RMB clearing bank. In this way, it shares capabilities with overseas banks, and the fund settlement occurs within the clearing bank's internal system. As in the above example, the funds are cleared within the Bank of China (between the overseas branch and the domestic head office).

3. NRA Account Model

The NAR model is where overseas enterprises directly open settlement accounts at domestic banks. The payment process of this model is almost identical to that of domestic enterprises. However, the process and procedures for overseas institutions to open NRA accounts at domestic banks are relatively complex.

RMB NRA accounts and OSA accounts (referring to "offshore accounts") are different in nature, NRA is a domestic account, OSA is an overseas account; NRA needs to pay interest tax, OSA has no interest tax; NRA has foreign exchange control, supervision belongs to the foreign exchange bureau, OSA has no foreign exchange control, supervision belongs to the banking regulatory commission.

NRA account supervision is relatively strict, subject to national foreign exchange control, and its use is also relatively single, so there are not many cross-border settlements in this model.

Of the above three models, the NRA account model is not widely used due to various policy and regulatory issues. Both the agent bank model and the clearing bank model have inherent deficiencies because they rely on the domestic CNAPS system, but the CNAPS was designed mainly to meet domestic business needs.

Because the participants in cross-border payments are not in the same economic entity, it will involve the impact of transaction time, policy and other factors, and the CNAPS system cannot handle these exceptions well.

And most domestic banks and overseas banks need to connect through SWIFT, and the control of SWIFT is in the hands of overseas institutions, so the risk of RMB cross-border settlement relying entirely on this system is also significant.

6.5.2 RMB Cross-Border Payment System

The above three traditional RMB cross-border settlement methods are unable to meet the growing demand for RMB cross-border settlement, coupled with the need for RMB internationalization, there is an urgent need for a new system to carry this service. Therefore, CIPS was born. CIPS stands for Cross-border Interbank Payment System. According to incomplete statistics, as of the end of April 2022, there were 1307 participants in the CIPS payment system, including 76 direct participants and 1231 indirect participants.

Banks both within and outside the country can directly access the CIPS system to enable the receipt and payment functions of the Renminbi. The overall architecture of CIPS can be understood as a Chinese version similar to SWIFT, which can free global Renminbi settlement from dependence on SWIFT. The relationship between CIPS and SWIFT is similar to that between UnionPay and VISA. CIPS specifically refers to the wholesale payment system for Renminbi cross-border payment and clearing business, aiming to further integrate existing Renminbi cross-border payment and settlement channels and resources, improve cross-border clearing efficiency, meet the needs of Renminbi business development in major time zones, enhance transaction security, and build a fair market competition environment. Taking direct interbank payment as an example, domestic and foreign companies engage in import and export trade, the commercial banks where both parties open accounts are directly connected, payments are made through the bank interface docked by the cross-border e-commerce platform, clearing and settlement of domestic and foreign banks are carried out through CIPS, and then foreign exchange settlement and sales are carried out through banks. CIPS is an independent payment system developed by the People's Bank of China, providing fund clearing and settlement services for Renminbi cross-border and offshore business of domestic and foreign financial institutions, and plays an important role in promoting the internationalization of the Renminbi.

6.5.3 Digital Renminbi

In terms of cross-border e-commerce export collection, by setting up a cross-border Renminbi collection account, direct Renminbi settlement business between domestic and foreign banks can be obtained, without the need to be included in foreign exchange verification management, the Renminbi for cross-border settlement does not need to enter the account to be checked, domestic sellers and foreign buyers place orders in Renminbi as the transaction currency, and declare customs in Renminbi. In recent years, China has vigorously promoted the application and development of cross-border Renminbi payment business in the field of cross-border e-commerce. The main advantages are as follows:

(1) Digital Renminbi strengthens transaction trust and reduces costs. The centralized management of digital Renminbi can achieve payment and settlement at the same time, which can improve the turnover efficiency of merchants' funds, help solve the liquidity problems of small and medium-sized enterprises, improve the speed of currency circulation and the efficiency of monetary policy implementation. The digital Renminbi currently adopts a zero-fee form in the pilot (there may be other costs in the future), which is beneficial to the settlement of merchants' funds.
(2) Cross-border Renminbi simplifies collection procedures and reduces payment costs. For cross-border trade income and expenditure with foreign currency declaration and Renminbi settlement or Renminbi declaration and foreign

currency settlement, enterprises should report trade credit and other reports to the foreign exchange bureau as required; for cross-border trade income and expenditure with Renminbi declaration and Renminbi settlement, enterprises do not need to report trade credit and other enterprise reports.

At present, the mainstream cross-border clearing mode in the world is through the SWIFT system led by the United States, and cross-border payment business has always faced problems such as high payment costs and long settlement cycles. The application of digital Renminbi can greatly reduce the handling fees and time costs of cross-border trade, HNA's Newborn Payment helps Hainan cross-border e-commerce to achieve digital Renminbi payment, and third-party cross-border payment manufacturers such as First Trust Easy Payment are actively exploring the application of digital Renminbi in cross-border payment scenarios.

The digital Renminbi has strong security, high efficiency, and low transaction costs in cross-border payments. The central bank will actively pilot the application and supervision of digital Renminbi in the field of cross-border payments in the future, and the pace of application of digital Renminbi in cross-border payment scenarios is accelerating.

6.6 Cross-Border Payment Influencing Factors, Enterprise Types and Regional Differences

6.6.1 Influencing Factors in Choosing Cross-Border Payment Methods

Different cross-border e-commerce platforms, different markets, and different consumer groups determine different cross-border payment methods. When conducting market activities in a cross-border e-commerce market, or planning to develop or enter a new cross-border e-commerce market, how to choose the appropriate cross-border payment method is of great significance. There are many factors that affect the choice of cross-border payment methods, and the following will introduce several important impression factors, which also need to be paid special attention to when engaging in cross-border e-commerce activities.

1. The Popularity and Coverage of Cross-Border Payment Methods

The popularity and coverage of cross-border payment methods are the basis and premise for choosing cross-border payment methods. Different cross-border payment methods such as credit card payment, cash on delivery, third-party payment platforms, etc., have different popularity rates in different global markets, and the regional coverage and business coverage of different cross-border payment methods are also different. For a certain market or type of market, the choice of cross-border payment methods will also be different. In developed areas such as Europe and America, the financial environment is relatively mature, e-commerce development and payment technology are relatively mature, so credit card payment and third-party payment have a higher popularity and coverage, thus becoming the preferred cross-border payment method in the cross-border e-commerce environment. In Africa, Latin America, Southeast Asia and other regions, the financial environment is relatively backward, and the popularity of credit cards is low, so the use of credit card payment, PayPal and other third-party payment tools will not be the first choice, and cash on delivery becomes a more common cross-border payment method.

2. Transaction Subject Usage Preference

In cross-border e-commerce transactions, there are differences in cross-border payment methods due to the payment habits, preferences, and overall environmental factors of the target area consumer group. This is a key focus of cross-border e-commerce activities and an important factor affecting the choice of cross-border payment methods. In the Middle East and Latin America, mobile payment development is faster, significantly higher than mature markets such as Europe and America, so mobile payment has become an important cross-border payment method. In developing markets such as Africa, Russia, and India, due to consumers' lack of trust in electronic payment tools, most consumers prefer to use cash on delivery, especially cash on delivery. When developing the Southeast Asian cross-border e-commerce market, cash on delivery is a must-have option, but general small and medium-sized sellers find it difficult to directly connect with local logistics providers, so choosing a cross-border e-commerce platform that provides cash on delivery services becomes an important choice. In Japan, where mobile phone usage is extremely high and the mobile payment ecosystem is relatively mature, mobile-based cross-border payment has become an important payment method in the Japanese cross-border e-commerce market.

3. The Cost of Using Cross-Border Payment Methods

Cross-border e-commerce sellers face more difficulties in payment recovery than domestic e-commerce sellers. Issues such as difficulties in overseas fund settlement, slow turnover, high withdrawal rates, and exchange rate risks all become significant problems restricting the recovery of payments in cross-border e-commerce. The cost of using cross-border payment methods becomes an important factor affecting the choice of cross-border payment methods. The cost of use includes time cost and capital cost, and the capital cost includes transaction fees, exchange rate costs, etc. Transaction fees need to be compared comprehensively. At present, the transaction fees for cross-border payments range from 1.7% to 5%. For example, PayPal, commonly used in the European and American markets, charges a receipt fee of $0.3 per transaction, a withdrawal fee of $35, a receipt fee of 3.4% to 4.4%, and a currency conversion fee of 2.5%, etc. With market competition, the fees of payment companies are constantly decreasing, aiming to attract more customers. For cross-border e-commerce transactions, because they involve commodity transactions with different countries, they will involve issues of currency exchange and exchange rates, which become one of the cost components of cross-border payment methods. Cross-border payment companies will issue multiple currencies to avoid users bearing the risk of exchange rate loss, adopt the method of direct debit in the user's own currency, and merchants need to convert currency from banks or payment companies, which will also generate currency conversion costs, generally ranging from 0.1% to 2.5%.

4. Features and Advantages of Cross-Border Payment Methods

As mentioned earlier, different cross-border payment methods have different advantages and disadvantages, which determine the different usage scopes of cross-border payment methods, as shown in Table 6.2. Different cross-border payment methods have different transaction times, fees, cooperation thresholds, and risks. The transaction entities engaged in cross-border e-commerce activities should choose suitable cross-border payment methods according to their own characteristics. Therefore, the characteristics and advantages of cross-border payment methods themselves have also become important influencing factors in the choice of cross-border payment methods under cross-border e-commerce transactions.

Table 6.2 Comparison of several cross-border payment methods

Category	PayPal	Bank transfer	Check	Western Union remittance	Credit card
Trading time	Real time	2–5 days	40–60 days	About 10 min	Real time
Service charge	2.4%–3.9% (at the same time, withdrawal service fees and other fees will be charged)	Over $30	Telecommunication fee + handling fee	More than $20 per transaction	2.2%–3.0%
Cooperation threshold	Low	Low	Low	Low	High
Risk	Risk of number theft	Risk of account information embezzlement	Risk of being falsely claimed and fraudulently claimed	The risk of being falsely claimed has been disabled by eBay and other websites	Risk of dishonor

6.6.2 *Types of Cross-Border E-Commerce Payment Companies*

The development of cross-border e-commerce promotes the development of cross-border payments, and traditional industries and related companies are involved in cross-border payment businesses. After several years of development, by sorting out the existing types of companies engaged in cross-border payment business, they can be summarized into the following categories:

(1) Traditional banks broaden product types and get involved in the cross-border payment market, such as online banking, cross-border bank transfer services of major banks, etc.;
(2) Professional credit card institutions are involved in cross-border payment business, such as Visa credit card, MasterCard, American Express card, etc.;
(3) Professional third-party payment companies are engaged in cross-border payment business, such as PayPal, Alipay, Tenpay, Yandex.Dengi, Qiwi Wallet, etc.;
(4) Social media add cross-border payment business, such as WeChat Pay, QQ Wallet, Facebook and Twitter, etc.;
(5) Mobile phone companies develop cross-border payment business, such as Apple's Apple Pay, Samsung's Samsung Pay, Xiaomi Pay, etc.;
(6) E-commerce platforms radiate cross-border payment business, such as Amazon Wallet, JD Wallet, Snapdeal, etc.;
(7) Internet companies are engaged in cross-border payment business, such as Google Wallet, NetEase Bao, etc.;
(8) Logistics companies provide cash on delivery services, such as international express companies, Chinese private express companies.

6.6.3 *Differences in Payment Habits in Different Regions*

1. North America

(1) United States.

The main online payment methods in the United States include Visa, MasterCard, American Express, Discover, PayPal, e-checks, bank transfers, Google Wallet, Amazon Wallet, Apple Pay, etc. Currently, American consumers mainly use credit cards. Since 2020, the "buy now, pay later" method has been on the rise, which is conducive to releasing suppressed consumer demand and is attracting more consumers to purchase high-end products and services. According to eMarketer data, the number of users in the US "buy now, pay later" installment payment service market grew by 81% in 2021, reaching 45 million people. PayPal launched this service in 2020, and Amazon also introduced the "buy now, pay later" payment method.

(2) Canada

Canadian consumers mainly pay with debit cards and credit cards. According to data from the United States International Trade Administration, 59% of Canadian shoppers use credit cards when shopping online, and 20% use PayPal. E-wallets are steadily growing and are expected to account for 27% of online payments by 2025. MasterCard is the preferred credit card in Canada, with a market share of 53.6%, followed by Visa at 41.3%, and American Express at 5.1%. Canadian consumers are interested in the "buy now, pay later" payment method for online shopping, with the highest interest among the 35–44 age group at 65.4%; the least popular among consumers over 65, accounting for 47%.

2. Europe

(1) Germany

Germans do not often use credit cards as a payment method. Online payment methods, such as PayPal, are also not commonly used by Germans. The most common payment method for Germans is still invoicing. Therefore, for businesses operating in Germany, it is important to offer customers different payment methods, such as credit cards, direct debits, PayPal electronic payments, and open invoice systems. Payment on invoice, installment payments, and cash on delivery are the main payment methods for the top 500 online shops in Germany, indicating that the "enjoy first, pay later" still has a large market in Germany. However, digital wallets have become one of the most popular payment methods among consumers, with PayPal dominating the market, followed by Apple Pay and Google Pay. It can be seen that German payment methods are moving towards digital wallets and mobile device payments.

(2) United Kingdom

According to Statista data, in 2021, the first place in UK e-commerce payments was e-wallets/mobile wallets, accounting for 32%; the second place was credit cards, accounting for 27%; the third place was debit cards, accounting for 24%. In terms of online shopping payment methods, credit cards are the most popular online payment method in the UK, with nearly 40% of online transactions using credit cards. When spending exceeds 100 pounds, Britons generally choose to pay with credit cards. This is because, according to the Consumer Credit Act and other related regulations implemented in the UK, large credit card payments will enjoy more perfect consumer protection, including full refunds. However, debit cards are also a common payment method, with more than 30% of online transactions being paid with debit cards. Another popular online payment tool in the UK is PayPal. These three payment methods cover most online transactions.

(3) France

The most popular and accustomed online payment method in France is indeed the credit card. In addition to Visa, MasterCard, and American Express, Carte Bleue is also a popular payment method in France. Carte Bleue is a cross-bank program in cooperation with local banks (often in partnership with Visa), which can be used as a debit card or a credit card. PayPal and similar digital payment methods are becoming increasingly popular in France, and digital wallets are also becoming popular. In addition, some French e-commerce merchants have stated that they also accept order payments from social media platforms.

(4) Italy

In Italy, card payments account for approximately 37%, while local wallets account for 54%, with Mybank (bank transfer) being particularly prominent. Mybank is an Italian local payment product based on real-time bank transfers, covering 227 banks in Europe and having over 30 million users. One of the main features of Mybank is that there is no need to register or create a new password; users only need to have a bank account to easily use Mybank. The most popular type of bank card in Italy is the prepaid card, partly because prepaid cards have better security and lower fees. The most popular credit cards are CartaSi, Visa, MasterCard, American Express, and Dinner Club. In Italy, smartphones are widely used, and people have a strong awareness of mobile payments. PayPal is an online payment method that Italian consumers recognize.

(5) Spain

The mainstream payment methods in Spain are credit cards (Visa, MasterCard), PayPal, and bank transfer apps (Klarna, Trustly). According to a survey by JPMorgan, credit cards are key to the Spanish market, accounting for the largest share of e-commerce payments, at 48%. However, this proportion is expected to decrease as the use of digital wallets and bank transfers increases. PayPal is the most popular digital wallet in Spain. In addition, there are also CaixaBank Wallet and BBVA Wallet in Spain. Meanwhile, thanks to the active promotion of bank transfer apps such as Klarna, Trustly, Bizum, and MyBank in 2022, bank transfer payments in Spain will grow at a compound annual growth rate of 50%.

(6) Russia

Russians prefer to use local e-wallets and debit cards for payment. In the Russian local payment market, the top four payment methods are Yandex payment, Webmoney, Qiwi, and PayPal. The proportion of bank online payments and e-wallet payments is also relatively high. Russians prefer cash payments, so local cross-border e-commerce platforms in Russia often use cash on delivery. In addition to e-wallets, common payment methods in Russia include bank transfers and cash payments. The commonly used online banks are mainly Sberbank, Alfa-click, etc. Russia has the fastest growth in cashless payments in the world, with the most commonly used online payments being QIWI, WebMoney, Yandex.Money, and Sberbank online bank transfers. In terms of cross-border payments, Russians use the international version of Alipay very frequently.

(7) Poland

The most common payment method in Poland is online bank transfer, with the number of people using online bank transfers being three times that of those paying with credit or debit cards. Data from PayU shows that over 80% of transactions are made through Pay-by-Link (PBL) bank transfers, allowing consumers to easily log into their bank accounts and obtain a one-time verification code to complete the purchase. Installment payments have also become an important payment method in Poland, providing a unique competitive advantage for merchants. A typical online payment method in Poland is PayU, which is used more frequently than PayPal in Poland.

3. Latin America

(1) Brazil

Online payments in Brazil are primarily made with credit cards and installment payments, accounting for over 93% of all online purchases in Brazil. 69% of users make online payments using credit cards. However, for sellers, it's important to distinguish between domestic and international credit cards. 49% of consumers are accustomed to using local credit cards such as Hiperchard and Elo, transacting in Brazilian Real (BRL); international credit cards, mainly Mastercard and Visa, account for 14%, and transactions can be made in both local and foreign currencies. However, only 20% of Brazilian buyers can use international credit cards, so it's crucial for merchants to accept local credit cards. At the same time, the method of installment payments should not be underestimated. In Brazil, 80% of e-commerce payments are made in installments, a method very popular among locals, especially among the 30% of Brazilians without a bank account. Pix is also one of the popular and rapidly growing payment methods in Brazil, very similar to Alipay/WeChat Pay in China, and currently, 70% of adult Brazilians have used Pix. The local payment brand Boleto occupies a significant share in Brazil and is the most popular payment method, mainly supporting offline cash payments. Boleto also supports mobile and web payments as well as bank transfers, and does not support chargebacks.

(2) Mexico

Cash still plays an important role in the payment field, but it is gradually shifting towards electronic payments. OXXO is Mexico's largest alternative payment method, which is a voucher-based payment method. As many people in Mexico do not have a bank account or credit card, this is a popular payment method in Mexico. Mexicans mainly use local credit cards, international credit cards, debit cards, and other payment methods. International credit cards such as Visa, Mastercard, and American Express dominate in Mexico. Mexicans prefer to make installment payments through credit cards or other methods.

(3) Argentina

In Argentina, 70% of online shopping is done through online payment methods. According to an AMI survey, the most common payment methods for e-commerce shopping in Argentina in 2021 are: credit cards (31%), electronic wallets (30%), debit cards (26%), cash vouchers (7%), bank transfers (2%), and other methods (4%). Pago Fácil is the most mainstream online payment method in Argentina, with a usage coverage of about 44%. As many people in Argentina do not have a credit card or prefer cash payments, Pago Fácil meets these buyers' payment needs as it is a cash payment method. For the Argentine market, there is a challenge in terms of payment: credit card fraud.

(4) Colombia

The penetration rate of international credit cards in Colombia has reached 38%, and unlike other countries, its payment vouchers only account for 10%, but bank transfers account for 21%, and the local bank transfer brand PSE is the most popular choice. Since PayPal withdrew from the Colombian market in 2015, a considerable number of users have chosen to use PSE since then. Its product feature is instant arrival, and it conforms to the local people's habit of using bank transfers. PSE also does not support chargebacks. Local payments are also a trusted and commonly used payment method by local residents in Colombia, such as efecty, which is a cash payment method that can provide remittance, payment, recharge, and other services.

4. East Asia

(1) Japan

The mobile payment market in Japan is continuously growing, making Japan one of the countries with the best development in mobile payment services. The main online payment methods include cash on delivery, credit card payment, bank card payment, and Alipay. Currently, cards (debit cards/credit cards/prepaid cards) are the main method of online payment for Japanese consumers, occupying 65% of the market share. The second place is online bank transfers, accounting for 14%; cash payments and electronic wallets account for 13% and 2% respectively. Konbini is a type of convenience store payment in Japan that is very popular. They accept cash payments for online transactions, especially popular among teenagers who do not have a bank account or cannot obtain credit. Electronic wallets only account for 2% of sales. The influential electronic wallets in Japan mainly come from branches of large e-commerce brands, such as Yahoo Wallet and Rakuten Wallet.

(2) South Korea

According to Rapyd data, the most popular payment methods in South Korea are electronic payment methods, such as Kakao Pay, Samsung Pay, local cards, international bank cards, bank transfers, etc. Koreans like to use digital payment methods such as electronic wallets and buy-now-pay-later, including deferred payment methods. Digital wallets like Kaokao Pay are providing deferred payment services for Korean consumers. Platforms like Coupang have also launched deferred payment services for consumers.

5. Southeast Asia and India

(1) Indonesia

Bank transfers, ATM transfers, online banking, and cash payments are common payment methods in Indonesia. Bank cards are the preferred payment method for

Indonesians, and most transactions prefer to use local bank cards. The Indonesian cross-border payment market is heavily regulated and quite closed. Gopay, OVO, DOKU, LinkAja are one of the mainstream electronic wallet payments in Indonesia, and OVO is one of the most commonly used electronic wallets in Indonesia.

(2) Malaysia

Malaysians prefer bank transfer apps, bank card payments, electronic wallets, online payment platforms, and cash, etc. Visa and Mastercard are the most commonly used payment methods, and more than 20% of Malaysians have credit cards. Malaysia's share in the card payment field is comparable to that of Indonesia, accounting for 32% of the total, but unlike Indonesia, which likes to use local bank cards, most of Malaysia's bank cards are international brands. However, Malaysia has a variety of local payment brands, among which the more famous ones are FPX and Touch n'Go.

(3) Thailand

Bank transfers are the most preferred payment method for Thais, followed by cash on delivery and electronic wallets. The credit card holding rate in Thailand is low, but the proportion of card payments still reaches 30%, of which debit cards account for 77%, but the proportion of cash payments also reaches 15%. For electronic wallets, PayPal is the most popular payment method for Thais; in terms of bank cards, the market is almost monopolized by Visa and Mastercard. Among local payment brands, Turemoney is one of the most famous companies.

(4) India

More and more Indians choose digital payments and credit cards to complete online shopping, but cash payment is still the main mode, in addition, the proportion of bank card transfers is not low. The buy-now-pay-later method is becoming more and more popular in India, such as Amazon Pay Latter launched by Amazon, which supports consumers to buy goods in installments.

6. Africa

(1) South Africa

The main payment methods in South Africa are cash, bank transfers, cards, and checks. Cash is the main payment method, followed by credit cards and online banking. Most of the income-earning population in South Africa does not have credit cards, and the credit card fraud rate is high. The South Africa Bank Transfer payment system is a payment method that almost every South African uses every day.

(2) Nigeria

The payment in Nigeria shows a trend of decreasing cash usage and increasing electronic and digital payments. Card payments account for 27% of the total (of which local card payments account for 65%), cash payments and bank transfers each have a market share of 24%, and electronic wallets account for 10%. Due to the presence of e-commerce giants such as Jumia and Konga, Nigeria's local payment brands are also quite active, with Paystack and Verve being particularly prominent.

7. Middle East

The use of credit cards in the Middle East varies greatly, with some countries still using cash as a means of circulation. Countries such as Kuwait, the UAE, Qatar, Saudi Arabia, and Oman have a high prevalence of credit cards, but due to concerns about undeliverable orders and a cautious attitude towards online shopping, Middle Eastern consumers prefer cash on delivery. However, emerging payment methods such as cryptocurrencies, facial recognition, and QR codes are also on the rise. Credit cards and mobile payments play a dominant role in the payment methods in the UAE and Israel.

8. Oceania

(1) Australia

The favorite payment method of Australians is card payment. Nearly half of online payments in Australia are completed through PayPal. The usage rate of online payments with credit cards and debit cards is also high.

9. China

In China, the most mainstream payment platforms are third-party payment platforms led by Alipay and Tenpay. These payments use a recharge mode to make payments and have inherited most of the online banking functions of banks. Therefore, in China, whether it is a credit card or a debit card, as long as the bank card has opened the online banking function, cross-border online shopping can be realized. However, the popularity of credit cards in China still needs to be improved, and most consumers use debit cards for payment. Then, credit cards are developing very fast in China, and their popularity is also soaring, especially among young white-collar workers in cities, it is very common to use credit cards for cross-border payments. In some economically developed cities, Visa and Mastercard credit card payments are very common, and the use of PayPal is also relatively high. In addition, QQ Wallet, WeChat Pay and other payment methods based on social networks are gradually becoming popular.

Chapter 7
Cross-Border E-Commerce Logistics Management

7.1 Concepts Related to Cross-Border Logistics

7.1.1 Concept of Cross-Border Logistics

Cross-border logistics refers to logistics services carried out between two or more countries. Cross-border logistics is a manifestation of the advanced stage of logistics service development. As the trading parties of cross-border e-commerce belong to different countries, goods need to be transported from the supplier's country through cross-border logistics to achieve spatial positioning, and finally logistics and distribution in the demander's country. According to the spatial displacement trajectory of goods, cross-border logistics is divided into three parts: export country logistics, international logistics, and import country logistics and distribution. Compared with domestic logistics, cross-border logistics involves the customs of the exporting country and the importing country, requires customs clearance and commodity inspection, and the work content is more complex, and few companies can handle and complete this part of the business on their own. The cross-border logistics market has heated up with the development of cross-border e-commerce. Cross-border logistics is different from traditional domestic logistics and international freight, its process is more complex, and there are more influencing factors. Cross-border logistics cannot avoid differences between countries and the connection of different logistics links in terms of hardware and software environment of logistics resources.

Cross-border logistics generated by cross-border e-commerce has become a new phenomenon in the modern logistics industry and has shown a booming development trend. With the development and further maturity of the cross-border e-commerce market, cross-border logistics companies will have huge room for growth and market, but also face huge challenges and crises. In the future cross-border e-commerce market, cross-border logistics companies should focus more on the role of global supply chain integrators, efficiently handling inventory, warehousing, sorting, order

X. Zhang, *Introduction to Cross-Border E-Commerce Ecosystem*,
https://doi.org/10.1007/978-981-96-1165-2_7

processing, logistics route optimization, logistics resource allocation, logistics distribution and other related links, to provide comprehensive global cross-border supply chain solutions for cross-border e-commerce.

7.1.2 Features of Cross-Border Logistics

Dependent on the development of cross-border e-commerce, cross-border logistics has some characteristics similar to domestic e-commerce logistics, but also has some different characteristics due to the influence of cross-border e-commerce.

1. Multiple Logistics Links

Compared with domestic e-commerce logistics, cross-border logistics, due to its cross-border nature, has a more complex process and more cumbersome operations. From the spatial scope of commodity circulation, cross-border logistics consists of three parts: logistics in the exporting country, international freight, and logistics in the importing country. Cross-border logistics includes logistics in the exporting country, international freight, logistics in the importing country, as well as customs and commodity inspection in the exporting country, customs and commodity inspection in the importing country, exchange rates, international finance, etc., as shown in Fig. 7.1.

Not only that, cross-border logistics in the logistics link of the exporting country will be subdivided into many links, including collection, packaging, sorting, transportation, warehousing, commodity inspection, customs clearance, etc. International freight includes pickup, port handover, documentation, insurance, transportation, etc. Logistics in the importing country includes customs clearance, commodity inspection, loading, warehousing, storage, sorting, logistics, distribution, etc.

2. Diverse Participants

Different participants are involved in each link of cross-border logistics, and these participants involve different fields, different industries, and different companies. The types of entities involved in cross-border logistics business include:

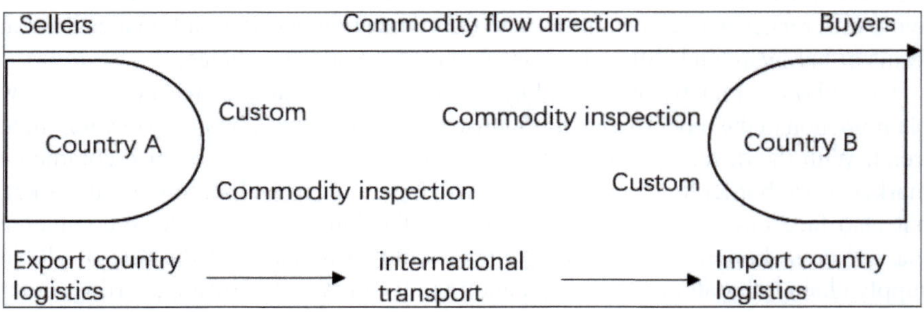

Fig. 7.1 Cross-border logistics flow chart

(1) Traditional retail companies, through the development of cross-border e-commerce business, their own business volume is enough to support the demand for cross-border logistics, have set up cross-border logistics networks, representative companies include Walmart, Home Depot, French Cdiscount, etc.;
(2) Traditional transportation and postal industry companies, in response to the demand of the cross-border e-commerce market, have increased their cross-border logistics business, representative companies include COSCO, Maersk, Universal Postal Union, etc.;
(3) Large manufacturing companies or large companies in traditional industries, with their existing logistics resources, use the logistics companies or logistics functional departments affiliated to the group, and with the expansion of their own cross-border e-commerce market, they start to get involved in cross-border logistics business, representative companies include Haier Logistics, Ande Logistics, etc.;
(4) Traditional e-commerce companies, with the expansion of cross-border e-commerce business, have stimulated the demand for cross-border logistics, have built their own logistics system in the domestic market, and tasted the advantages brought by self-built logistics, and then spread it to the cross-border logistics market, self-built cross-border logistics network, representative companies include JD Logistics, Alibaba's Cainiao Logistics, Amazon, Russia's Ulmart, etc.;
(5) Traditional courier companies do not want to miss the cross-border logistics market, have cut into the cross-border logistics business, representative companies include UPS, FedEx, SF Logistics, Pony Express, etc.;
(6) Emerging cross-border logistics companies, which have focused on the cross-border logistics market since their inception, include representative companies such as Brazil's Intelipost, Axado, Loggi, and D4 Logistics.

3. Long Logistics Cycle

According to a customer satisfaction survey by Focalprice, it was found that the biggest complaints about cross-border e-commerce are concentrated in logistics, with the long logistics cycle being a key point of customer complaints. The characteristics of cross-border trade make the industrial chain and links of logistics longer, coupled with the cycle of customs clearance and commodity inspection, resulting in a much longer logistics cycle for cross-border e-commerce than domestic e-commerce. In cross-border logistics, the issue of transportation and delivery time is prominent, as short as half a month to a month, and as long as several months, and during peak shopping seasons such as Christmas, the logistics time will be even longer. Many e-commerce businesses are hindered by logistics and delivery, and with the time for customs clearance and commodity inspection, the cycle of cross-border logistics is even longer, which has become a barrier to the development of China's cross-border e-commerce.

4. High Logistics Risk

Cross-border e-commerce involves international transactions and cannot avoid local political, intellectual property, regional customs, policy changes, and other factors. Many factors, such as the Russo-Ukrainian conflict, Brazil's high tax and welfare, Islamic countries' religious beliefs, and local protectionism in Southeast Asia, will have a deep impact on cross-border e-commerce logistics. Taking the exchange rate risk as an example, when a country's currency depreciates or appreciates, the tax rate will change, thereby indirectly leading to a reduction in the profits of cross-border e-commerce logistics.

7.1.3 Cross-Border Logistics Operation Process

Cross-border logistics allows goods to flow from the seller to the buyer, through various modes of transportation, to achieve the spatial displacement of goods across borders, including the final delivery link. Cross-border logistics is an important link and element in the cross-border e-commerce ecosystem and is an important guarantee for the realization of cross-border e-commerce transactions. Different cross-border e-commerce models produce different cross-border logistics operation models. Overall, the operation model of cross-border logistics is that when the seller receives an order, they will arrange for the corresponding logistics company to carry out activities such as export country customs and commodity inspection, international freight, import country customs and commodity inspection, and then enter the logistics of the import country, until the goods are delivered to the consumer, at which point the cross-border logistics activities end.

Whether it is cross-border export e-commerce business or cross-border import e-commerce business, according to the direction of goods flow, it will involve export, international transportation, and import links. According to the three main links of cross-border logistics, the operation process of cross-border logistics is further divided into the operation process of export country logistics, the operation process of international segment logistics, and the operation process of import country logistics. Each logistics link has its own operation process and core nodes.

1. Operation Process of Export Country Logistics

According to the direction of goods flow in cross-border logistics, cross-border logistics first involves the logistics link of the export country. According to the key activities involved in cross-border logistics, the operation process of export country logistics is shown in Fig. 7.2. The logistics operations at the export country stage are mostly from the supplier to the cross-border e-commerce company, and then to the customs organization, with the goods passing through multiple logistics nodes. Among them, the key nodes are the warehousing link of the supplier, the logistics transportation

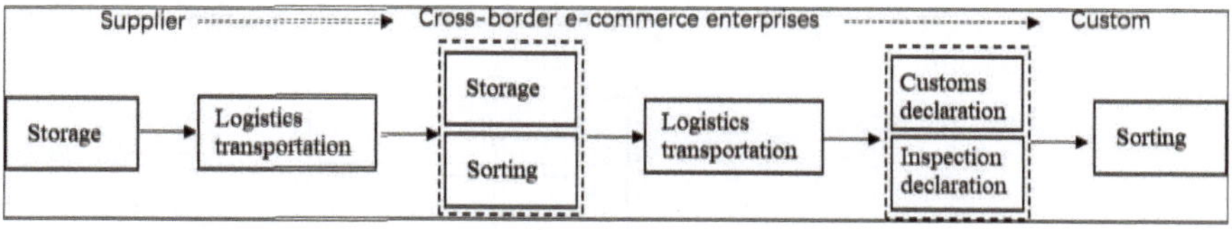

Fig. 7.2 Operation process of export country logistics

link from the supplier to the cross-border e-commerce company, the warehousing and sorting link of the cross-border e-commerce company, the logistics transportation link from the cross-border e-commerce company to the customs sorting center, the customs declaration and inspection link of the goods at the customs, and the sorting link of the goods at the customs sorting center. Depending on the different business content, the logistics links will increase, and the logistics operation process will become more complex.

The operation process of cross-border e-commerce logistics differs from domestic logistics, and there are essential differences. The biggest difference between cross-border e-commerce logistics and domestic general e-commerce logistics is cross-border, the traded goods need to go through customs import and export, and the way goods enter and exit determines the operation mode and complexity of cross-border logistics. In the logistics link of the exporting country, although it also includes the traditional domestic e-commerce logistics operation process, the difference is more focused on the operation of logistics at the customs link, including the operation content of customs declaration and inspection, and the goods sorting operation content of the customs sorting center.

2. International Logistics Operation Process

After the goods pass through the logistics stage of the exporting country, they will exit the country through air, sea or land ports, and then enter the international logistics operation link. Depending on the countries involved in cross-border goods transactions, international logistics operations will involve different modes of transportation, mainly including air transportation, sea transportation, road transportation, rail transportation, international multimodal transport, etc. When the goods arrive at the customs of the importing country through international transportation, cross-border e-commerce companies also need to carry out the customs declaration and inspection of the goods, so that the goods can pass through the customs of the importing country and enter the territory of the goods importing country. The international logistics operation process is shown in Fig. 7.3.

3. Importing Country Logistics Operation Process

After the goods pass through the customs link of the importing country, they will be sorted at the customs sorting center. After the goods are sorted, they are transported to the warehousing center of the logistics carrier in the importing country, and then sorted and transported according to the location of the consumer who purchased the goods. Similar to the domestic e-commerce logistics operation

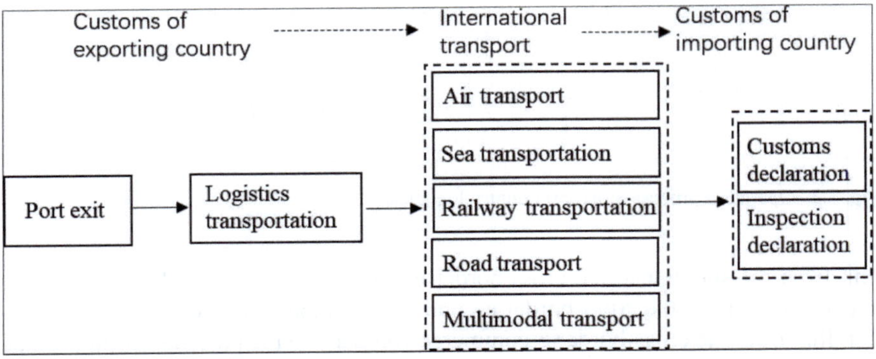

Fig. 7.3 International logistics operation process

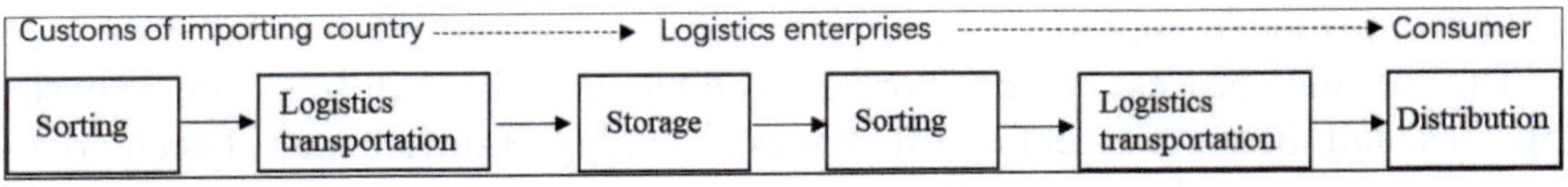

Fig. 7.4 Importing country logistics operation process

process, cross-border logistics needs to go through the distribution link to deliver the goods to the consumers, thus completing all the operation processes of cross-border logistics. These logistics operations are all realized and completed within the consumer's national borders. Relative to the country where the cross-border e-commerce company is located, this part is also called the logistics of the importing country. The logistics operation process of the importing country is shown in Fig. 7.4.

7.2 Types of Cross-Border Logistics

With the gradual transition from "overseas shopping" or "purchasing agent" mode to cross-border e-commerce mode, the cross-border logistics mode is also gradually becoming standardized, legalized, and diversified. In the development process of cross-border e-commerce, international postal parcels (especially international postal small packets) and international express delivery play an extremely important role, and these two types have the largest usage proportion among many cross-border logistics modes. Driven by the development and evolution of cross-border e-commerce, market demand has stimulated the emergence of various logistics modes, and the cross-border logistics mode is no longer limited to international postal parcels and international express delivery. The new type of cross-border logistics mode led by overseas warehouses is gradually attracting attention and being applied to the cross-border e-commerce market. According to the emergence and development process of cross-border logistics mode, international postal parcels and international express delivery are regarded as traditional cross-border logistics modes, and the cross-border logistics modes that have emerged in recent years, such as overseas warehouses, are regarded as new cross-border logistics modes.

7.2.1 Traditional Cross-Border Logistics Operation Mode

1. International Postal Parcels

Before introducing the specific channels of the post office, cross-border e-commerce operators need to understand an organization, namely the Universal Postal Union (Universal Postal The Universal Postal Union (UPU), also known as the "World Postal Union," is an intergovernmental international organization that negotiates international postal affairs. Its purpose is to organize and improve international postal services, develop international cooperation in postal matters, and provide postal technical assistance requested by member countries within its capabilities. The UPU has established the principle of free transit of international mail, unified international mail handling procedures and tariff standards, simplified international postal accounting settlement methods, and established arbitration procedures for disputes among national postal departments. It is because of this organization that we can send a package or letter from one country to other countries and regions through the global postal system.

International postal parcels refer to the import and export transportation of goods through the Universal Postal Union, often using personal mail packages for shipping, and using the postal system as a carrier for cross-border logistics of goods. In the cross-border e-commerce market, international postal parcel methods include large packages and small packages, among which postal small packages are most widely used due to their fast timeliness and low prices. International postal small packages are widely used in current cross-border e-commerce and are the most common cross-border logistics model for overseas shopping and overseas purchasing. In the Universal Postal Union, the most used by cross-border e-commerce are China Post, Singapore Post, Hong Kong Post, Royal Mail, Belgium Post, Russian Post, German Post, Swiss Post, etc. The advantages of international postal small packages are obvious, they are cheap and convenient for individuals to clear customs; but the disadvantages are also significant, mainly long delivery time, high package loss rate, and difficulty in tracing progress for non-registered items. In terms of timeliness, although most international postal small packages claim to be 15 ~ 30 days, almost more than 80% of the packages take more than 30 days to deliver, and if it encounters peak seasons or special holidays like Christmas, the logistics cycle will be even longer. In terms of package loss rate, consumers who often use international postal parcels will have a high probability of encountering package loss. After a package is sent out, although there is customs clearance information, the subsequent information disappears until it is finally found that the goods have not been delivered at all. If you need to track the logistics trajectory, you need to use the registered mail method, and registered mail needs to add registration fees on the basis of the original price, which is also a significant cost expenditure. International postal parcels are suitable for light, small goods, and have high restrictions on the volume, weight, shape, etc. of the goods, such as special goods containing electricity, powder, liquid, etc. cannot be cleared through normal methods in the postal channel.

2. International Express

Another common cross-border logistics model in cross-border e-commerce is international express delivery. International express delivery refers to the logistics and distribution activities between two or more countries or regions carried out by international express companies. Global international express companies mainly include UPS, FedEx, DHL, etc. International express delivery generally charges for goods based on weight and volume, usually charging the higher of the two, and has high requirements for goods packaging. International express delivery can choose different channels for goods transportation and express delivery according to different customer needs, such as region, type of goods, volume, weight of goods, etc. International express delivery and international postal parcels complement each other, the advantages of international postal parcels are the disadvantages of international express delivery, and the disadvantages of international postal parcels are generally the advantages of international express delivery. International express delivery has the advantages of high express delivery timeliness, low loss rate, traceability, etc. The global network of international express delivery is relatively complete, capable of providing auxiliary services such as customs declaration, inspection, insurance, etc., supporting goods packaging and warehousing services, providing door-to-door service and goods tracking service. However, the price of national express delivery is relatively high, especially the additional fees charged in some countries or remote areas are astonishing. International express delivery will encounter policy restrictions in some countries, especially in terms of the type of goods, which will become prohibited or restricted goods in some countries. In the United States, some goods are listed in the international express delivery prohibition list, such as fresh, canned meat and meat products, plant seeds, vegetables, fruits, non-canned or smoked fish and caviar, etc. To meet the rapidly growing needs of cross-border e-commerce, some international express companies have launched special service products, such as China Post Express and Alibaba's AliExpress jointly launched ePacket, which charges far less for parcels under 2 kg sent cross-border than the regular EMS price, and the delivery time is still consistent with EMS products.

7.2.2 New Cross-Border Logistics Operation Model

1. Overseas Warehouse

Overseas warehouse, commonly known as overseas warehousing, is a cross-border logistics model that has emerged in recent years. It refers to cross-border e-commerce companies renting or building warehouses outside the seller's country, especially in the buyer's country, transporting the goods to be sold to this warehouse in advance through international freight, and then displaying and selling the goods on the cross-border e-commerce platform. After receiving consumer orders, the goods are shipped, logistics and distribution activities are carried out from this warehouse. The development and demand innovation of cross-border e-commerce has promoted the emergence of overseas warehouses, which is an effective solution to the logistics dilemma of cross-border e-commerce and a breakthrough in the development path of cross-border logistics. Since the emergence of the overseas warehouse model, it has received much attention, and more and more companies engaged in cross-border e-commerce business have established overseas warehouses to solve the cross-border logistics problems they face. Amazon and eBay have established overseas warehouses in various parts of the world through different models, including cooperation with governments, cooperation with enterprises, leasing models, self-built models, and have quickly established overseas warehouses in Australia, Latin America, China, and Western Europe.

Overseas warehouses can concentrate goods for large-scale goods transportation, improving efficiency and helping to reduce logistics costs. The use of overseas warehouses can effectively solve the disadvantages and shortcomings of international postal parcels and international express delivery, such as logistics timeliness, logistics costs, customs clearance and commercial inspection, returns and exchanges, local preferences, etc., and can also reduce the risks brought by different countries in terms of exchange rates, taxes, culture, customs, language, etc. Specifically, overseas warehouses have the following significant advantages.

(1) Overseas warehouses can significantly reduce logistics costs

In modern logistics, the warehouse is a key node connecting buyers and sellers. By setting up overseas warehouses, cross-border e-commerce companies place this node overseas, which not only reduces logistics costs, but also facilitates the development of overseas markets. According to the volume of market business, cross-border e-commerce merchants can transport goods in bulk to overseas warehouses. As cross-border e-commerce has characteristics such as small batches and multiple batches, through bulk transportation, the frequency of transportation, customs clearance, and commercial inspection can be reduced, significantly reducing the costs in these links. The scale of bulk also effectively reduces the risk in various links of logistics, achieving the purpose of significantly reducing the logistics cost of cross-border e-commerce. Data from Russian E-mail shows that overseas warehouses can reduce about 60% of the logistics cost of cross-border e-commerce.

(2) Overseas warehouses help to shorten transportation and distribution cycles

Overseas warehouses provide cross-border e-commerce with one-stop services such as warehousing, sorting, packaging, and distribution. Through bulk transportation, the overall logistics time of goods is greatly shortened. Overseas warehouses can also meet the local delivery of the buyer's location, thereby shortening the order response cycle. When the buyer places an order, the cross-border e-commerce company can respond quickly at the first time, promptly notify the overseas warehouse to sort and package the goods, and improve the logistics response time. By combining the logistics characteristics of the location of the overseas warehouse, the goods can be accurately and timely delivered, shortening the delivery cycle.

(3) Overseas warehouses can avoid risks such as exchange rates, politics, and culture

Through overseas warehouses, cross-border e-commerce companies can achieve localized operations, which is conducive to breaking local protection barriers. Local warehouses for distribution are easily trusted by buyers, reducing resistance to local consumption habits and culture. Through the established overseas warehouses, cross-border e-commerce companies keep the received currency in the account as much as possible, do not settle the exchange in the short term, and use the currency to pay for the rent or operating costs of the overseas warehouse. This operation can compensate for the adverse effects caused by exchange rate changes.

(4) Overseas warehouses can handle returns and exchanges

Overseas warehouses can realize local returns and exchanges. When customers need to return or exchange goods, the goods can flow back to the local overseas warehouse, thereby avoiding the customs clearance and logistics links of the goods returning to the country. Not only does it make returns and exchanges possible, but it can also avoid secondary customs clearance and commercial inspection, secondary long-distance transportation, saving a lot of time and cost. Delivering and shipping from overseas warehouses can reduce logistics time, improve the accuracy of delivery, reduce the damage rate of goods during transportation, and fundamentally reduce the probability of returns and exchanges.

There are certain risks in overseas warehouses. Overseas warehouses require huge investment and refined management. First, leasing, construction, and operation of warehouses require manpower, material resources, and financial resources; second, goods need to be transported in bulk to overseas warehouses in advance, which requires extremely high expectations for early consumption and predictions of the quantity and type of goods, otherwise there will be inventory and backlog due to poor sales after the goods are delivered. In addition, due to market changes, there will be risks of capital backlog and unsalable goods. If they flow back to the country, they will become import activities of goods. In addition to international freight costs, various import fees need to be paid; finally, overseas warehouses will face political, legal, social and other risks in the host country.

After several years of development and improvement, the overseas warehouse model has undergone updates and changes. The following summarizes several common overseas warehouse models.

(1) Platform Overseas Warehouse Model

The platform overseas warehouse refers to the overseas warehouse built and operated by cross-border e-commerce platform companies, providing cross-border logistics service business for sellers on the cross-border e-commerce platform, including goods warehousing, sorting and packaging, transportation, collection, customer service and product return and exchange processing and other one-stop service processes. Representative platform overseas warehouses include Amazon FBA (Fulfillment by Amazon). Amazon's overseas warehouse. Sellers on cross-border e-commerce platforms display their products on the platform and ship them to overseas warehouses in the destination country in advance. Consumers place orders through the cross-border e-commerce platform, and the platform's overseas warehouse logistics system completes the subsequent sorting and delivery process. Taking Amazon's FBA overseas warehouse as an example, based on its cross-border logistics network, rich logistics experience, and intelligent management system, Amazon's FBA overseas warehouse has become the largest overseas warehouse operator in the global cross-border market. Its overseas warehouses are spread all over the world, and its warehouse operation management and logistics distribution system are very mature. FBA overseas warehouses can help cross-border e-commerce companies increase product exposure, which is conducive to increasing the traffic and sales of cross-border e-commerce companies. At the same time, Amazon's FBA overseas warehouse charges fees based on the warehouse usage space per cubic foot, and will charge long-term inventory storage fees for slow-selling products. Therefore, FBA overseas warehouses are suitable for small and light export companies. Although the cost of FBA is high, it can get more traffic support from Amazon.

(2) Self-operated Overseas Warehouse Model

Self-operated overseas warehouses refer to overseas warehouses established and operated by cross-border e-commerce sellers themselves, providing only logistics services such as warehousing, transshipment, distribution, and delivery for their own products. The entire cross-border e-commerce logistics system is controlled and managed by the export cross-border e-commerce company itself, which is more flexible. The disadvantage is that the seller needs to solve problems such as warehousing, customs declaration, and logistics transportation by themselves. The construction cost and risk of self-built warehouses are relatively large. Moreover, if the volume of goods transported is not large, it is difficult to get a price advantage in transportation. Self-operated overseas warehouses require a large amount of investment and require export cross-border e-commerce companies to have strong control and operational capabilities of overseas logistics systems. Therefore, self-operated overseas warehouses are suitable for cross-border e-commerce companies with a larger market share and stronger strength.

(3) Third-party Overseas Warehouses

Third-party overseas warehouses refer to overseas warehouses built and operated by third-party logistics companies. They are logistics platforms that provide multiple cross-border e-commerce companies with customs clearance, inbound quality inspection, order receipt, order sorting, multi-channel delivery, and subsequent transportation logistics services. Third-party overseas warehouses emphasize more on the construction and operation by third-party logistics companies. The cooperation model between cross-border e-commerce companies and third-party overseas warehouses mainly has two types: one is rental, in this case, there will be multiple fees such as operation, rental, and transportation; the other is cooperative construction, only transportation fees are incurred, but there is a certain amount of capital investment in the early stage. Third-party overseas warehouses have advantages in first-leg customs clearance and inventory management, attracting more and more sellers to use, or to use in conjunction with platform overseas warehouses.

(4) Public Overseas Warehouses

A public overseas warehouse refers to a storage facility that is invested in or operated by a company abroad, and can provide customs clearance, warehousing logistics, marketing display, returns and exchanges, and after-sales maintenance services for cross-border e-commerce companies and foreign trade companies. The concept of a public overseas warehouse is more generalized, and it overlaps with self-operated overseas warehouses, platform overseas warehouses, and third-party overseas warehouses, but there are also some differences. The difference from third-party overseas warehouses is that its construction or operation is no longer limited to third-party logistics companies, and its main body is broader; the difference from self-operated overseas warehouses and platform overseas warehouses is that it needs to highlight the shared use of the warehouse with other companies, especially cross-border e-commerce companies and foreign trade companies. The construction of a public overseas warehouse requires high standards, in addition to certain scale construction area requirements, it also requires an independent research and development or third-party information management system, with basic order management modules, logistics modules, and warehouse management modules, capable of docking customer, product, warehousing, distribution and other information; it can provide domestic collection, international freight, overseas shelving, terminal distribution, returns and other cross-border comprehensive logistics services, sign cooperation agreements with mainstream express companies in the host country, and have logistics distribution channels that radiate the local market overseas; familiar with the customs policies and regulations of the destination country and related requirements, provide one-stop customs clearance services such as customs declaration, tax payment, pickup, and transshipment; provide offline product display services, build their own e-commerce platforms or cooperate with cross-border e-commerce platforms, help cross-border e-commerce companies and foreign trade companies expand marketing channels, assist companies in overseas brand promotion, etc.

(5) Virtual Overseas Warehouse

A virtual overseas warehouse, also known as a virtual warehouse, can be seen as an evolved model of an overseas warehouse, but it is different from the traditional overseas warehouse model. The virtual overseas warehouse is a model between domestic direct delivery and overseas warehouse delivery. Its operation mode is: when an order is generated on the cross-border e-commerce platform, the back-end transport label is printed in the system, and it is sent to the destination country using the first leg solution of international express, which is responsible for customs clearance in the destination country, and the package is sent to the virtual overseas warehouse in the destination country, and then it is sent to the overseas warehouse through various channels for unpacking and distribution. The virtual overseas warehouse is a place for cross-border e-commerce sellers to transit packages. Its feature is that the origin shown online is the destination country of the goods, but the actual goods are sent directly from the country where the cross-border e-commerce seller is located. Different from traditional overseas warehouses, cross-border e-commerce virtual overseas warehouses do not generate warehousing, leasing, etc., thereby reducing warehousing costs, and compressing the intermediate time cost, and the transportation efficiency is greatly improved. The virtual overseas warehouse can control the timeliness of the entire process according to the platform's timeliness requirements; support returns and exchanges in overseas warehouses, solve the problem of malicious returns; sellers do not need to stock up, no inventory risk, no financial pressure, etc.

2. Border Warehouse

A border warehouse is a cross-border logistics model derived from the concept of an overseas warehouse. The difference between a border warehouse and an overseas warehouse lies in the different geographical locations of the warehouses. An overseas warehouse is a warehouse built outside the country where the seller of the cross-border e-commerce transaction is located, while a border warehouse is a warehouse built in the neighboring country of the country where the buyer of the cross-border e-commerce transaction is located. A border warehouse refers to a warehouse on the border of the neighboring country of the country where the goods are imported, where goods are delivered to this warehouse in advance through leasing or construction, and a series of activities such as product display, browsing, ordering, processing, payment, and customer service are carried out through the cross-border e-commerce platform, and cross-border logistics transportation and distribution are directly carried out from this warehouse through offline logistics.

According to the geographical location of the warehouse, border warehouses can be divided into two types: relative border warehouses and absolute border warehouses. Absolute border warehouses refer to the warehouses located in the seller's country, where the cross-border e-commerce transaction entity is located, and the warehouse location is adjacent to the buyer's country. For example, China establishes warehouses in cities near the China-Russia border within China, such as Harbin; relative border warehouses refer to the warehouses located in the border cities or regions of the buyer's neighboring countries when the countries of the cross-border e-commerce transaction entities are not adjacent, to meet the cross-border logistics business needs generated by cross-border e-commerce transactions, such as cross-border e-commerce transactions between China and Brazil, warehouses are set up in border cities near Brazil in neighboring countries such as Argentina, Colombia, Paraguay, and Peru.

The relative border warehouse is a relative concept. It belongs to the category of border warehouses relative to the buyer's country and belongs to the category of overseas warehouses relative to the seller's country. Border warehouses can avoid some risks of overseas warehouses and are a new type of cross-border logistics model generated in response to domestic protectionism and the development of cross-border e-commerce business. Due to factors such as political instability, harsh tax policies, currency depreciation, and domestic inflation in some countries, the emergence and development of border warehouses have been stimulated. Border warehouses are particularly advantageous in some free trade zones. For example, Brazil's domestic protectionism and harsh tax policies restrict the development of cross-border e-commerce and cross-border logistics, but by using the advantages of the South American Free Trade Agreement and establishing border warehouses in neighboring countries of Brazil, risks can be avoided and South American and Brazilian cross-border e-commerce business can be promoted. Border warehouses have advantages that overseas warehouses cannot achieve, such as avoiding political, tax, currency, and legal risks of the importing country; they can take advantage of regional policies, such as the South American Free Trade Agreement, North American Free Trade Area, etc.

3. International Logistics Dedicated Line

The international logistics dedicated line is a new type of cross-border logistics model that has emerged in the context of the development of cross-border e-commerce. The international logistics dedicated line refers to the cross-border logistics model formed in two or more countries or regions, where the transportation route, transportation time, logistics start and end points, and transportation tools are all fixed. For cross-border e-commerce, the international logistics dedicated line can play the function of long-distance cross-border transportation, has a high degree of scalability, and can achieve economies of scale through the dedicated logistics model, which is of great significance for reducing cross-border logistics costs, especially for cross-border e-commerce companies with fixed markets, it is an effective cross-border logistics solution. Depending on the different regional routes, there are many types of international logistics dedicated lines. Taking China as an example, they can be divided into China-Russia dedicated lines, China-US dedicated lines, China–Europe dedicated lines, China-Australia dedicated lines, etc. Depending on the different transportation methods, international logistics dedicated lines are divided into air dedicated lines, port dedicated lines, railway dedicated lines, land bridge dedicated lines, and multimodal transport dedicated lines. The dedicated lines that have been opened mainly include Zhengzhou-Europe Block Trains, Japan OCS, Europe GLS, traditional Asia-Europe international routes, etc. The timeliness of the international logistics dedicated line is better than that of international postal parcels, but weaker than international express delivery; the logistics cost of the international logistics dedicated line is lower than that of international express delivery, but higher than that of international postal parcels. International logistics dedicated lines can provide convenient customs clearance services. The international logistics dedicated line has obvious regional limitations and cannot adapt to the logistics demand without geographical restrictions generated by cross-border e-commerce, which will cause the cross-border logistics dedicated line to fail to become one of the main modes of cross-border logistics. For cross-border e-commerce companies targeting a certain country or region, the international logistics dedicated line is a relatively good cross-border logistics solution. The international logistics dedicated line will become a solution for cross-border e-commerce logistics to tap into fixed markets, and can also become an intermediate link and turnover link in cross-border logistics. When the business volume can support it, by developing multiple international logistics dedicated lines to form an international logistics dedicated line network, the frequency of use and overall value of the international logistics dedicated line can be increased.

4. Bonded Area and Free Trade Zone Logistics

In the context of the development of cross-border e-commerce, the value of free trade zones and bonded areas is highlighted, and countries around the world are accelerating the construction of free trade zones and bonded areas. Relying on the logistics services of bonded areas or free trade zones has become a new type of cross-border logistics model in the cross-border e-commerce market. Bonded area or free trade zone logistics refers to the pre-shipment of goods to the bonded area or free trade zone warehouse through international freight, displaying goods, traffic, placing orders, processing, payment and other activities through the cross-border e-commerce platform. After processing the online order, the goods are sorted, packaged, and shipped through the offline bonded area or free trade zone warehouse to complete the final delivery and other logistics activities.

The logistics model of the Free Trade Zone or Bonded Zone generally belongs to the "logistics first, order later" approach. The logistics model of the Free Trade Zone or Bonded Zone combines the advantages of scaled logistics, cargo consolidation logistics, and localized logistics. It helps to shorten logistics time, improve logistics efficiency, reduce logistics costs, and also take advantage of the resource benefits of the bonded zone or free trade zone. Logistics in the bonded zone or free trade zone can enjoy the preferential policies and comprehensive advantages of the bonded zone or free trade zone, mainly reflected in logistics, customs clearance, commodity inspection, payment and receipt of foreign exchange, tax refunds, etc. It also simplifies the cumbersome procedures and procedures of cross-border e-commerce and cross-border logistics. For example, Amazon has established a free trade zone logistics warehouse in the Shanghai Free Trade Zone, using the Shanghai Free Trade Zone as the entrance for cross-border e-commerce transactions, introducing a global product line, and sending goods to the free trade zone logistics warehouse in advance. When consumers place orders, the goods are dispatched from the free trade zone logistics warehouse, which can achieve centralized international freight, customs clearance and commodity inspection, reducing cross-border logistics costs, shortening logistics time, and improving logistics and distribution efficiency. The logistics model of the bonded zone or free trade zone is more suitable for daily consumables such as maternity and baby products, food, cosmetics, or goods with many models, and giant e-commerce companies with large sales data analysis capabilities. In addition, during large-scale promotional events such as "Double 11" and "Black Friday", this model brings great convenience to solving the congestion problem of clearing a large number of goods.

5. Consolidation Logistics

Cross-border e-commerce belongs to the category of e-commerce. Based on the cross-time and space boundary characteristics of the Internet, its consumption is more dispersed, the single order volume is small, and the product types are diverse. With the rapid development of cross-border e-commerce, consolidation logistics has emerged. The emergence of the consolidation logistics model is to reduce the high cost of cross-border logistics. The consolidation logistics model generally belongs to the "order first, logistics later" approach, suitable for various product demands with different sales volumes. Logistics providers can shorten the overall logistics time to the greatest extent through system response, inventory management, and efficient customs clearance, and also have a significant competitive advantage in cost performance. Consolidation logistics refers to first transporting goods to local or local storage centers or distribution centers. When a certain quantity or scale is accumulated, the goods are transported to overseas buyers through international freight modes in cooperation with international logistics companies; or the goods sent from various places are first gathered and then distributed in batches; or cross-border e-commerce companies with similar product attributes or types form strategic alliances to establish a common cross-border logistics operation center, using the concept of scale optimization and complementary advantages to achieve the purpose of reducing cross-border logistics costs. Although the logistics model of the bonded zone or free trade zone is similar to the consolidation logistics model and can generally be classified into the category of consolidation logistics, consolidation logistics is not equivalent to the logistics model of the bonded zone or free trade zone. Consolidation logistics can not only centralize storage before carrying out cross-border e-commerce activities, but also centralize logistics and distribution after carrying out cross-border e-commerce activities. The warehouse of consolidation logistics is not limited to the bonded zone or free trade zone, and has already left the limited geographical space category.

6. Third-Party Logistics

Third-party logistics refers to the logistics function undertaken by a third party other than the trading entity. The third-party logistics company adopts the contract commissioning model to undertake the logistics demand generated by the transaction. In domestic e-commerce transactions, self-built logistics can be regarded as first-party logistics, such as JD.com, Alibaba's Cainiao Logistics, Haier's Ririshun Logistics in China, and Ulmart's self-built logistics, Amazon Logistics, Walmart Logistics, etc. abroad. Second-party logistics is undertaken by the buyer. Third-party logistics is undertaken by professional third-party logistics companies. In cross-border e-commerce, the process and environment are more complex, self-built logistics requires high investment, high requirements, and high risks. Although some cross-border e-commerce companies are also adopting the self-built logistics model, such as JD.com, Yangmatou, etc., due to factors such as capital, the complexity of cross-border logistics, and various risks and obstacles, the vast majority of cross-border e-commerce companies, in addition to using international postal parcels and international express delivery, are gradually beginning to turn to the third-party logistics model, cooperating with the Universal Postal Union system, international express companies, or professional third-party cross-border logistics companies. In cross-border logistics, there will be a phenomenon of multiple models or multiple third-party logistics companies cooperating, and there will also be a phenomenon of coexistence of self-built logistics and third-party logistics.

7. Fourth-Party Logistics

Fourth-party logistics is an entity independent of the transaction parties and professional third-party logistics providers, undertaking goods logistics and distribution business, providing logistics consulting, logistics planning, goods transportation, logistics information systems, supply chain management and other comprehensive activities for the buyers and sellers of goods transactions, and third parties. It is a supply chain integrator that provides comprehensive and comprehensive supply chain solutions by managing its own resources and external coordinate data, capabilities, and technologies.

Fourth-party logistics emphasizes the ability to integrate supply chain resources. Through its influence and voice in the entire supply chain, it solves logistics needs as the basis, integrates various internal and external resources, and realizes logistics information sharing and full utilization of social logistics resources. With the development and maturity of cross-border e-commerce, cross-border logistics is more complex, and services are no longer limited to the demand for cross-border spatial displacement of goods, and many value-added service needs will be generated. A batch of fourth-party logistics companies have emerged to provide richer cross-border logistics services for the cross-border e-commerce market. For example, Axado cooperates with more than 150 logistics companies worldwide to integrate the fragmented cross-border logistics market and provide a one-stop logistics solution for the demand side. Global integration of logistics service resources not only provides dedicated line logistics services, but also provides one-stop comprehensive service items such as shopping cart construction, source distribution, online promotion, channel management software services, online payment, global logistics and warehousing, and gradually involves big data, information technology and financial value-added services.

7.2.3 Cross-Border Logistics Comparative Analysis

By analyzing the characteristics of various cross-border logistics models in terms of timeliness, cost, applicability, and current usage rate, we can have a clearer understanding of various types of cross-border logistics models, as shown in Table 7.1. Among the main cross-border logistics models, international postal parcels and international express delivery are used earlier and are the main cross-border logistics usage models. International postal parcels benefit from the logistics network system of the Universal Postal Union, with the densest network worldwide, capable of radiating to nearly 200 countries or regions worldwide. Among the cross-border logistics models,

Table 7.1 Comparison of cross-border logistics models

Mode	Timeliness	Cost	Applicability	Current usage
International postal packet	Slowest	Lowest	Wide	Highest
International Express	Fastest	High	Wide	Highest
Overseas warehouse	Faster	Lower	Wide	Higher
Border warehouse	Faster	Lower	Significant limitations	Low
International logistics line	Faster	Lower	Significant limitations	Low
Free Trade Zone Logistics	Faster	Lower	Significant limitations	Higher
Collection Logistics	Commonly	Lower	Significant limitations	Low
Third-party logistics	Uncertain	Uncertain	Wide	Higher
Fourth-party logistics	Uncertain	Uncertain	Wide	Higher

the cost of international postal parcels is the lowest, and the corresponding timeliness is the slowest. The cross-border logistics cycle is basically more than a month, sometimes even several months, and there are problems such as lost packages and lost goods. International express delivery is based on mature global international express companies, such as UPS, DHL, FedEx, EMS, etc., and its usage rate in the cross-border e-commerce market is also very high, mainly due to its fast logistics speed and timeliness.

Overseas warehouses have emerged in recent years and have developed rapidly, becoming an excellent logistics solution for many cross-border e-commerce companies. Overseas warehouses can also effectively solve localization and return and exchange needs, and their usage is on a rapid upward trend. Third-party logistics and fourth-party logistics benefit from professional advantages, have a wide range of applications within the same country, and therefore have high development prospects. Their logistics timeliness and cost vary depending on different situations, company and product needs. Models such as bonded areas or free trade zone logistics with significant scale advantages, international logistics dedicated lines, and cargo consolidation logistics have certain advantages in terms of logistics timeliness and cost, but they have significant limitations in applicability. These limitations are not only reflected in geographical and temporal limitations, but also exist in terms of companies and products. There is no absolute advantage or disadvantage between different cross-border logistics models, and it is necessary to determine according to different needs. Different cross-border logistics models also have their best application range.

7.3 Cross-Border E-Commerce Customs Clearance

Customs, as an indispensable key link in cross-border e-commerce, involves a lot of customs clearance knowledge. As a cross-border e-commerce seller, it is necessary to understand the basic system and precautions of customs goods supervision. Goods supervision is an important management authority of the customs on behalf of the state at the port, according to import and export laws, regulations and policies to supervise the legal import and export of goods and transport tools, and is also the basis for the customs to complete the collection of tariffs, stop smuggling violations, and compile customs statistics. The declaration, inspection, taxation, and release of the transport tools and their cargo entering and exiting constitute a unified whole of cargo supervision that is mutually restrictive and relatively independent. There are two customs involved in cross-border e-commerce: one is the export customs of the exporter, and the other is the import customs of the consumer.

7.3.1 Cross-Border E-Commerce Export Customs

In cross-border e-commerce exports, as long as the seller complies with customs laws and regulations, does not transport prohibited goods explicitly prohibited by customs, and handles import and export customs procedures, the documents declared by the consignor for import and export goods are consistent with the actual import and export goods, that is, the single goods match, generally there are no major problems. The following briefly introduces the information about cross-border e-commerce export declaration:

Some cross-border e-commerce companies in some ports have been able to achieve one-time customs declaration through the cross-border e-commerce customs clearance service platform, and customs, taxation, inspection and quarantine, foreign exchange, market supervision and other departments can simultaneously obtain cross-border e-commerce product information through this platform, realizing the whole process supervision of products.

(1) Cross-border e-commerce export customs clearance process

- Record on the cross-border e-commerce service platform;
- After the goods are sold, e-commerce, logistics, and payment companies submit order, payment, and logistics three-single information to the cross-border e-commerce service platform;
- The cross-border e-commerce service platform completes the three-single comparison, automatically generates the goods list, and sends the list data to the export country's electronic port;
- The goods are transported to the cross-border e-commerce supervision warehouse;
- After the customs verifies the single goods match through the cross-border e-commerce service platform, the goods are released for export;
- The e-commerce company applies for a tax refund from the tax bureau with the customs declaration form.

(2) Customs declaration documents

Generally, traditional foreign trade export customs clearance documents include invoices (Invoice), packing lists (Packing List), customs declaration form. In cross-border e-commerce, due to the fragmentation of orders, these formal documents are not usually used. For example, the customs information of postal parcels is directly displayed on the waybill.

Only when sending commercial express, the courier company will ask the seller to provide the invoice of the goods. Invoices are divided into proforma invoices (PROFORMA INVOICE) and commercial invoices (COMMERCIAL INVOICE). In theory, the invoice used for customs declaration must be a commercial invoice, but in actual operation, a proforma invoice can be used. The content covered by the two is basically the same, the main difference is: on the one hand, the names are different; on the other hand, the proforma invoice is more like an estimate document, not as formal as a commercial invoice.

The invoice generally contains the following content:

- Invoice wording and sender's company header (English)
- Sender's company name, address (English) and phone number
- Recipient's company name, address (English) and phone number
- Waybill number and invoice number
- Trade terms (such as FOB, CFR, CIF, etc.)
- Weight of goods
- Size or volume of goods
- Detailed description of the item name (Chinese and English)
- Quantity of goods
- Unit price and declared total price (currency unit: US dollars)
- Country of origin
- Customs code (required by some courier companies)
- Company seal of the sender (required by some countries)

Precautions:

- The invoice must be a printed original (not handwritten), photocopies, faxes are invalid;
- There should be no traces of modification (must be stamped after modification).

7.3.2 Cross-Border E-Commerce Destination Country Import Customs

Global cross-border trade is booming, the "Belt and Road" opens the "dream space", and strengthens the process of the world economic community. In the process of economic globalization, customs policies on import trade in various countries also vary.

1. Customs Detention

The most common problem encountered in the destination country is detention. When encountering problems such as goods being detained, don't be too nervous, first understand the reason for the detention of the goods, because the customs regulations of each country and region are different. When detention occurs, the relevant customs department will give you an explanation, which contains the reason for the detention, and the sender or recipient must cooperate with the customs to provide relevant documents.

(1) Reasons for goods being detained by customs or not allowed to clear customs

- The description of the goods is not detailed or clear, and a proof letter needs to be provided again, specifically explaining the name and purpose of the goods;
- The declared value of the goods is too low (customs has reason to suspect tax evasion);
- International express cargo documents are incomplete, necessary documents such as invoices, packing lists, import licenses, and 3C certifications are required;
- Sensitive goods, items that are prohibited or restricted for import and export by the country;
- The recipient's conditions do not allow (such as lack of import rights);
- Exceeding the minimum duty-free amount for imports in the destination country;
- Other relevant policies stipulated by the local country.

Generally, most are due to the relevant policies of the local country in the first three items. Once the goods are detained, the sender or recipient should cooperate with customs as much as possible and provide relevant documents. Generally, customs will evaluate the goods, and as long as it is consistent with the sender/recipient's statement, the goods can be released after the clearance procedures are completed.

(2) Handling methods

- If the declared value is too low and the goods are detained, negotiate with the customer to pay the customs duties and retrieve the goods from customs; if the customs duties are not high, consider sharing with the buyer;
- If the goods are detained due to incomplete procedures, such as personal imports, customs require import rights, find a company with import rights to act as a customs clearance agent;
- If relevant certification procedures are required, provide them to customs if possible; if not, the goods cannot be cleared;
- You can apply to customs for the return of goods. According to international practice, goods that cannot be cleared can apply for return to the place of shipment or a third-party trade port. If applied, they can be returned.

(3) How to avoid customs detention as much as possible

- To avoid customs detention, for general packages, try to select gift, but do not directly write gift in the declared product name. Relatively speaking, personal packages have a lower chance of being inspected by customs. To avoid high customs clearance fees after detention, the declared value can be written a little less, but not too much lower than the actual value, because the detention rate of valuable items is high. In addition, after customs detention, the customs clearance fee is calculated based on the declared value. The higher the declared value, the higher the customs clearance fee.

- Understand the policies of various countries. For example, although Australia is easy to clear customs, battery products are not allowed by customs, so try not to send battery or electromagnetic products to Australia. If you have to sell products with batteries, you can tell the customer clearly that you will not send the battery, only the product.
- Choose a safe delivery method. DHL has a high detention rate, followed by FedEx and UPS; relatively safe delivery methods are airmail registered parcels and EMS. In addition, even if EMS is detained by customs, it can still be returned to the place of shipment for free. Especially for countries with strict customs such as Russia and Brazil, small packages and EMS have absolute advantages in customs clearance.

2. Tariff Thresholds and Duty-Free Amounts in Various Countries

The minimum duty-free declared amount refers to the declared dollar amount of eligible shipments that is less than the specified amount, which can be exempted from formal customs declaration and no need to pay customs duties or taxes.

(1) United States

At the beginning of 2016, the United States raised the minimum duty-free declaration amount for inbound shipments from \$200 per shipment to \$800. This means that most shipments imported into the United States with a value less than \$800 can be exempted from formal customs declaration and import duties. This adjustment will effectively promote trade development, reduce costs, and speed up the circulation of goods. In particular, Asian exporters can benefit from this by reducing paperwork to speed up the clearance of goods and shorten the transportation time to the United States.

Threshold: \$800.

Composition of the comprehensive tariff: DUTY (duty) + ADV (customs clearance miscellaneous tax).

DUTY = value of goods * tax rate.

(2) European Union

The European Union starts taxing packages that are higher than 22 euros. Because the duty-free declaration amount is relatively low, in the EU region, packages often get inspected due to low declaration. For member countries of the EU region such as Spain, France, Norway, Sweden, etc., packages higher than 22 euros will be taxed. From past data, a small number of packages have been inspected, and the safety factor of small packages and EMS is relatively high. Germany is a relatively special country in the EU region, and the inspection intensity of customs is greater than other EU countries, and EMS is often returned due to customs reasons.

Composition of the comprehensive tariff: VAT = (declared value to customs + freight + DUTY) * 19%

DUTY = (value of goods + 70% freight) * product tax rate

(3) United Kingdom

UK: Duty will be charged when the declared value is more than 18GBP.

Threshold: 15 pounds.

Composition of the comprehensive tariff: VAT(**) + DUTY (duty) + ADV (customs clearance miscellaneous tax).

VAT = (declared value to customs + freight + DUTY) * 20%

DUTY = value of goods * product tax rate.

(4) Australia

The inspection of imported packages is relatively relaxed, and packages less than 1000 Australian dollars are exempt from duty, except for some prohibited and raw wood products, which are easy to clear customs.

Threshold: 1000 Australian dollars.

Composition of the comprehensive tariff: DUTY + GST + ADV (customs clearance miscellaneous tax).

GST = UK VAT (declared value to customs + freight + DUTY) * 10%

DUTY = value of goods * tax rate.

(5) Russia

According to a report by the Russian media "News", in October 2016, the Russian Customs General Administration proposed to the Russian Ministry of Economic Development to reduce the tax-free amount of imported goods purchased online and to tax international mail packages imported online in stages. Previously, the Russian Federal Customs exempted goods purchased within a month in inbound packages, with a value not exceeding 1000 euros and a weight not exceeding 21kg. The proposal of the Russian Customs General Administration is to reduce this tax-free import amount from 1000 euros per month to 22 euros. However, this proposal is still controversial and has not yet been approved by the Russian Ministry of Economic Development. In addition, Russia is a very special country, with many corruption issues in customs, and express delivery can only go through EMS.

(6) Brazil

The main channel to Brazil is still the postal channel, such as postal parcels from various countries, which are relatively simple to clear customs. Sending parcels to Brazil via commercial express has always been one of the most headache-inducing issues for cross-border e-commerce sellers. If you send parcels to Brazil via commercial express, the following conditions will apply:

- The recipient's tax number is required, there are two types of tax numbers: CNPJ (company tax number- XX.XXX.XXX/XXXX-XX) and CPF (personal tax number- XXX.XXX.XXX/XX). If the recipient is an individual, provide the CPF, if the recipient is a company, formal customs declaration is generally required.
- Brazilian customs implements a simplified tax system for imported goods (such as imported goods or gifts purchased from the internet, transported to Brazil via mail or international express) that are declared to be worth less than 3000USD,

have no resale purpose, and have not been formally cleared. The tax threshold is around 50USD, import duties are levied on the basis of the simplified tax system, all are levied at 60% of the declared value of the goods, and an additional 18% of the destination country tax (ICMS TAX) is also levied locally.
- If the declared value of the parcel is inaccurate, it may lead to Brazilian customs forcibly detaining, forcibly returning, or imposing hefty fines.
- When the recipient is an individual, there may be a situation where Brazilian customs deems the goods to be for commercial use, prohibits importation, and requires forced return. This usually happens when an excessive number of items are sent to the same person, and the above judgment may even depend on the subjective judgment of Brazilian customs. For example, if 10 identical items are sent to the same recipient, they may be deemed to be goods for resale, and Brazilian customs will prohibit importation and force a return. Therefore, for personal shipments to Brazil, it is recommended to reasonably allocate the quantity of the same goods in the same package and the shipping time.

Due to the differences in customs policies of various countries, sellers need to have a general understanding of the relevant information before shipping, in order to facilitate the smooth clearance of goods. Relevant information can be consulted with other sellers, freight forwarders, etc.

7.4 Cross-Border E-Commerce Customs Supervision Mode

7.4.1 Introduction to Cross-Border E-Commerce Customs Supervision Code

The General Administration of Customs of China added codes 9610 and 1210 for customs supervision in 2014, added code 1239 in 2016, and added codes 9710 and 9810 in 2020, thus forming five basic cross-border e-commerce business modes, namely: 9610, 1210, 1239, 9710 and 9810 cross-border e-commerce modes. According to the different directions of goods flow, it can be divided into cross-border import and cross-border export, among which the cross-border e-commerce import business modes include: 1210 online shopping bonded import mode, 1239 online shopping bonded import A, 9610 direct mail import mode. Cross-border e-commerce export business modes include: 1210 export business mode, 9610 export business mode, 9710 export business mode, 9810 export business mode.

(1) 9610 Cross-border E-commerce Mode

9610, fully named "Cross-Border Trade E-commerce", also known as "E-commerce", is applicable to domestic individuals or e-commerce enterprises that carry out transactions through e-commerce trading platforms and adopt the "list verification and release, summary declaration" mode to handle customs clearance procedures for e-commerce retail import and export goods (excluding e-commerce retail import and export goods through customs special supervision areas or bonded supervision places). The list verification and release refers to: import e-commerce enterprises first push the order information of the imported goods on the trading platform to the cross-border e-commerce public service platform where the business is located, and match it with the payment slip and waybill to complete the list declaration. After the customs electronically audits and releases the "list", the actual goods are released, solving the problem of fewer orders and more batches for cross-border retail imports, facilitating the actual operation of enterprises and regulatory departments, and greatly improving the efficiency of customs clearance. (2) 1210 Cross-Border E-commerce Model 1210, fully named "Bonded Cross-Border Trade E-commerce", also known as "Bonded E-commerce", refers to cross-border e-commerce import enterprises stocking cross-border e-commerce import goods in customs special supervision areas. After domestic consumers place orders and generate orders, the goods purchased by consumers are cleared through customs in small parcels and delivered to domestic buyers. It is applicable to domestic individuals or e-commerce enterprises that carry out cross-border transactions on e-commerce platforms approved by customs and e-commerce retail import and export goods entering and exiting through customs special supervision areas or bonded supervision places (retail import and export goods traded between customs special supervision areas, bonded supervision places and areas outside (places outside) through e-commerce platforms are not applicable to this supervision method). Bonded warehouses refer to warehouses approved by customs for the storage of imported goods and are not subject to customs laws and import control regulations. Imported goods stored in bonded warehouses are exempt from customs duties if re-exported, and must pay customs duties if they enter the domestic market. (3) 1239 Cross-Border E-commerce Model 1239, fully named "Bonded Cross-Border Trade E-commerce A", also known as "Bonded E-commerce A". It is applicable to cross-border e-commerce retail import goods entering through customs special supervision areas or bonded logistics centers (Type B) by domestic e-commerce enterprises. Compared with the 1210 supervision method, the 1239 supervision method is applicable to cross-border e-commerce retail import goods entering through customs special supervision areas or bonded logistics centers (Type B) by domestic e-commerce enterprises. Goods in the list of cross-border e-commerce retail import goods are exempt from submitting permit documents to customs; direct purchase goods are supervised according to personal goods requirements, and online shopping bonded goods need to be supervised according to goods requirements when entering the "first line" area, and refer to personal goods supervision requirements when exiting the "second line" area. (4) 9710 Cross-Border E-commerce Model 9710, fully named "Cross-Border E-commerce Enterprise Direct Export to Enterprise", also known as "Cross-Border E-commerce B2B Direct Export", is applicable to goods directly exported by cross-border e-commerce B2B. 9710 refers to domestic enterprises reaching a transaction with foreign enterprises through a cross-border e-commerce platform, and directly exporting goods to foreign enterprises through cross-border logistics. The 9710 supervision model has multiple advantages compared to traditional foreign trade exports, namely: simplified declaration procedures, priority for inspection, priority for transshipment procedures, reducing enterprise customs clearance costs while greatly improving the customs clearance time of export enterprises. (5) 9810 Cross-Border E-commerce Model The full name of 9810 is “Cross-border E-commerce Export Overseas Warehouse”, also known as “Cross-border E-commerce Export Overseas Warehouse”, which is applicable to goods in cross-border e-commerce export overseas warehouses. 9810 refers to domestic enterprises first exporting goods to overseas warehouses through cross-border logistics, and then delivering them to overseas buyers after transactions are completed through cross-border e-commerce platforms. Domestic enterprises deliver exported goods to overseas warehouses through cross-border logistics, including Amazon FBA warehouses/Walmart WFS warehouses, third-party overseas warehouses, or self-built overseas warehouses. After transactions are completed through cross-border e-commerce platforms, goods are delivered from overseas warehouses to buyers, and relevant electronic data is transmitted according to customs requirements.

7.4.2 *Cross-Border E-Commerce Customs Supervision Business Process*

As mentioned in Chap. 3, by the end of May 2023, the General Administration of Customs of China has successively added 9610, 1210, 1239, 9710 and 9810 cross-border e-commerce customs supervision modes. The concepts of these five modes have been introduced in Chap. 3, and this section focuses on sorting out the business processes of these five cross-border e-commerce customs modes.

1. 9610 Business Process

Since 9610 is divided into imports and exports, their business processes are introduced separately.

(1) 9610 Export Business Process

The specific 9610 export business process is as follows:

① Advance filing: Before the export of cross-border trade e-commerce goods, e-commerce platforms, e-commerce enterprises, payment companies, and logistics companies need to file in the customs enterprise management system. The e-commerce platform needs to record pre-sale goods on the cross-border clearance platform.

② Online declaration: After the consumer places an order online, the e-commerce platform, payment company, and logistics company respectively send the electronic order, payment voucher, and logistics waybill electronic data to the cross-border clearance platform.

③ After the e-commerce enterprise delivers the retail goods to the customs supervision area, the e-commerce enterprise or customs declaration agency should declare the exit list to the cross-border clearance platform.

④ The cross-border clearance platform compares the exit list with the electronic order, payment voucher, logistics waybill, and product filing information. If the exit list comparison is successful, it automatically ends; if the comparison is unsuccessful, manual review will be conducted.

⑤ Convenient customs clearance: After approval, the cross-border clearance platform sends data to the express on-site sorting equipment for physical inspection.

⑥ Quick verification and release: The staff quickly verifies and releases the export goods through the express on-site sorting equipment. For goods that do not need to be opened for inspection, they are directly released after the "same screen comparison" is correct; goods that need to be opened for inspection should be manually inspected.

⑦ Summary declaration: During the summary declaration period, the e-commerce enterprise summarizes the released but not summarized outbound list, the cross-border clearance platform generates the official export declaration form according to the business rules, applies to the customs through the electronic port, and the customs automatically reviews and clears. The enterprise declaration form is used as proof to handle foreign exchange settlement and tax refund procedures.

(2) 9610 Import Business Process

The operation process of the 9610 import mode is as follows:

① Consumers place orders to purchase goods on the cross-border e-commerce platform.

② The platform places orders to purchase goods from overseas merchants based on the order information and arranges overseas logistics for delivery.

③ Goods are imported through overseas logistics to reach the domestic market and enter the supervised warehouse of the cross-border e-commerce platform.

④ The cross-border e-commerce platform takes the goods out of the supervised warehouse and entrusts a domestic logistics company for delivery.

⑤ Consumers sign for the goods and make payment.

⑥ The platform settles the payment to the overseas merchants based on the order information, and carries out customs declaration, tax payment, etc., according to the tax rate and tax type.

2. 1210 Business Process

Since 1210 is divided into import and export, their business processes are introduced separately.

(1) 1210 Export Process

The specific process of 1210 export business is as follows:

① Overseas merchants store their goods in overseas warehouses, and then deliver the goods to the sales location through the warehouse partner.

② Overseas consumers can choose their favorite products and place orders through websites or shopping apps, etc.

③ The sales platform will contact the overseas warehouse in time according to the sales volume and inventory situation, extract goods from it, and hand them over to the local logistics company.

④ The courier company delivers the goods to the overseas consumers.

(2) 1210 Import Process

The specific process of 1210 import business is as follows:

① Establish a computer management system that meets the requirements of customs supervision, and exchange electronic data on the Internet according to the requirements of customs.

② Enterprises participating in cross-border e-commerce retail imports should register or register their company information with the local customs in advance.

③ Enterprises participating in cross-border e-commerce retail imports should go to the local electronic port to handle the data access procedures of the "Cross-border E-commerce Import Unified Edition Information System".

④ Set up a dedicated cross-border logistics account book; the same warehousing company needs to set up one or more account books according to the requirements of customs supervision, recording the entry, exit, and transfer of goods.

⑤ The tax withholding agent should handle the tax guarantee for imported goods of online shopping before starting the business at the local customs.

⑥ Enterprises participating in cross-border e-commerce retail imports should handle the procedures for the import and export of online shopping bonded imported goods in advance, the procedures for the first-line entry of goods, and the procedures for the second-line exit of goods.

3. 1239 Business Process

The 1239 business process is similar to 1210. The difference is that 1210 can only be piloted in the special customs supervision areas (including comprehensive bonded zones, bonded port areas, bonded zones, etc.) or bonded logistics centers (Type B) in the national pilot cities and the whole island of Hainan; while 1239 is carried out in special areas or logistics centers outside the pilot cities.

4. 9710 And 9810 Business Process

Both 9710 and 9810 are cross-border e-commerce export modes. The difference is that 9710 belongs to cross-border e-commerce B2B direct export, and 9810 belongs to cross-border e-commerce export overseas warehouse. Their export business processes are similar, as shown in Fig. 7.5.

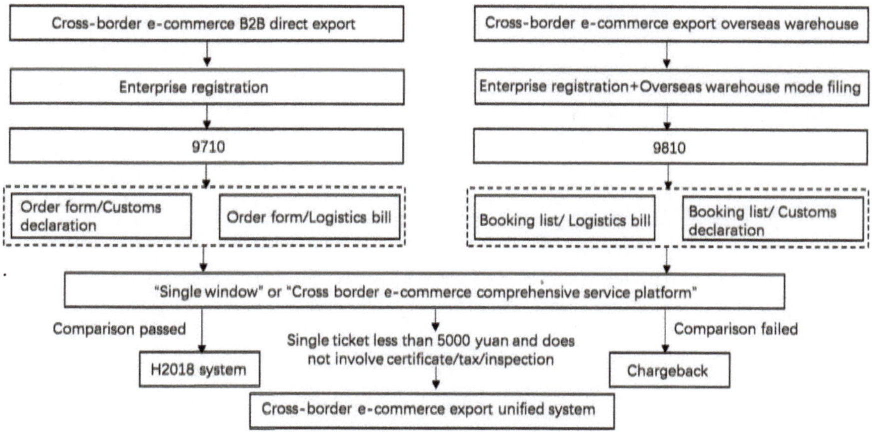

Fig. 7.5 9710 and 9810 Export Process

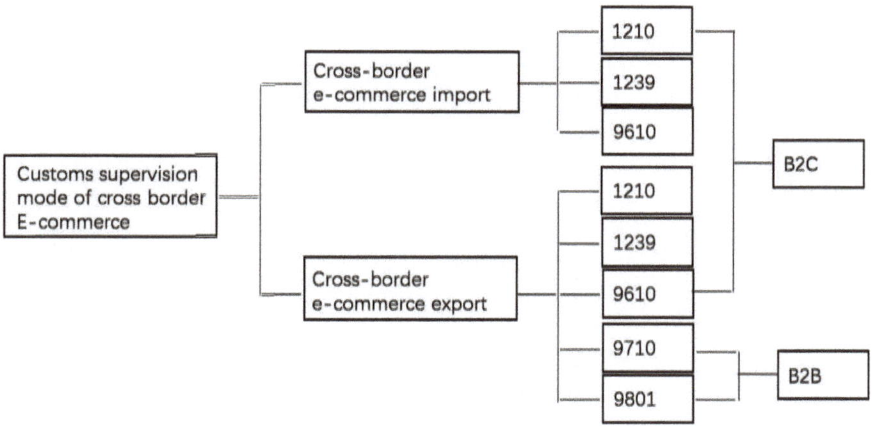

Fig. 7.6 Comparison of cross-border e-commerce customs supervision modes

7.4.3 Comparison of Cross-Border E-Commerce Customs Supervision Modes

As shown in Fig. 7.6, the cross-border e-commerce customs supervision mode is classified according to import and export. Cross-border e-commerce imports include 1210, 1239, and 9610, and cross-border e-commerce exports include 1210, 1239, 9610, 9710, and 9810; looking at the type of trading entity, 1210, 1239, and 9610 belong to the B2C category, and 9710 and 9810 belong to the B2B category.

Chapter 8
Cross-Border E-Commerce Warehousing and Distribution Management

8.1 Cross-Border E-Commerce Warehousing Management

8.1.1 Basic Concepts of Cross-Border E-Commerce Warehousing

1. Concept of Cross-Border E-Commerce Warehousing

To understand the concept of warehousing, we first analyze the terms "warehouse" and "storage". A "warehouse" is a building or site for storing goods, such as buildings, large containers, caves, or specific sites, with the function of storing and protecting goods. "Storage" refers to the collection for future use, which includes collection, custody, storage, and delivery for use. Combining the meanings of "warehouse" and "storage", "warehousing" can be understood as the act of using a warehouse to store items that are not needed for immediate use. Therefore, warehousing refers to the custody of goods before their use. It is an intermediate link between supply and consumption before the goods reach the customer. Warehousing is part of the logistics system, and its main function is to store goods (raw materials, parts, work-in-progress, finished products, etc.) at the place of production, consumption, or somewhere in between, and provide managers with information about the status, conditions, and handling of stored goods.

Warehousing management refers to the activities of storing goods in a warehouse and managing, controlling, etc., the goods stored in the warehouse, that is, the planning, organization, command, supervision, and regulation of the warehousing, custody, and outbound operations of goods. Through warehousing management, warehousing operations are arranged and organized in a certain order in space and

X. Zhang, *Introduction to Cross-Border E-Commerce Ecosystem*,
https://doi.org/10.1007/978-981-96-1165-2_8

time, so that the entire warehousing process can proceed in an orderly and continuous manner. The purpose of warehousing management is to achieve rationalization of warehousing, that is, to achieve warehousing functions in the most economical way, and its essence is to invest the least while ensuring the realization of warehousing functions.

Cross-border e-commerce warehousing refers to the use of information management technology to achieve the warehousing functions required for cross-border e-commerce business, mainly including the storage, selection, repackaging, distribution, etc., of goods, as well as the corresponding links before the goods reach the consumer.

2. Content of Cross-Border E-Commerce Warehousing Management

Cross-border e-commerce warehousing management includes the following aspects.

(1) Site selection and construction operations of the warehouse. This includes the principles of warehouse site selection, determination of warehouse construction area, arrangement of internal transportation roads and operations, etc.
(2) Selection and configuration of warehouse facilities and equipment. According to the characteristics of various warehouse operations and the logistics characteristics of stored goods, appropriate warehouse facilities and equipment are selected and related management is carried out.
(3) Procurement management. According to the demand situation and the quantity of inventory items, use reasonable methods to determine the types and quantities of items that need to be purchased into the warehouse.
(4) Inventory control. According to the demand of the enterprise and the market, use reasonable procurement methods to store an appropriate quantity of goods.
(5) Warehouse business management. Organize and manage the business work of goods inbound inspection, warehouse layout, in-warehouse custody, outbound inspection, etc.

From the perspective of decision-making, warehousing management usually makes the following decisions.

(1) Ownership decision of the warehouse. Whether to use self-operated warehousing or public warehousing.
(2) Decision on centralized or decentralized warehousing. Decide how many warehouses need to operate.
(3) Decision on the size and location of the warehouse. Two other warehousing decisions closely related to the number of warehouses and centralized or decentralized warehousing decisions, namely the decision on the size and location of the warehouse.
(4) Warehouse layout decision. Decide the layout of the internal aisles, shelves, equipment, and all other space-occupying implementations in the warehouse.
(5) Decision on the types and quantities of inventory. The types and quantities of goods stored in different warehouses.

3. Functions of Cross-Border e-commerce Warehousing

With the advancement of technology and the improvement of social productivity, the mode of large-scale social production gradually appears, products are unprecedentedly rich, and people's living standards are gradually improving. The demand for warehousing from social production and people's lives has greatly increased both in quantity and quality, and the function of warehousing has therefore greatly expanded, specifically the following five.

(1) Storage and custody

Storage and custody are the most basic functions of warehousing. Due to the need for storage and custody, warehousing is generated and further developed, and it must have the necessary space to accommodate items. Warehouse capacity is one of the basic parameters of warehousing. During the custody process, it should be ensured that the items are not lost, damaged, or deteriorated, and there needs to be a sound custody system, reasonable loading and unloading handling equipment, and correct operating methods to ensure that the items will not be damaged during the loading and unloading handling process.

(2) Regulate supply and demand, create time value

From the perspective of production materials, the continuity law of production and consumption varies greatly due to different products, and the rhythm of production and consumption cannot be completely consistent. From the perspective of living materials, the improvement of residents' consumption level gradually weakens the seasonal law of demand for living goods, so the seasonality of many food productions must be resolved through warehousing.

Warehousing plays a buffering, regulating, and balancing role in the logistics system, and together with transportation, it constitutes the central link of logistics. Corresponding to transportation, warehousing is an activity aimed at changing the time state of "things", overcoming the time difference between production and demand to achieve better utility. Items may need to stay for a certain period of time before entering the production field, during the production field process, before entering the circulation field from the production field, or during the circulation field process, which forms warehousing. Warehousing plays an important role in social reproduction.

(3) Adjust transportation capacity

The transport capacity of various transport tools varies greatly. Waterway transport, railway transport, road transport, air transport, and pipeline transport have their own characteristics and requirements. The transshipment between different transport methods or within the same transport method may result in situations that do not match the transport capacity. These differences in transport capacity need to be adjusted and connected through warehousing (warehouses or freight yards, etc.).

(4) Reduce logistics costs

Scientific and reasonable warehousing decisions and warehousing management can effectively reduce the overall warehousing costs and logistics costs, thereby realizing the rationalization of the enterprise or social warehousing system.

(5) Distribution and circulation processing

Modern warehousing, in addition to storage and custody as the main functions, is also developing towards circulation processing and distribution. Modern warehousing has gradually evolved into a multifunctional logistics distribution center that integrates circulation processing and distribution. Modern warehousing not only has the function of storage and custody of goods facilities, but also adds sorting, distribution, packaging, circulation processing, information processing and other functions. This not only expands the functional range of warehousing, but also improves the comprehensive utilization rate of items, and at the same time promotes the rationalization of logistics, facilitates customers, and improves service quality.

8.1.2 Cross-Border E-Commerce Warehousing Operation Process

The cross-border e-commerce warehousing operation process refers to the operation links that goods must go through from the start of storage to the process of delivery, which are interconnected in a certain order. According to their operation order, they mainly go through transportation, unloading, sorting, inspection, storage, storage, maintenance, loading and unloading handling, sorting, packaging and shipping, etc. Each link is not isolated, they are interconnected and mutually constrained. The start of the next operation depends on the successful completion of the previous operation, and the completion effect of the previous operation also directly affects whether the next operation is successfully completed. Because in the warehousing process, there are connections within each link, and it requires a certain amount of manpower and material resources, and the warehousing cost accounts for a large proportion of the logistics cost, so it is necessary to conduct a thorough and detailed analysis and reasonable organization of each warehousing operation process.

For different goods, due to their different characteristics, the operation links included in the warehousing operation process, the operation content of each link, and their connection order may not be the same. Therefore, when organizing warehousing operations, it is necessary to analyze the specific operation process, with the aim of reducing as many operation links as possible, shortening the handling distance and operation time of goods, improving the efficiency of storage and delivery, and reducing warehousing costs.

Specifically, the warehousing operation process is mainly divided into three parts: inbound operation management, in-warehouse operation management, and outbound operation management, as shown in Fig. 8.1.

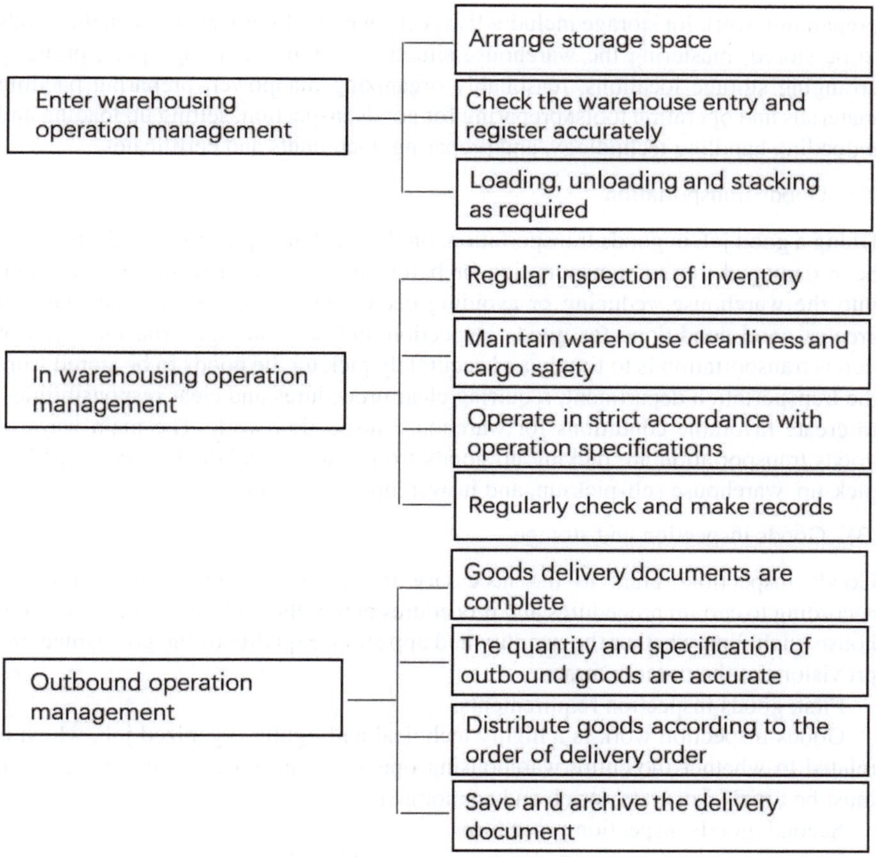

Fig. 8.1 Warehousing operation process

1. Inbound Operation Management

Inbound operation management is an important link in warehousing management, and doing a good job in goods storage is the premise of warehousing management. At the same time, the level of inbound operations directly affects the efficiency and benefits of the entire warehousing operation. The inbound operation process includes pre-storage preparation, goods transportation, and goods inspection and storage.

(1) Pre-storage preparation

The preparation work before goods storage is mainly to arrange storage locations for the goods and commodities that are about to be stored according to the procurement plan and the provisions of the order contract, and to organize related manpower and material resources to complete the storage operation. Its main purpose is to ensure that goods can be stored on time and to ensure the smooth progress of storage work. The preparation work for storage includes 9 aspects, namely familiarizing with the goods to be stored, mastering the warehouse situation, making a storage plan, properly arranging storage locations, reasonably organizing manpower, preparing padding materials and operation tools, preparing for goods inspection, setting up loading and unloading handling technology, and preparing documents and certificates.

(2) Goods transportation

Doing a good job in goods transportation, on the one hand, prevents goods that have been damaged during transportation or before transportation from being brought into the warehouse, reducing or avoiding economic losses; on the other hand, it creates good conditions for goods inspection and later storage. The main job of goods transportation is to timely and accurately pick up the goods to be stored from the transportation department, requiring clear procedures and clear responsibilities, to create favorable conditions for warehouse inspection work. The main ways of goods transportation are picking up goods from stations and docks, dedicated line pick-up, warehouse self-pick-up, and in-warehouse pick-up.

(3) Goods inspection and storage

Goods inspection refers to the necessary inspection of the transported goods according to certain procedures and procedures before they officially enter the warehouse, including whether the quantity and appearance quality of the goods meet the provisions of the order contract.

First, goods inspection requirements.

Goods inspection work is a highly technical and tightly organized job, which is related to whether the entire warehousing operation can proceed smoothly, and it must be timely, accurate, strict, and economical.

Second, goods inspection procedures.

① Acceptance preparation. First, upon receiving the arrival notice, the warehouse arranges acceptance personnel according to the characteristics and quantity of the goods, including professional technical personnel and loading and unloading personnel; next, it is necessary to collect and familiarize with the relevant standards and contracts of the goods to be inspected; then prepare the necessary inspection tools; finally, call the necessary loading and unloading machinery to assist in acceptance.

② Document verification. These documents include the warehouse acceptance form, a copy of the order contract, quality certification of the goods, packing list, shipping order, transport document, etc.

③ Physical inspection. Physical inspection is the core of the acceptance work. The warehouse is generally responsible for the acceptance of the appearance quality and quantity of the goods. For some incoming materials that need to be inspected for internal quality and performance, the warehouse should actively cooperate with the inspection department to complete the acceptance work.

Third, physical acceptance.

Physical acceptance refers to checking whether the packaging, quantity, and appearance quality of the goods are consistent with the warehouse documents, that is, verifying whether the quantity of goods is consistent with the warehouse vouchers, whether the quality of the goods meets the requirements, and whether the packaging of the goods ensures the safety of the goods during storage and transportation. The inspection methods for goods include packaging inspection, quantity inspection, quality inspection, and sampling inspection.

Fourth, warehouse handover.

After the goods pass the quantity and quality inspection, the management personnel arrange for unloading, warehousing, and stacking, while handling the handover procedures, accepting the goods and related documents, and signing the relevant documents, clarifying the responsibilities of the transportation department and the warehouse, and the warehouse-related personnel carry out the goods' bookkeeping, card making, and file establishment to successfully complete the warehouse handover work.

2. In-Warehouse Operation Management

The in-warehouse operation management of goods is an important link in warehouse operation management and is one of the key links to reduce warehousing costs. In-warehouse operation management includes in-warehouse goods maintenance and custody, inventory work, order processing work, picking work. Among them, inventory work is an important content of in-warehouse operation management, which refers to the operation of counting the quantity in various storage places in order to effectively control the quantity of goods.

First, the purpose of inventory work.

The purpose of inventory work is to check the actual inventory quantity, and through profit and loss adjustment to make the inventory book quantity consistent with the actual inventory quantity; help enterprises calculate asset profit and loss; discover problems in warehousing through inventory.

Second, the content of inventory work.

① Check quantity. Check the actual quantity of goods in the warehouse by counting, and verify whether the inventory book data is consistent with the actual inventory quantity.

② Check quality. Check whether the quality of the goods in the warehouse has changed, whether it has exceeded the expiration date or shelf life, whether there is a long-term squeezing phenomenon, and if necessary, it must be technically inspected.

③ Check storage conditions. Check whether the storage conditions are in line with the storage requirements of various goods, such as whether the stacking of goods is stable, whether the temperature and humidity in the warehouse meet the requirements, etc.

④ Check safety. Check whether various safety measures and fire-fighting equipment and equipment meet safety requirements.

Third, the inventory work process.

The process of inventory work is usually inventory planning, pre-inventory preparation, determining inventory time, determining inventory methods, organization and training of inventory personnel, cleaning up the inventory site, inventory, finding out the reasons for the differences in inventory, and handling of inventory results.

Fourth, inventory methods. The main inventory methods are book inventory and field inventory.

3. Outbound Operation Management

Warehouse outbound operation management refers to various activities carried out according to the outbound voucher, which involves distributing the required goods to the demanding department. The outbound operation of goods is also known as the delivery business, which involves a series of operations such as picking, sorting, packaging, and delivering the goods to the transportation department or the owner, based on the outbound voucher issued by the business department or the owner of the enterprise.

The outbound of goods must follow the "first in, first out" principle to make warehouse management efficient and orderly. Regardless of the method of outbound, the following procedures should be followed for good management.

(1) Order review. The voucher for the outbound of goods, whether it is a material requisition, a material dispatch note, or an outbound note, should be signed or stamped by the relevant business department. When the warehouse receives the order or outbound note, it should check the content of the document, such as whether the seals on the document are complete, and whether there are any alterations. After verifying that there are no errors, the name, specifications, quantity, etc. of the goods listed on the outbound voucher should be fully checked against the warehouse books. After confirming that there are no errors, the outbound information processing and picking operations can be carried out.
(2) Outbound information processing. After completing the review and entry of the outbound documents, the outbound information of the goods is processed, including the arrangement of first in, first out, and the inspection of inventory quantity, etc.
(3) Picking. According to the customer's order requirements or the warehouse's outbound plan, the goods should be sorted out as quickly and accurately as possible. Picking is divided into manual picking and automatic picking.

   ① Manual picking. All the operation processes are carried out manually according to the picking documents or other picking information. After the picking operation is completed, the workers put the goods ordered by each customer into the marked containers in each area, waiting for shipment.

   ② Automatic picking. This method of picking uses an automatic sorter. The automatic sorter uses a computer and recognition system to classify the goods. This method is not only fast and labor-saving, but also accurate, especially suitable for warehouses or distribution centers with a variety of goods and busy business.
(4) Delivery inspection. During the delivery inspection, the picked goods are verified according to the customer information and train number, and the quality and quantity of the goods are checked according to the relevant information, and the status and quality of the goods are inspected. The delivery inspection is key to ensuring that the documents and goods match, avoiding errors, and improving

service quality. It is a further confirmation of whether there are errors in the picking operation, so it must be carefully checked to prevent errors.

(5) Loading. The process of moving the sorted goods onto the vehicle according to the delivery route arrangement, time arrangement, and loading diagram.

(6) Delivery information processing. After receiving the customer's confirmed outbound note and delivery note, the completed outbound information is entered into the system. The outbound document is the basis for collecting payment from customers, and timely updating of the in-stock information of goods is also the basis for ensuring that the inventory information is accurate.

8.2 Cross-Border E-Commerce Distribution Overview

8.2.1 The Connotation of Cross-Border E-Commerce Distribution

Distribution refers to the logistics activities of picking, processing, packaging, dividing, assembling, etc. of items within a reasonable economic area, and delivering them to a designated place on time according to customer requirements.

Cross-border e-commerce logistics distribution refers to a kind of international commercial logistics activity that completes cross-border e-commerce transactions by reaching transactions and making payment settlements through cross-border e-commerce platforms, delivering the prepared goods to the recipient safely and accurately at the specified time and place according to the requirements of domestic and foreign consumers with the help of cross-border logistics. Cross-border e-commerce logistics distribution is a special and comprehensive activity form in cross-border e-commerce logistics, which closely combines commercial flow and logistics, and is a logistics form that includes several functional elements of logistics.

8.2.2 Basic Steps of Delivery

Delivery operation is the process of sorting out goods according to user requirements and sending them to the designated location on time and in the right quantity. The delivery operation is the core content of the distribution center's operation, so the rationality of the delivery operation process and the efficiency of the delivery operation will directly affect the normal operation of the entire logistics system. Overall, delivery is composed of three steps: stock preparation, goods sorting, and delivery, each of which contains several specific and detailed activities.

1. Stock Preparation

Stock preparation refers to the series of activities to prepare goods, which is a basic step in delivery. Stock preparation includes two specific activities, namely, gathering goods and storing goods.

The first is gathering goods. Under different economic systems, gathering goods (or organizing sources of goods) is completed by different actors. If the manufacturing company directly carries out the delivery, then there will be two situations for gathering goods: one, it is directly undertaken by the delivery company providing the delivery service, usually by ordering or purchasing goods from the manufacturing company; the other, choosing to separate commercial flow and logistics for delivery, ordering, purchasing and other activities to gather goods are usually done by the owner of the goods (such as the manufacturing company), and the delivery organization is only responsible for receiving and gathering goods, and the ownership of the goods belongs to the principal (the demander of the delivery service). However, no matter how different the specific practices are, in terms of overall activities, gathering goods is composed of a series of activities such as ordering (or purchasing), receiving, gathering, and related inspection, settlement, etc.

The second is storing goods. Storing goods is a continuation of purchasing and receiving activities. In delivery activities, there are two forms of goods storage: one is temporary storage; the other is reserve storage (including insurance reserve and turnover reserve). Temporary storage is to store a small amount of goods in the sorting area according to the requirements of sorting and distribution processes. This form of goods storage is set up to adapt to the needs of "daily distribution" and "just-in-time delivery". The amount of such storage has a great impact on the convenience of the next step, but it does not affect the overall benefits of storage activities. Reserve storage is determined according to the requirements of delivery activities for a certain period and the arrival situation of the source of goods (arrival cycle). It is the resource guarantee for the continuous operation of delivery. There are two specific forms of goods reserves used to support delivery: turnover reserve and insurance reserve. However, no matter which form of reserve, relatively speaking, the quantity is quite large. Therefore, whether the goods reserve is reasonable or not will directly affect the overall benefits of delivery.

2. Sorting Goods

Sorting goods is an important part of delivery and is also an important sign differentiating it from general delivery. Sorting includes activities such as goods sorting, distribution, and packaging. Goods sorting uses appropriate methods and means to sort out (or select) the goods needed by users from the stored goods. There are generally two ways to sort goods: one is picking, and the other is seeding.

Picking-style sorting is like picking fruit in an orchard. The specific method is: the operator pulls the collection box (or sorting box) and walks around the neatly arranged warehouse shelves, picking out and loading into the collection box the variety, specifications, quantity, and other goods required by the customer as listed on the delivery note. Under normal circumstances, each pick is only for one customer; under special circumstances, it can also be for two or more customers. At present, automated sorting technology has been promoted and applied, and the labor efficiency of sorting operations has been greatly improved due to the installation of automated sorting facilities.

The sowing-style sorting of goods is similar to the sowing operation in the field. The specific method is: to concentrate a large number of the same kind of goods to the shipping yard, then take out the goods according to the sending amount of each cargo space, and put them into each cargo space representing the user until the distribution is completed. In order to transport the goods intact and facilitate the identification of equipped goods, some goods that have been sorted and assembled need to be repackaged, and labels need to be affixed to the packaging, recording the variety, quantity, recipient's name, address, and arrival time of the goods, etc.

3. Delivery

Delivery is the core of the distribution center and an extension of the stock preparation and sorting process. In the movement of logistics, the phenomenon of delivery is actually the transportation (or delivery) of goods, so it is often represented by transportation. However, the transportation that constitutes the distribution activity (some people call it "distribution transportation") is quite different from the "main-line transportation" usually mentioned. Because the delivery (or transportation) in the distribution needs to face many customers and needs to move in multiple directions, therefore, in the delivery process, often on the basis of comprehensive planning, a scientific, shorter distance freight route is formulated, and the nearest, fastest, and safest transportation method is chosen as the main transportation tool.

4. Circulation Processing

In the distribution process, according to user requirements or the characteristics of the distribution object (product), sometimes it is necessary to process the goods (such as steel cutting, wood sawing, etc.) before the distribution in order to improve the quality of distribution and better meet user needs. The goods processing integrated in the distribution is a special form of circulation processing, and its main purpose is to make the goods distributed fully adapt to user needs and improve the utilization rate of resources.

8.2.3 The Relationship Between Distribution and Transportation

Transportation is a logistics activity that uses equipment and tools to transport items from one location to another. It includes a series of operations such as collection, distribution, handling, transshipment, loading, unloading, and dispersion.

Both distribution and transportation are line activities. Logistics activities can be divided into two categories according to whether the items move in position, namely line activities and node activities. Logistics activities that cause position movement are called line activities, otherwise they are node activities. Node activities are carried out in a place within an organization, not for the purpose of creating spatial utility, but mainly for creating time utility or form utility, such as loading, unloading, handling, packaging, storage, circulation processing, etc., carried out in factories, warehouses,

Table 8.1 The difference between distribution and transportation

Item	Transport	Distribution
Scope of activities	Large scale, such as between countries, regions, cities, etc	Generally limited to one region or one city
Nature of transportation	Line Haul	Branch line transportation, regional transportation and terminal transportation
Nature of goods	Few varieties and large quantities	More varieties and less batches
Means of transport	Heavy tonnage transportation tools such as large-scale train or railway transportation and waterway transportation are used	Small trains are used, and the carrying capacity is generally no more than two tons
Management focus	Efficiency first	Service first
Ancillary functions	Only handling and bundling	Many, mainly including loading and unloading, storage, packaging, sorting, circulation processing, order processing, etc

logistics centers or distribution centers, are all node activities. The difference between the two is shown in Table 8.1.

The complementary relationship between distribution and transportation, although they are both line activities, but due to functional differences, they cannot replace each other, but form a relationship of mutual dependence and complementarity. It is impossible to meet the above requirements with only transportation or only distribution, because according to the principles of transportation scale and distance, large-scale, long-distance transportation is reasonable, but it cannot meet the requirements of dispersed consumption; although distribution has the characteristics of small batch and multiple batches, it is not suitable for long-distance transportation. Therefore, they must cooperate with each other, complement each other's strengths, and achieve the ideal goal. In the logistics system where transportation and distribution coexist, transportation is in front of distribution, first realizing the long-distance position transfer of goods through transportation, and then handed over to distribution to complete the short-distance transportation.

8.2.4 The Role of Cross-Border E-Commerce Distribution

1. Cross-Border E-Commerce Distribution is an Important Component of Cross-Border E-Commerce

With the development of network technology and electronic technology, electronic intermediaries have been introduced as tools into production, exchange, and consumption, ushering humanity into the era of e-commerce. Internet banking, business platforms, and logistics companies constitute the three pillars of e-commerce operations, and are also the three main entities connecting production enterprises and consumers in the era of cross-border e-commerce. E-commerce is the product of the integration of the network economy and logistics, created jointly by the network economy and modern logistics, and can be described by the formula: E-commerce = Online information transmission + Online transactions + Online settlement + Logistics distribution. Cross-border logistics distribution naturally becomes the foundation and important component of cross-border e-commerce.

2. Cross-Border E-Commerce Distribution Provides Reliable Assurance for the Realization of Cross-Border e-commerce Advantages

Cross-border e-commerce has the advantages of convenience, speed, and efficiency. Without leaving home, one can purchase high-quality, affordable, popular, and high-end products from abroad. However, without a cross-border logistics distribution system that matches cross-border e-commerce, the advantages of convenience, speed, and efficiency brought by cross-border e-commerce are difficult to realize.

3. Cross-Border E-Commerce Distribution is a Marketing Method for Businesses to Face Customers

Cross-border e-commerce distribution provides an opportunity for merchants and customers to communicate face-to-face, helps both parties to enhance understanding and communication, eliminates customers' doubts about virtual enterprises and online shopping, establishes a good image of the enterprise in the minds of customers, and at the same time, cross-border logistics distribution can also help enterprises understand the real needs of customers and serve customers better.

8.3 Cross-Border E-Commerce Distribution Business Process

The basic process of cross-border e-commerce distribution includes the following operations: procurement, handling and unloading, storage, order processing, sorting, replenishment, distribution, and delivery. The process is shown in Fig. 8.2. Distribution operation is the core content of the operation of the distribution enterprise or department, so the rationality of the distribution operation process and the efficiency of the distribution operation will directly affect the normal operation of the entire logistics system.

When receiving a user order, the order is first processed according to its nature, and then the "picking" operation is carried out according to the processed order information to take out the goods required by the user from the warehouse. Once it is found that the remaining stock in the picking area is too low after picking, the

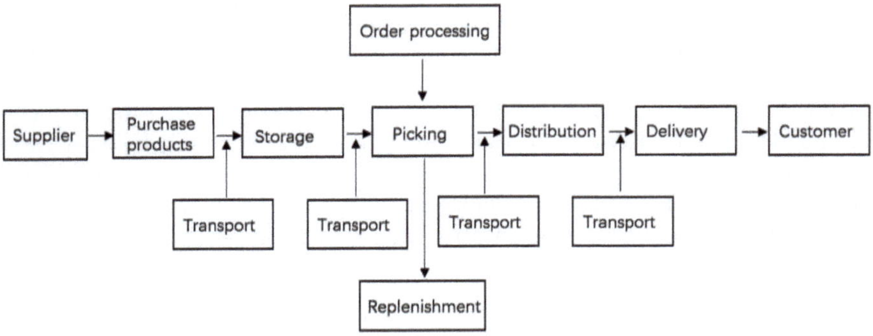

Fig. 8.2 Basic distribution process diagram

"replenishment" operation must be carried out from the storage area. If the stock in the storage area is lower than the specified standard, goods will be ordered from the supplier. The goods picked from the warehouse can be prepared for "delivery" after sorting. Once all delivery preparations are ready, the driver can load the goods on the delivery vehicle and carry out the "delivery" operation to the user. In addition, in all operations, it can be found that as long as it involves the flow of goods, the process must be carried out by "handling".

The distribution operation process involves many operation links. Here, the procurement operation, order processing, picking operation, replenishment operation, distribution operation, delivery operation, return adjustment operation, and information processing are introduced in detail.

8.3.1 *Procurement Operation*

The basic process of the procurement operation is shown in Fig. 8.3.

The content of determining the procurement target generally includes: mastering the arrival date, variety, and quantity of goods; coordinating the traffic problems of incoming and outgoing trucks in conjunction with berthing information; planning the parking position of the truck for convenient unloading and handling; planning the temporary storage location in advance.

Goods acceptance is the process of inspecting the quality and quantity of products. Acceptance work is generally divided into two types: the first is to first receive the goods, and then notify the unit responsible for inspection to carry out the inspection work; the second is to first inspect the quality by the inspection department, and after deeming it qualified, notify the storage department to handle the receipt procedures.

1. Standards for Goods Acceptance

In order to accurately and timely accept goods, it is necessary to clarify the acceptance standards. In actual work, the following standards can be used to accept goods:

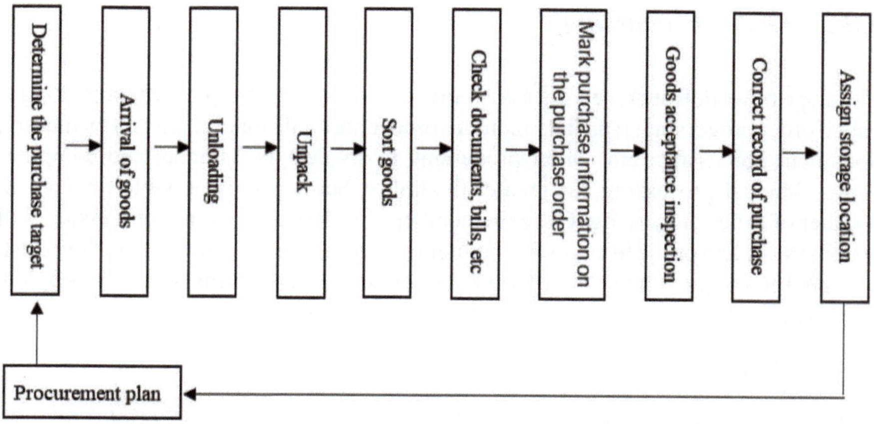

Fig. 8.3 Procurement operation process

(1) The specific requirements and conditions stipulated in the purchase contract or order;
(2) The specifications or diagrams in the purchase contract;
(3) The qualified samples at the time of bargaining;
(4) The national quality standards or international standards for various products as the standards for accepting goods.

2. Content of Goods Acceptance

When accepting goods, the main tasks are quality acceptance, packaging acceptance, and quantity acceptance.

(1) The main purpose of quality inspection of incoming goods is to find out the quality status of incoming goods, so as to timely discover problems, clarify responsibilities, and ensure that the goods in the warehouse meet the order requirements.
(2) The specific content of packaging acceptance mainly includes whether the packaging is safe and firm, whether the packaging signs and marks meet the requirements, and whether the quality of the packaging materials is good.
(3) In daily operations, overages and shortages in the quantity of incoming goods are common phenomena, which directly relate to the inventory control and current asset management of the distribution center. Therefore, quantity acceptance is a very important part of the incoming operation.

After the goods arriving at the distribution center are confirmed by acceptance, a "acceptance form" must be filled out, and the relevant incoming information must be timely and accurately logged into the inventory information management system to timely update the relevant data of the inventory goods. The purpose of logging in the goods information is to provide a basis for management and control in subsequent operation links.

8.3.2 Order Processing

The stage of work from receiving a customer order to starting to prepare for picking is called order processing. It usually includes order data confirmation, inventory inquiry, document processing, etc. Order processing is divided into manual and computer forms. Manual processing has greater flexibility, but it is only suitable for a small number of order processing. Once the number of orders is large, the processing will become slow and prone to errors. Computer processing is fast, efficient, and low-cost, suitable for a large number of order processing, so the latter form is mainly adopted. The basic content and steps of order processing are shown in Fig. 8.4.

1. Accepting Orders

Order acceptance is the first step in order processing. With the changes in the circulation environment and the development of modern technology, customers now tend to order at a high frequency and require fast delivery. Therefore, the way to accept customer orders has gradually evolved from traditional manual ordering and acceptance to electronic ordering, which directly sends and receives order data between computers. Electronic ordering replaces the traditional manual writing, input, and transmission of orders with electronic transmission. It converts order data from paper data to electronic data and transmits it through a communication network.

2. Confirmation of Goods Quantity and Date

After receiving the order, the first step is to confirm the name, quantity, and date of the goods, that is, to check whether the name, quantity, delivery date, etc. are missing, miswritten, or do not meet the company's requirements. Especially when there is a problem with the delivery time or the delivery time has been delayed, it is necessary to reconfirm the order content with the customer or correct the delivery time. Similarly, if you accept orders through electronic ordering, you must also check and confirm the received order data.

3. Confirmation of Customer Credit

Regardless of how the order is transmitted to the company, the delivery system must check the customer's financial status to determine whether they have the ability to

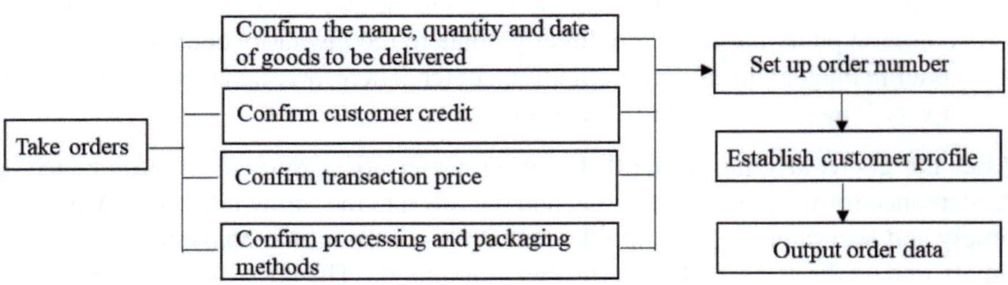

Fig. 8.4 Basic content and steps of order processing

pay the account payable for the order. The usual practice is to check whether the customer's accounts receivable have exceeded their credit limit. If the customer's accounts receivable have exceeded their credit limit, the system automatically issues a warning, allowing the input staff to decide whether to continue inputting their order information or reject their order. If the sales department discovers a problem with the customer's credit, the order will be returned to the sales department for further investigation or order cancellation.

4. Order Form Confirmation

Although the distribution center integrates the functions of traditional wholesalers and efficient logistics information processing, it still needs to adopt different practices according to different customer needs when facing more trading objects. In accepting orders, it manifests as having various forms of order transactions, so the logistics center should adopt different transactions and processing methods for different customers.

(1) General Transaction Order

The general transaction order is the order that picks, departs, sends, and collects payment after receiving the order. The processing method is to input the information into the order processing system after receiving the order, and process it according to the normal order processing procedure. After the data processing is completed, pick, depart, send, and collect payment operations are carried out.

(2) Indirect Transaction Order

The indirect transaction order is a transaction order where the customer orders from the distribution center and is directly delivered to the customer by the supplier. The processing method is to pass the customer's departure information to the supplier for distribution after receiving the order. It should be noted that the customer's delivery note is self-made or commissioned by the supplier, and the shipping information should be checked and confirmed.

(3) Cash Sale Transaction Order

The cash sale transaction order is a transaction order that trades with the customer on the spot and directly gives the goods. The processing method is that after the order information is input, the goods have been given to the customer at this time, so the order information no longer participates in picking, shipping, sending, etc., and only needs to record the transaction information.

(4) Contract Transaction Order

The contract transaction order is a transaction with the customer to sign a distribution contract, such as signing a certain period of regular delivery of a certain quantity of goods. The processing method is to input the delivery information into the system for shipping and delivery on the agreed delivery day; or to input the order information of the contract content from the beginning and set the delivery time for each batch, so that the system automatically generates the required order information on the agreed date.

5. Order Qualification Confirmation

For different customers (wholesalers, retailers), different order quantities may correspond to different selling prices, so the system should check when inputting prices. If the input price does not match (input error or salesperson accepts the order at a reduced price, etc.), the system should lock it for supervisor review.

6. Processing Packaging Confirmation

Whether the goods ordered by the customer require special packaging, splitting, labeling, or related gift packaging, etc., the system must make a special confirmation record.

7. Setting Order Number

Each order must have a separate order number, which is generally designated by the control unit or cost unit. In addition to facilitating cost calculation, it is also conducive to all related work such as manufacturing and distribution. All work instructions and progress reports should be accompanied by this number.

8. Establishing Customer Files

Detailed recording of the customer's situation can not only benefit the smooth progress of this transaction, but also increase future cooperation opportunities.

9. Order Data Processing Output

After the order data is processed as described above, it can start to suppress the shipping documents and start subsequent logistics operations.

8.3.3 Picking Operation

The picking operation is the central link in the distribution operation. Picking, as the name suggests, is the process of picking goods from their storage locations or other areas as quickly and accurately as possible based on customer order requirements or the operation plan of the distribution center. The important elements of the picking operation system include picking units, picking methods, picking strategies, picking information, picking equipment, etc.

The picking operation in the distribution operation not only has a large workload and complex processes, but also requires short operation time, high accuracy, and good service quality. The picking operation process is: making picking operation documents—arranging picking paths—assigning picking personnel—picking.

The time consumed by the entire picking operation mainly includes the following four parts: the time for the order or delivery note to be processed into picking instructions; the time for walking or handling goods; the time to accurately find the storage location of the goods and confirm the picked goods and quantity; the time to complete the picking and classify the goods.

The simplest way to divide the picking operation is to divide it into order picking, batch picking, and composite picking. Order picking is picking according to each order; batch picking is accumulating multiple orders into a batch, forming a picking list after summarizing, and then picking goods according to the instructions of the picking list, and then determining which orders are suitable for order picking and which are suitable for batch picking, and then adopting different picking methods.

8.3.4 Replenishment Operation

The replenishment operation is the work of moving goods from the warehouse storage area to the picking area. Its purpose is to ensure that goods can be delivered to the designated picking area in a timely manner with guaranteed quality and quantity. The basic process of the replenishment operation is shown in Fig. 8.5.

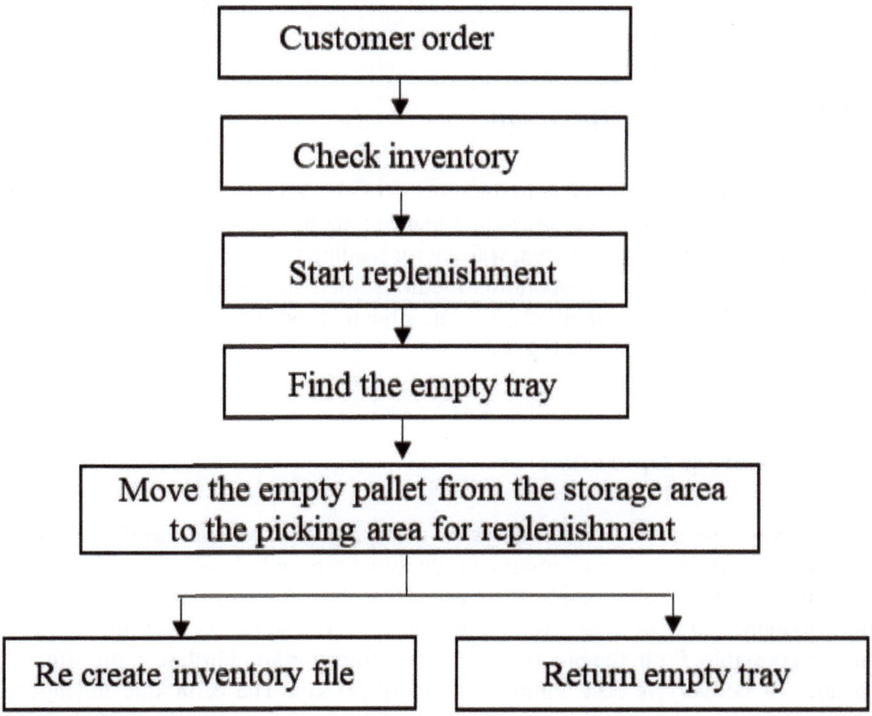

Fig. 8.5 General replenishment operation process

The replenishment methods mainly include whole box replenishment, pallet replenishment, and replenishment from the upper shelf to the lower shelf. The timing of replenishment mainly includes batch replenishment, timed replenishment, and random replenishment.

Batch replenishment refers to the replenishment quantity obtained by calculating the total picking quantity of the required goods by the computer every day and querying the inventory quantity in the dynamic management area, so as to replenish it in one go before picking to meet the daily picking quantity. This principle of one-time replenishment is more suitable for situations where the daily operation volume does not change much, there are not many urgent orders, or each batch picking quantity is large.

Timed replenishment is to divide each day into several time points, and the replenishment personnel check the inventory of goods on the shelves in the dynamic management picking area during the period, and replenish them in time if they are insufficient. This method is suitable for distribution centers with fixed batch picking times and more urgent processing.

Random replenishment refers to dedicated replenishment personnel who inspect the inventory of goods in the dynamic management picking area at any time, and replenish them at any time if they find them insufficient. This method is suitable for situations where each batch picking quantity is not large, there are many urgent orders, and the daily operation volume is not easy to grasp in advance.

8.3.5 Distribution Operation

The distribution operation refers to the process of checking the picked and classified goods, loading them into containers and marking them, and then transporting them to the distribution preparation area, waiting for loading and sending. The distribution operation can adopt manual operation methods, man–machine operation methods, and automated operation methods, but the organization methods are different. Its operation process is shown in Fig. 8.6.

8.3.6 Delivery Operation

The delivery operation is the process of using delivery vehicles to deliver items ordered by users from manufacturers, production bases, wholesalers, distributors, or distribution centers to the users. Delivery is usually a short-distance, small-batch, high-frequency form of transportation. It aims to serve and satisfy customer needs as much as possible. From the practice of delivery transportation in Japan, the effective distance of delivery is best within a radius of 50 km. The economic mileage of distribution centers and logistics centers in our country is about 30 km. Delivery is the end transportation and branch transportation in transportation. Therefore, how to

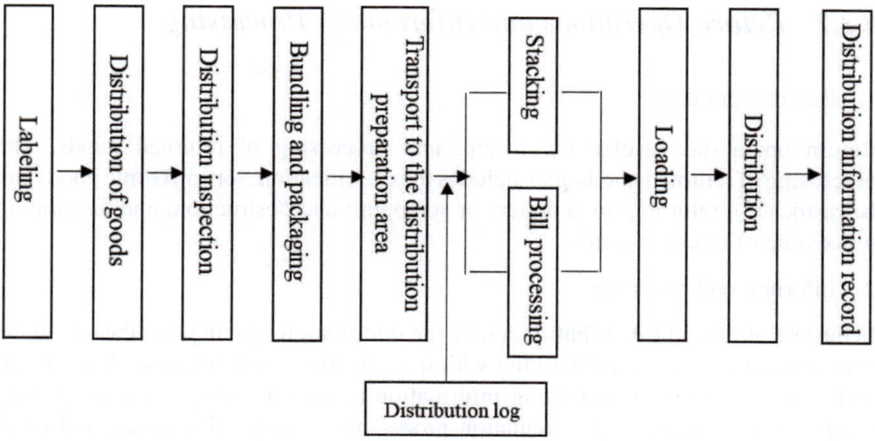

Fig. 8.6 Distribution operation process

concentrate vehicle dispatch, combine the best routes, determine the delivery order, and complete vehicle loading are the main problems that need to be solved in the delivery organization of distribution activities. The delivery operation process is shown in Fig. 8.7.

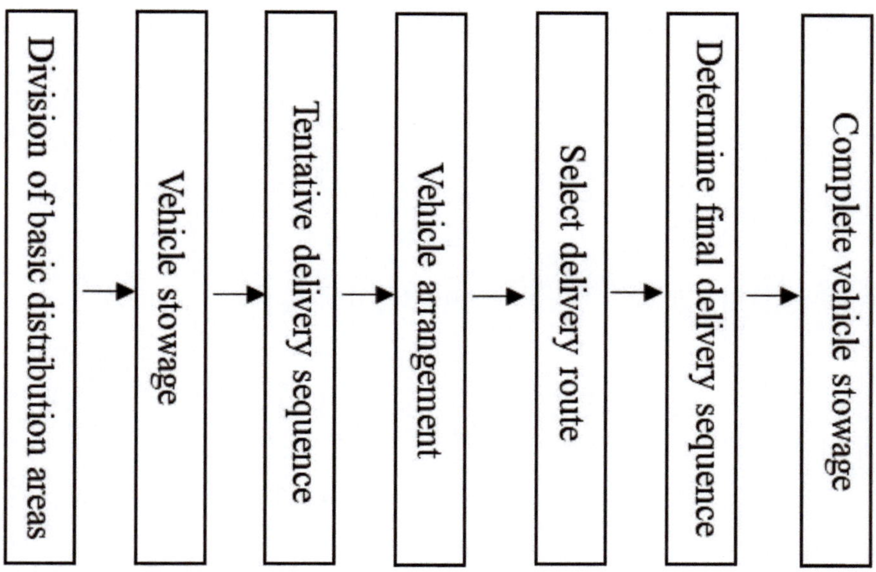

Fig. 8.7 Delivery operation process

8.3.7 *Return Operations and Information Processing*

1. Return Operations

Return operations involve the receipt and processing of returned goods. The processing of returned goods also includes the classification, sorting (some goods can be restocked), returning to suppliers or scrapping and destruction, and accounting processing of returned goods.

2. Information Processing

In the operation of the distribution center, the information system plays the role of the central nervous system, networking with manufacturers, wholesalers, chain stores, and other customers, transmitting information to various subsystems, integrating receiving, storage, picking, circulation processing, sorting, distribution and other logistics activities, coordinating and commanding the efficient operation of various logistics equipment and facilities. The operation of the distribution center includes three "flows", namely logistics, capital flow, and information flow. The specific functions of the logistics information system include: mastering the current situation, accepting orders, instructing shipments, organizing distribution work, settling costs, managing daily business, replenishing inventory, and communicating with the outside world.

Chapter 9
Cross-Border E-Commerce Marketing Management

9.1 Cross-Border E-Commerce Product Management

Cross-border marketing needs to use products as carriers. In the sense of marketing, a product refers to anything that can be provided to the market to satisfy people's certain desires and needs, including physical objects, services, etc. Before the emergence of e-commerce, to do a good job in international marketing, product strategy is related to the success or failure of international marketing. Before a product enters the international market, it needs to go through thorough international market research, choose suitable products for the target country and region, and push it to the international market with a perfect product promotion plan. Different from traditional international marketing, cross-border marketing uses developed e-commerce platforms and Internet marketing methods, uses data-driven methods in product selection, and scientifically selects products. For the selected products, use cross-border e-commerce platforms or social media and other Internet marketing methods to quickly test on a small scale. Once the test results are relatively ideal, you can expand the scope for cross-border marketing. For new product development, cross-border marketing can also use data to accurately develop new products from market demand, user groups, and other data.

9.1.1 The Connotation of Product Strategy

The product strategy of cross-border marketing is the basis of the cross-border marketing mix strategy. Product strategy refers to a series of specific implementation strategies adopted by enterprises in the marketing mix to gain a competitive advantage in the production and sales process of products, including the positioning of cross-border marketing products, product brand strategy, standardization strategy,

X. Zhang, *Introduction to Cross-Border E-Commerce Ecosystem*,
https://doi.org/10.1007/978-981-96-1165-2_9

differentiation strategy, new product development strategy, product selection strategy, etc.

The rapid development of cross-border e-commerce has brought about fundamental changes in cross-border marketing methods. Cross-border marketing can better utilize the dividends brought about by the advancement of the Internet and e-commerce technology, thereby breaking through the limitations of traditional international marketing in terms of region, information transmission and acquisition, marketing methods, and the impact on consumer psychology and decision-making. Compared with traditional international marketing, the product strategy of cross-border marketing has four advantages.

1. Cross-Border Marketing Greatly Shortens the Marketing Cycle of Products

Traditional international marketing, in terms of product selection, requires preliminary international market demand surveys, which in itself has a time cost. After selecting a product, it is necessary to formulate a product promotion strategy for the target country, including media selection, and then design the product's trademark and packaging in the local language. After the product is launched, it is necessary to comprehensively evaluate the market feedback in the target country's region. The entire process will result in a longer international marketing cycle. Cross-border marketing, with the help of the Internet and e-commerce technology, can greatly shorten the marketing cycle, whether it is from product selection, product promotion strategy, or collecting market feedback from the target country's region, all can be done through network data for quick data-driven decision-making.

2. Cross-Border Marketing Reduces the Marketing Cost of Products

Cross-border marketing has an innate advantage in obtaining market and user data in the target country's region, with fast acquisition speed and low cost. With the help of cross-border e-commerce platforms and Internet marketing media, products can be market-tested through low-cost content marketing strategies.

3. Cross-Border Marketing Lowers the Threshold for Companies to Engage in International Marketing

For traditional international marketing, pushing a product to the international market requires sufficient financial strength and brand strength as a support. This is unimaginable for small and micro enterprises. Cross-border e-commerce platforms and Internet marketing platforms greatly lower the threshold for companies to engage in international marketing. On platforms like Amazon and AliExpress, an unknown, or even unbranded product suddenly becoming a hit is no longer a novelty.

Different user groups have different needs, especially as international users are increasingly pursuing personalization. For users, the focus on brands has decreased, while the creativity and individuality of products have become the first choice for users' purchase decisions. As long as the product highlights individuality in design, it will win the favor of international users. This is precisely the strength of small and micro enterprises, which gives them an opportunity.

4. Cross-Border Marketing Quickly Collects Market Feedback and Adjusts Product Strategies in a Timely Manner

Compared with traditional international marketing, cross-border marketing can quickly collect market feedback through online questionnaires, existing data analysis, user online review analysis, etc., and adjust product strategies in a timely manner based on market feedback. This allows for low-cost, quick market trial and error, which is something traditional international marketing cannot do.

9.1.2 Classification of Cross-Border Marketing Products

1. The Connotation of Cross-Border Marketing Products

Product strategy is formulated around the product. For products, Philip Kotler proposed the three basic levels of core products, tangible products, and additional products; Richard Hes further developed Kotler's theory, believing that in addition to these three basic levels, products also include expected products and potential products. Therefore, products are understood from these five levels.

(1) Core Product

The core product refers to the core functions or values of a product that consumers value most when purchasing a product. In cross-border marketing, even for the same product, when it is pushed to consumers in different countries or regions, the core of the product that consumers focus on will change. For example, for the same smartphone, when targeting economically backward areas such as Africa, consumers may value the practical functions and cost-effectiveness of the phone the most; when targeting economically developed areas such as Singapore, entertainment functions may be the focus of people's attention.

(2) Tangible Product

Tangible products refer to the appearance, shape, packaging, brand, color, material, and other tangible things of a product that consumers can intuitively see when purchasing a product. In international marketing, products can reach consumers through offline stores such as stores, shopping malls, supermarkets, etc., and consumers' feelings about tangible products are more intuitive. For example, when a consumer buys a dress, they can not only observe the style, but also touch the fabric, try it on, and understand the product effect in all aspects. Limited by geographical conditions, cross-border marketing is more often completed online and in contact with users. Through cross-border e-commerce platforms and social media platforms, products are delivered to consumers in countries or regions, and consumers' feelings about tangible objects of products are no longer so intuitive, so it is particularly important to reflect the details of the product through product pictures, and even convey some tangible information to consumers through pictures or videos of real-life usage scenarios.

(3) Additional Product

Additional products refer to the intangible services attached to the product. In cross-border marketing, additional products usually include the product's shipping policy (such as whether free shipping is available), return and exchange policy (whether no-reason return and exchange is supported within a certain period), product use training, installation services, product warranty policy, extended warranty policy, etc. It is worth noting that in developed countries or regions such as Europe and America, users will also pay attention to some policies of the product in protecting user privacy.

(4) Expected Product

The expected product refers to the content that consumers expect before using the product, that is, the content that can surprise consumers. In cross-border marketing, surprises are created for consumers by adding gifts outside the product, through some marketing activities on social media before the product reaches the user's hands, and so on.

(5) Potential Product

The potential product refers to the new needs that consumers may have after purchasing and using the product. For example, after a user purchases a certain brand of smartphone, it may stimulate the user's need to purchase the professional version (non-standard version) of the earphone accessory for the phone, or the need to purchase a personalized phone case for the phone.

2. Cross-Border Marketing Product Positioning

Cross-border marketing product positioning refers to the process of producing or selecting corresponding products to meet different consumer needs according to different consumer needs in different countries or regions during the cross-border marketing process, and establishing a specific image in the consumer's mind through various marketing means during the marketing promotion process. In simple terms, it is to give users in different countries or regions a reason to buy a product in cross-border marketing.

Because the products of cross-border e-commerce platforms or other cross-border sales channels are very rich, they provide enough choice space for cross-border consumers. Therefore, it is very important to accurately position the product for different consumers in different countries or regions, and convey this positioning to consumers through text descriptions, pictures, videos, etc. The core of positioning lies in the comparison with similar products, usually using the following methods:

(1) Price comparison positioning method: Emphasize to price-sensitive users that the price is cheaper.
(2) Product difference comparison positioning method: Emphasize the differences between similar products.
(3) Core function enhancement positioning method: Emphasize to consumers that the core function of the product is more prominent.

(4) Value Delivery Positioning Method: What kind of use value can it bring to consumers.
(5) Feature Segmentation Positioning Method: Positioning a specific feature of the product, highlighting its uniqueness.
(6) Competitive Positioning Method: Emphasizing features superior to main competitors.

3. Standardization and Differentiation Strategies of Cross-Border Marketing Products

(1) Product Standardization Strategy

Product standardization refers to providing the same standard products to users in different countries and regions in cross-border marketing, that is, the performance, specifications, materials, etc. of the product adopt a consistent standard. Product standardization strategy is quite common in the field of fast-moving consumer goods, such as the most common Coca-Cola, the same formula worldwide. In cross-border marketing, product standardization strategy is also very common, especially for small and medium-sized enterprises, product standardization can greatly reduce R&D and production costs.

The advantages of product standardization strategy are as follows: mass production, reducing production costs; establishing a unified brand image in different countries and regions, which is conducive to brand establishment and promotion; reducing product R&D costs; reducing market marketing costs.

The disadvantage of product standardization is also obvious, that is, it cannot meet the different needs of consumers in different countries and regions.

(2) Product Differentiation Strategy

Product differentiation strategy refers to providing different products to consumers in different countries and regions in cross-border marketing to meet their different needs. Product differentiation strategy will increase production and marketing costs, because it needs to produce different products for different countries and regions, and adopt different marketing strategies. This strategy is more common in some personalized products in cross-border marketing. For example, in the category of mobile phone cases, by printing different patterns, colors, and appearances on the phone cases to meet the personalized aesthetic needs of consumers in different countries and regions, thereby achieving differentiated production and marketing.

Cross-border enterprises in cross-border marketing, whether to choose standardization or differentiation strategy, not only need to consider the product characteristics and operating conditions of the enterprise itself, but also need to consider the market differences in different countries and regions, consumer demand characteristics, use conditions restrictions, the competitive environment of the target market and other factors.

4. Product Brand Strategy

Product brand refers to the characteristics used to identify products, including names, terms, signs, patterns, or symbols, as well as combinations of these characteristics, usually including the brand name and brand logo of the product. The purpose of the product brand strategy is to distinguish the product from competitors' products, occupy a place in the consumer's mind, and thereby reduce the marketing cost of developing new customers.

Building a product brand can achieve four functions, including identification, value-added, decoration, and promotion. Take the value-added function as an example, a typical example is the brand value of Coca-Cola. The world's largest communication group WPP and Kantar Millward Brown released the "2018 BrandZ™ Top 100 Most Valuable Global Brands" ranking in London, UK. Coca-Cola's brand value of $79.964 billion ranked 14th globally.

For cross-border marketing companies, the following brand strategies are usually adopted: (1) Multi-brand strategy, operating two or more competing product brands at the same time; (2) Unified brand strategy, that is, one brand encompasses all products under the company; (3) Family brand strategy, different series of products use different brands, but all carry the family brand mark; (4) Brand reconstruction strategy, this situation often occurs when consumer preferences undergo fundamental changes or competitors launch powerful brands, that is, the market environment undergoes huge changes, forcing companies to actively or passively adopt product brand reconstruction strategies; (5) Brand internationalization strategy, which can adopt different strategies such as using a unified brand, partially changed brand, or completely different brand depending on the specific situation in different countries and regions.

9.1.3 Selection of Product Strategy

In the early stage of cross-border marketing, it is necessary to fully analyze the needs of foreign consumers in order to correctly choose the product positioning strategy; for cross-border traders (as opposed to manufacturers), the correct product selection strategy directly determines the success or failure of cross-border marketing; in the process of cross-border marketing, it is necessary to reasonably adopt product standardization or product differentiation strategies to push products to different countries or regions; if new needs are discovered in the process of cross-border marketing, the correct new product development strategy needs to be adopted; running through the entire cross-border marketing process is also the product's brand strategy.

1. New Product Development

In cross-border marketing, due to the fact that it targets consumers in different countries and regions, and there are large differences between individual consumers, when existing products are difficult to meet consumer needs, or new demand points in the target market are discovered during the promotion process of the original product, new product development is needed.

It should be noted that the new product development mentioned here refers to the new product development of manufacturing enterprises. In the field of cross-border marketing, for traders (as opposed to manufacturers), new product development actually refers to the product selection mentioned below. The so-called new product, in the cross-border marketing environment, refers to the fact that the manufacturing enterprise has changed the function or shape of the product, which is different from the original product, or the manufacturing enterprise has made revolutionary innovations to the product, producing products that are not available on the market, all of which belong to new products. The purpose of developing new products is to meet consumer needs and provide new benefits or value to consumers.

New products usually include the following categories: (1) Innovative brand-new products; (2) Upgrades of original products; (3) Improved products of the original product, which have been partially improved, but not to the extent of upgrading; (4) Imitation products of competitors, which is a common practice for companies to cope with market competition; (5) Products that are redeveloped due to mistakes in product positioning.

In cross-border marketing, due to the convenience of cross-border e-commerce platforms and social media marketing platforms, and the agility of the Internet marketing environment, many business opportunities are fleeting. Once the best launch timing is missed, companies often lose the initiative, and in the fully competitive environment of cross-border e-commerce platforms, losing the initiative often means failure.

The new product development process in cross-border marketing has undergone huge changes compared to traditional international marketing. The new product development process in cross-border marketing is usually:

The first step, analyze market environment data and user demand data

Targeted collection of market environment data and user demand data from the target country is made possible by cross-border e-commerce platforms and social media platforms. In traditional international marketing, data collection alone requires a longer period. By studying the product categories on cross-border e-commerce platforms, we can uncover unmet user needs by examining the sales and user reviews of products in the same category in the target country or region. For example, for a women's office suit, there are many negative comments about the style of the suit in the user comment area. These comments can be collected and analyzed to find the pain points of user needs, and then targeted new product development can be carried out. At this stage, the market environment and user demand data that need to be collected include: ① demographic data of the target user group, such as age group, income level (consumption ability), gender ratio, occupational characteristics, etc.; ② consumer behavior data, such as consumption preferences, personal style, hobbies, consumption cycle, consumption decision path, etc.; ③ national and regional characteristics, such as climate, religion, cultural characteristics, taboos, economic development level, population density, etc.; ④ competitive product analysis, including the number of similar products on the market, brand influence, hot-selling products of the same brand, product selling points, etc.; ⑤ industry data, such as the life cycle of the industry to which the product belongs, market competition, number of market players, characteristics of leading players, market saturation, market structure, product category structure, growth space, etc.; ⑥ user demand pain point analysis, which unmet user pain points can be analyzed in detail through user comments. After collecting enough data, clean, analyze, and summarize the data to form a core set of market and user demand data to assist decision-making. The second step is to conceive new product ideas based on the data analysis from the first step, or to imitate and improve existing products on the market. For products that are not yet on the target market and need to be completely innovatively produced, product idea conception, idea collection, and final product design drafts need to be carried out; for products that are not yet on the target country's market but are already owned by the company, consideration needs to be given to adapting the product for the target market based on the data analysis results from step ①; for products that are already on the target market and are in a product life cycle stage that can be considered for new entry, an imitation new product development strategy can be adopted. The third step is to produce a concept product and test it on a small scale in the market to gauge market reaction. Cross-border marketing and social media marketing environments provide excellent practice for small-scale testing of new products. Producers can target e-commerce platforms or social media platforms to launch small-scale concept products, or even just launch them to social media fan communities first, to collect and test user feedback. The fourth step is to improve the concept product based on the collected user feedback. Based on the feedback collected from a small group of users, improvements can be made to the shortcomings of the concept product. For example, if users feedback that the product color is too monotonous, multiple colors can be produced (which colors can also be collected from user opinions) to meet user needs. The fifth step is to expand the testing range and finalize the concept product. After small-scale testing or improvement, if relatively ideal user feedback is obtained, the testing range can be expanded, such as expanding the product promotion range on cross-border e-commerce platforms or social media platforms, collecting a larger sample size of user opinions, making rapid improvements based on user opinions, and finally finalizing the concept product. The sixth step is mass production and large-scale market promotion. After the concept product is finalized, it enters the mass production stage. The company can mass produce the product and carry out large-scale market new product introductions and promotions. Although the above steps are numerous, with the convenience of communication between the internet and users and the agility of internet feedback, companies can achieve rapid iterative development of new products.

2. Product Selection Strategy

The correct product selection strategy is crucial to the success or failure of cross-border marketing. On the user communication sections of various cross-border platforms, product selection is always a hot topic. Creating a best-selling product is the dream of most sellers. So, what is the correct product selection strategy in cross-border marketing?

(1) Factors to Consider in Product Selection Strategy at the Macro Level

For cross-border marketing, product selection at the macro level should first consider whether the product is suitable for cross-border sales. The content to consider includes: ① Whether the market potential is large enough; ② Whether the profit margin is high enough; ③ Whether after-sales services such as on-site installation are required? Obviously, this is not suitable for cross-border marketing, and operations need to be simple, such as clothing, digital 3C, etc.; ④ Whether it can reflect differentiation, especially in design? For example, bottled water is difficult to reflect design differentiation; ⑤ Adverse factors in international logistics, such as long cycles (fresh products require cold chain logistics), whether it is fragile? Is it very heavy, a large weight means high shipping costs; ⑥ Whether it is suitable for the religious and cultural factors of the target country; ⑦ Whether it violates the laws and regulations of the target country, and whether there may be intellectual property infringement issues; ⑧ Whether it violates platform rules, which may lead to the product being quickly removed or even the store being banned.

Of course, the above factors are not absolute. For example, the cross-border marketing of industrial products is now in full swing, and some industrial products require on-site installation services. This does not mean that cross-border e-commerce cannot be done. This is just a suggestion for macro-level regular considerations.

(2) Data Required for Product Selection Strategy

A significant advantage of cross-border marketing over traditional marketing is that it allows for scientific product selection through data. In the process of product selection, we need to collect data in the following areas: ① Potential user data of the product, including age, gender, income level, location, occupation, etc., potential user consumption characteristics data, including user consumption preferences, consumption decision-making path, media exposure, etc.; ② Data of the industry to which the product belongs: the life cycle stage of the product, products in the decline stage of the life cycle have no future, the sales cycle of the product, whether the planned time to market is off-season or peak season; market saturation, whether there are already enough sellers in the product market, it is difficult to enter again; ③ Product competition environment data: sales, volume, average customer price, product pricing, product structure, etc. of the TOP sellers in the same industry; hot-selling product data, TOP sales products in the same industry, product sales, main purchasing user characteristics, marketing methods, etc.; competitors, who are the main target competitors? What cross-border marketing strategies have these competitors adopted, and what are their strengths and weaknesses; ④ Data of the category attributes of the product: total sales of the category, number of sellers in the category, total transactions of the category, average customer price of the category, number of sub-categories, sales, volume, number of sellers, etc. of each sub-category, growth space of the category, average promotion cost of the category, etc.; ⑤ Product key attribute data: product material, what materials are used by competitors; product style, appearance of competitors, temperament positioning, consumer evaluation; product specifications, specifications and dimensions of competitors, whether there are special specifications; price range, pricing range of competitors; product style, description of competitors' styles; product color, what colors are high-selling competitors; product selling point refinement, what are the core selling point refinements of competitors; product function, performance, description of competitors' functions and performance; product packaging, what features are on the packaging of competitors; product repurchase rate, repurchase rate of competitors; product sales combination, combination sales strategy adopted by competitors when selling products; ⑥ Industry TOP seller store data: store decoration style, store brand, brand popularity, social media exposure, store sales, volume, hot-selling products, store copywriting style, store positioning, store differentiated operation strategy, store marketing strategy; ⑦ Product suppliers: competitor supplier survey, target supplier capability assessment, including production capacity, quality management capability, new product R&D capability, warehousing and logistics capability.

(3) Product Selection Strategy

The core of the cross-border marketing product selection strategy is to differentiate the positioning of stores and products on cross-border e-commerce platforms, or to differentiate the positioning of products through content marketing in social media marketing, to avoid homogeneous price competition. This is mainly reflected in the following aspects:

First, store positioning: differentiation strategy

Based on the analysis of competitor stores mentioned above, differentiate the positioning of the store, highlight the features of the store that are different from competitor stores, and make a difference in store decoration, copywriting style, and category planning.

Second, data-driven product selection strategy

Use data-driven product selection tools to collect the above product information, scientifically select products, and create hot-selling explosive products.

Third, user pain point product selection strategy

Collect product user pain points through social media, classify and organize user pain points, and select products for user pain points that have not been satisfied.

Fourth, product combination strategy

In cross-border marketing, a product matrix can be created by expanding related products around a certain explosive product and implementing a product combination sales strategy.

(4) Product Selection Tools

First, Google Trends (https://trends.google.com/trends/)

Google Trends is a very good product selection tool. By entering product keywords, you can view the user search trends of the product over a certain period of time, thereby judging the market prospects of this product. For example, search for DIY tools, Chalk Paint, you can see that it has been on the rise in the US market in recent years.

Second, use product classification or tracking tools

Jungle Scout is an Amazon Listing tracking tool that can help us classify products on the platform when selecting products, and can help us quickly locate listings.

Especially this product can not only be used for Amazon, but also for other e-commerce platforms.

Third, subscribe to some foreign content about market trends

The Cool Hunter: Global creative product recommendations, with high authority in cross-border marketing.

Trend Watching: Provides consumer trend intelligence worldwide

Fourth, view different B2B platforms or competitors' social media accounts

9.1.4 Product Strategy Management

In the formulation and implementation process of cross-border marketing product strategy, what kind of product strategy to adopt at what time, how to ensure that the product strategy can be well executed, especially when cross-border marketing faces multiple cross-border e-commerce platforms or multiple social media marketing matrices, how to better manage becomes the key to whether the product strategy can be implemented.

In product strategy management, multi-platform product management and product lifecycle management in cross-border marketing are the links where problems are more likely to occur. The following will focus on how to do a good job in multi-platform product management and product lifecycle management in cross-border marketing.

1. Multi-platform Product Management

The cross-border e-commerce industry has made great strides in recent years. Both import and export cross-border e-commerce have taken shape, and many excellent platforms have emerged. For example, on the import side, there are self-operated B2C models like NetEase Koala, platform B2C models like Tmall International, and platform C2C models like Taobao Global Purchase. In addition, Yangmatou innovatively adopted the C2C buyer live broadcast format, and Xiaohongshu is a community import e-commerce.

Of course, for sellers, export cross-border e-commerce platforms are more important. At present, the more popular platforms internationally include Amazon, AliExpress, Wish, and eBay. When selling, export sellers may operate on multiple platforms at the same time. Here is a discussion on multi-platform product management for these four major cross-border e-commerce platforms.

2. Scope of Multi-platform Product Management

Product management: product selection, new product listing, product listing and delisting, product violation handling, etc.

Order management: management of product order information, order execution, etc.

Logistics management: product delivery, returns and exchanges, freight management, etc.

Product inventory management: inventory management, procurement management, inventory operation, etc.

Customer relationship management: including customer relationship maintenance, complaint handling

Supply chain management: supplier relationship management, channel management

Multi-platform management: multi-platform linkage, multi-platform joint holiday promotions, etc.

3. The Role of Multi-platform Management

Enhance the professionalism of single platform management

Improve management efficiency

Clarify division of labor, improve team communication efficiency

Improve customer satisfaction

4. Multi-platform Management Details

(1) Product Information Management

Synchronization of product information across multiple platforms, when product information is updated on one platform, it is simultaneously updated on other platforms

Management of products from different warehouses and different batches

Management of shipping policies for products from different warehouses and channels

Maintenance of basic product information

Management of products in multiple languages and currencies

Management of product promotions

Product price management, real-time price adjustments and synchronization

(2) Order Information Management

Collection and summary of orders from different platforms

Processing of orders from different platforms

Management of order status on different platforms, such as handling when a user cancels an order

Integration of order processing and logistics handling on different platforms to prevent missed or incorrect orders

Order statistics and settlement

(3) Logistics Management

Splitting and logistics distribution of different product categories in a single order

Logistics management of different sales channels

Logistics distribution management of different products on different platforms

Sorting of goods and matching of logistics information in different countries
Logistics handling of returned and exchanged goods

(4) Inventory Management

Inventory management, inventory information statistics, timely replenishment
Product order forecasting, preparing stock in advance based on the forecasted order volume
Collection of post-sale complaints from buyers about the product and packaging, communication with manufacturers

(5) Supply Chain Management

Supplier management
Supplier incentives
Supplier expansion
Communication with suppliers

(6) Customer Relationship Management

Maintenance of customer relationships
Handling of customer complaints
Handling of negative information on social media
Management of member relationships, VIP customer relationships

(7) Multi-platform Linkage Management

Management of holiday promotions across platforms
Daily linkage management across multiple platforms
Handling of account issues, such as when an account is reported
Handling of account and store bans

5. Lifecycle Management

Every product has lifecycle attributes, and it is very important to enter the market at a reasonable point in the product lifecycle. A product on sale has issues with lifecycle management. The so-called product lifecycle refers to the time cycle from when a product is launched to when it finally exits the market. The product lifecycle is divided into four stages: introduction, growth, maturity, and decline, which is a common classification in cross-border marketing.

9.2 Cross-Border E-Commerce Price Management

Pricing strategy is a crucial strategy in the marketing mix. In a narrow sense, price refers to the amount of money people pay to obtain a certain product or service, while in a broad sense, price not only includes the monetary expenditure paid by consumers, but also other expenditures, such as time and energy. The price of a product often becomes a key factor in the success of a transaction, or at least one of the key factors, and due to its high flexibility and diverse influencing factors, pricing strategy becomes a difficult point in the product marketing mix strategy. When formulating a pricing strategy, not only the company's costs and profits need to be considered, but also the consumer's acceptance ability; in cross-border marketing, the acceptance ability of consumers in different countries and regions for pricing needs to be considered. In addition, the issue of currency exchange rates in different countries and regions also further complicates pricing.

The development of internet and e-commerce technology has made pricing strategies more flexible and more difficult to formulate. Compared with traditional international marketing, pricing strategies in cross-border marketing are more immediate, such as temporary price changes during promotions need to be completed immediately. In addition, it is also more transparent, the pricing of competing products on e-commerce platforms is clear at a glance, and pricing strategies also become more transparent. Due to the characteristic of cross-border e-commerce platforms that prices can be changed at any time, the flexibility of pricing strategies is also higher.

9.2.1 *The Connotation of Pricing Strategy*

Pricing strategy refers to the strategy of cross-border enterprises to determine the product price scientifically and reasonably based on the analysis and research of costs, demand, and competition conditions, in order to achieve cross-border marketing goals.

For enterprises, they hope to achieve marketing goals through product pricing. Although this marketing goal ultimately points to profit, it is not solely aimed at current profit, but also implies that the enterprise hopes to achieve continuous marketing of products through reasonable pricing. The goal of maximizing current benefits and market share, and optimizing product quality is achieved through flexible pricing strategies.

1. Factors Affecting Pricing Strategy

In cross-border marketing, the factors that affect the pricing strategy mainly include the following aspects: (1) Cost factors, which determine the minimum pricing of the product, mainly include the following aspects, such as: the production cost of the product, management cost, intermediate link costs in cross-border marketing such as logistics costs, distribution costs, tariffs, currency exchange rate fluctuations, cost increases caused by inflation; (2) Marketing promotion factors, such as: holiday promotions and discounts, marketing expenses brought by participating in activities on cross-border e-commerce platforms, paid promotions, membership operations and other daily activities promotions and discounts, price policy changes on cross-border e-commerce platforms; (3) Market demand factors, which determine the maximum pricing of the product, such as: if supply falls short of demand, then the price is high; if supply exceeds demand, then the price is low; (4) Market competition factors, reflecting the flexibility of pricing, such as: competitors adjust prices, new competitors join or competitors withdraw from competition; (5) Government regulatory actions in the target country of cross-border marketing, such as: tax policies, tariff policies, interest rates, anti-dumping measures taken, etc.

2. Scientific Pricing Through Data Analysis

Cross-border e-commerce platforms and social media platforms provide a convenient and comprehensive marketing environment for cross-border marketing. However, due to their characteristics such as three-dimensional information transmission and round-the-clock communication with consumers (consumers can comment at any time), pricing strategies have become more flexible, and the difficulty of reasonably formulating pricing strategies has increased. So, how to scientifically and reasonably formulate pricing strategies in cross-border marketing? The three-dimensional transmission and round-the-clock communication characteristics of cross-border e-commerce platforms and social media platforms have increased the difficulty of pricing, but their transparent and open platform characteristics have also provided us with convenience for quickly obtaining public data. Therefore, data analysis has become a sharp tool for scientific pricing.

In the daily management of cross-border marketing, it is necessary to dynamically collect price-related data on cross-border platforms and social media platforms, which usually include:

(1) Data of Competitors and Competitive Products

Sales, volume, average customer price, product pricing, etc. of TOP merchants in the same industry

Hot-selling product data in competitive products, product sales, pricing, average customer price, etc.

Pricing range of competitive products

Packaging and estimated packaging costs of competitive products

Competitor's marketing promotion activities, estimated activity costs

Competitor's combination marketing strategy, which products participate in combination sales, their respective pricing

Data of the product's category attributes: total sales of the category, number of merchants, average customer price

Number of subcategories, sales, volume, number of merchants, average promotion cost of each subcategory, etc.

Consumer feedback on competitor product pricing on e-commerce platforms and social media platforms

(2) Consumer Feedback Related to Price

Consumer feedback on pricing and shipping costs on e-commerce platforms

Consumer feedback on promotional discount prices on e-commerce platforms

Consumer feedback related to pricing on social media platforms

Consumer feedback related to pricing on professional review websites

Through the collection of the above data, after screening and retaining data with higher credibility, the data is analyzed. Long-term data collection can form a competitor price curve, which can conveniently monitor the price fluctuations of competitors and competitive products, and can predict the price trends of competitors or market competitive products based on historical prices, thereby adjusting pricing strategies in advance.

Furthermore, cross-border marketing companies can integrate the above data curves and influencing factor data to infer a price prediction formula. This formula can also take into account factors such as daily exchange rate fluctuations, making pricing strategies more scientific, reasonable, and controllable.

9.2.2 Selection of Pricing Strategy

1. Selection of Pricing Strategy

In international marketing, it is believed that the core factors affecting price are three, namely cost, demand, and competition. In cross-border marketing, in addition to these three factors, there is another important factor, namely the marketing promotion factors of the Internet environment such as e-commerce and social media. Therefore, in the choice of pricing methods, they often make flexible choices based on these four factors. Pricing strategy is the application of pricing methods under different conditions.

(1) Cost-Oriented Pricing Method

First, comprehensive cost pricing method

The comprehensive cost pricing method refers to the consideration of not only the production cost of the enterprise itself when pricing a product, but also the usage and maintenance costs of consumers, and these factors are comprehensively considered for pricing.

Second, cost-plus pricing method

The cost-plus pricing method is a well-known pricing method, which is based on the unit cost of the product and the expected profit of the product as an addition to set the price.

The unit cost of the product includes many costs, in addition to the production cost, there are also operating costs, such as sales, management, promotion, transportation, taxation, etc.

The pricing formula for a single product is: product price = product cost * (1 + cost markup rate)

The cost markup rate is the expected profit markup. For example, if the expected profit is 35%, then the price of a single product is: price = cost * 1.35

Third, target profit pricing method

The pricing formula is: unit product sales price = (total cost + target total profit) / total sales volume

The target profit pricing method is based on the total cost of the enterprise and the total sales volume within a certain calculation period, as well as the target total profit to calculate the unit price of the product.

(2) Demand-Oriented Pricing Method

The demand-oriented pricing method starts from market demand and prices according to market demand.

First, differential pricing method

The price is set according to the different demands caused by the differences in the actual target country's region, target user group, product, and consumption time.

For example, when the fidget spinner has become popular in the United States, and some other Asian countries just know what a fidget spinner is, it is necessary to price differently for the United States and countries outside the United States.

Second, reverse pricing method

According to the price of similar products on the target country's market, estimate the retail price of the product, and then subtract the commission of the e-commerce platform, tariffs, shipping costs, etc., to reverse the product's ex-factory price.

(3) Competition-Oriented Pricing Method

Cross-border marketing will refer to the price of competitors to price, this is the competition-oriented pricing method.

First, follow the market pricing method

The price is set according to the average price of the product in the target country, and this pricing method can also effectively avoid triggering vicious price competition.

Second, competitive pricing method

When the enterprise comprehensively considers its own strength and the comparison of the strength of competitors, and believes that it can compete with competitors, it can adopt the competitive pricing method, that is, to keep a close eye on competitors, the price is lower than competitors, thereby defeating competitors from the price strategy.

(4) Marketing-Oriented Pricing Method

Cross-border e-commerce platforms or social media platforms, holiday promotions, and daily promotional activities are everywhere. Therefore, the marketing-oriented pricing method is a pricing method different from traditional international marketing.

First, holiday promotion pricing method

Holiday promotions are usually major promotional activities led by cross-border e-commerce platforms. In product pricing strategies, prices are usually much lower than the daily selling prices during non-promotion periods, generally priced slightly higher than the cost price. The goal is to rush sales in the short term, and it is also very helpful for accumulating and improving the store level.

The holiday promotion pricing method is a strategy of small profits but quick turnover, and even the sales volume of a company participating in a promotion can achieve the annual sales target.

Second, Discount Pricing Method

This involves driving sales by participating in or initiating activities on e-commerce platforms or social media platforms. These activities often come with some discount promotions.

Third, Product Bundle Pricing Method

This involves bundling popular products and slow-moving products for sale in the store, using popular products to drive marketing activities for slow-moving products. When pricing, concessions are made on popular products as a selling point.

2. New Product Pricing Strategy

New products, due to their recent entry into the market, await large-scale market validation. Therefore, pricing cannot simply be compared to the prices of other mature products. Therefore, new products require some unique pricing strategies, including skimming pricing strategy, penetration pricing strategy, and moderate pricing strategy.

(1) Skimming Pricing Strategy

Skimming pricing strategy refers to setting the price of a new product far above the cost, in order to maximize profits in the short term and recover the investment as soon as possible.

The advantage of the skimming pricing strategy is that it facilitates rapid investment recovery. When the product sales enter a new stage, there is enough room for price reduction, and it is also convenient to control market demand through high prices. Usually, for mass consumer goods with a large market capacity, even if the price is high, there are still enough users to pay. Another situation is that the company has sufficient technical barriers, such as patent protection, even if the price is set very high, competitors will find it difficult to intervene in a short time. Both of these situations are suitable for the skimming pricing strategy.

Many digital products like to use the skimming pricing strategy. When a new product is launched, a higher price is set. The well-known Apple iPhone is an example of this. After a period of sales, the price falls back to the normal price, and when the next generation of new products is launched, the price is further reduced.

The disadvantage of the skimming pricing strategy is also quite obvious. High prices mean high profits, which will inevitably stimulate and encourage new competitors to join and intensify competition. At the same time, a high pricing strategy is not conducive to quickly occupying the market and expanding the market scope.

(2) Penetration Pricing Strategy

The penetration pricing strategy is usually suitable for companies with strong financial strength and sufficient brand awareness. When a new product is launched, the company can quickly open up the market, expand the market scope, increase market share, and take the lead to form market barriers to prevent or delay competitors from joining.

The advantage of the penetration pricing strategy is that it can quickly open up and occupy the market, increase market share, and take a position in the consumer's mind in advance. Consumers have a mental cost of choosing products. Once a product successfully occupies a position in the consumer's mind, it greatly increases the chance of being chosen by the consumer at the time of purchase. This pricing strategy is commonly used in the field of fast-moving consumer goods or daily necessities that are sensitive to consumer prices. For example, some mineral water companies and dairy companies will use strong market promotion methods, including penetration pricing strategies, when new products are launched.

The disadvantage of the penetration pricing strategy is the slow cost recovery. Since the price is set low from the beginning, it is difficult to raise the price later. Also, it may leave an impression in the consumer's mind that the price is low due to low quality.

(3) Moderate Pricing Strategy

As the name suggests, it is a pricing method that is relatively moderate. Compared to the previous two aggressive pricing methods, the mild pricing strategy is less likely to cause a drastic market reaction and is more stable.

Companies with relatively low strength and brand recognition usually adopt a mild pricing strategy when launching new products, in order to avoid stimulating competitors and considering costs.

3. Other Pricing Strategies

(1) Psychological Pricing Strategy

Consumers have some similar psychology when shopping. Summarizing consumer psychology and pricing accordingly is the psychological pricing strategy. Psychological pricing strategies include: prestige pricing strategy, odd–even pricing strategy, and bait pricing strategy.

The so-called prestige pricing strategy is to set prices far higher than similar products on the market in cross-border marketing, based on consumers' admiration for international brands and well-known brands in the industry. The premise of this pricing method is that the company's brand recognition is extremely high, common in the luxury or gift industry, such as Hermès bags, Parker pens, etc.

The odd–even pricing strategy is also a pricing based on consumer psychology. After making formal modifications to the price of the product, it can cater to consumers' desire for low-cost and affordable consumption. The common ones are integer plus decimal and ending with 9, such as pricing a product expected to be 10 as 9.99. This pricing method is common in offline supermarkets and clothing discount activities in shopping malls, and this technique is also used by cross-border marketing sellers.

The bait pricing strategy refers to setting the price of a product far lower than the market price to attract consumers, making consumers think that the price of similar products is lower than the market price. In fact, some of the other products are higher than the market price, to make up for the loss of low-priced goods. This pricing method is often used by offline large supermarkets such as Walmart.

(2) Discount and Allowance Pricing Strategy

In cross-border marketing, discount and allowance pricing strategies are often used in cross-border promotions, such as major holiday promotions or event promotions. There are various ways of promotional discounts, such as cash discounts, buy-one-get-one discounts, seasonal specials, trade-in promotions, etc.

In cross-border promotions, cash discounts mean that the seller gives a certain discount on the basis of the original price. With the change of cross-border promotion methods, in the major promotion activities of cross-border platforms, sellers often have to participate in e-commerce platform category promotions after giving discounts on the basis of the original price, which involves double or multiple discounts. Sellers need to take these factors into account when pricing. In addition to direct discounts, cash discounts also include full reduction discounts, such as a reduction of 50 for every 200 spent, to encourage consumers to buy more.

Quantity discounts are also common in cross-border marketing, manifested as buy-one-get-one-free activities, such as buy 5 get 1 free, that is, consumers get 1 free product for every 5 products purchased.

Seasonal discounts are relatively easy to understand and are common in clothing with distinct seasons. For example, in summer, discounts are offered on down jackets worn in winter. In cross-border marketing, off-season and season-changing discounts are common. Off-season discounts refer to the aforementioned discounts on clothing worn only in winter during summer; season-changing discounts refer to discounts during the change of seasons, such as discounts on winter goods in spring and discounts on summer goods in autumn. In cross-border marketing, it is important to note that the seasons and climate changes in different target countries are often different. A typical example is tropical African countries, where the demand for winter clothing is relatively small.

New replacement discounts refer to a pricing strategy where merchants discount the price of already sold goods, and consumers get a certain discount when buying new products from the merchant by offsetting the discounted price of the old product.

In addition to the above pricing strategies, there are also geographical location pricing strategies, transfer pricing strategies, etc. One factor that cannot be ignored in cross-border marketing is the cost and delivery time of freight. International freight often becomes a large part of the cost of cross-border marketing, especially for heavier goods. Now more and more companies are opening overseas warehouses to reduce freight costs and shorten delivery times. For merchants who open overseas warehouses, geographical location factors must be considered when pricing. Transfer pricing strategies are based on considerations such as reasonable tax avoidance.

9.2.3 Management of Pricing Strategies

In cross-border marketing, due to the transparency of prices on cross-border e-commerce platforms, the competition between similar products is becoming increasingly fierce, which requires higher and higher response times to price changes. At the same time, the increasingly diverse and frequent promotional activities on cross-border e-commerce platforms also make the company's pricing strategy sufficiently flexible, which requires an effective pricing strategy management mechanism. The management of pricing strategies is usually reflected in price adjustment strategies and multi-platform price management in cross-border marketing.

1. Price Adjustment Strategy

In traditional international marketing, price adjustment is a systematic project, influenced by various factors, such as the increase in production costs caused by the rise in raw materials and labor wages, inflation factors or changes in supply and demand relationships, such as the emergence of supply exceeding demand or demand exceeding supply. Companies are very cautious about price adjustments because they will bring a series of changes to the market and consumers, some of which are even unpredictable. Incorrect price adjustment strategies can even bring devastating blows to the company.

In cross-border marketing, because cross-border e-commerce platforms make prices transparent, the prices of competitors or competitive products are clear at a glance. Cross-border e-commerce platforms often carry out full-platform promotional activities, and price adjustment has become a very common pricing strategy in cross-border marketing.

(1) Factors Influencing Price Adjustment Strategy

In cross-border marketing, the factors influencing the price adjustment strategy are both similar and different from traditional international marketing.

First, the cost factors of the enterprise

Changes in the macroeconomic environment in which the company operates lead to changes in the company's production costs, such as rising raw material prices, rising labor wages, and inflation, all of which will lead to an increase in the company's production costs. In this case, in order to maintain profits or sustain the business, the company will be forced to raise prices.

However, in the cross-border marketing environment, since there may be sellers from different countries selling the same product on the same e-commerce platform, the macroeconomic conditions of different countries are different. The rise in labor wages in the country where the company is located does not mean that labor wages in the country where other competitors are located are also rising. Therefore, in this situation, a price increase often means being at a competitive disadvantage.

Second, changes in the supply and demand of products

In traditional international marketing, when a certain product is in short supply, a price increase is often the best choice. However, in cross-border marketing, due to the transparent pricing of cross-border e-commerce platforms, even if the product is in short supply, it depends on whether competitors have adopted a price increase strategy. On the other hand, due to the flexibility of cross-border marketing pricing strategies, even if the wrong price increase strategy is chosen, it can still be quickly corrected to minimize the impact.

In cross-border marketing, more often than not, the supply of products exceeds demand, and the same product has multiple competitors, so even if the supply exceeds demand, it does not necessarily mean that prices need to be reduced. This is distinctly different from traditional international marketing. However, when the supply of products in the entire market is clearly excessive, price reduction becomes a trend.

Third, promotional factors

In cross-border marketing, promotions are a very common marketing method. Whether it's a platform-wide promotion on a cross-border e-commerce platform or a promotional event initiated by the cross-border seller itself, it will be accompanied by price adjustments, usually in the form of profit concessions to boost sales, such as discounts, buy one get one free, etc. Essentially, they all involve giving up a certain amount of profit to increase sales volume. For example, the discount promotion activity on the eBay platform.

During the promotion process, price adjustments are extremely flexible. This requires companies to formulate price adjustment rules for promotional activities in advance to avoid arbitrary price adjustments that could lead to losses. Companies can formulate price adjustment rules based on the form of the activity, such as a unified rule for platform-wide promotions, and another rule for periodic promotions, such as weekend promotions; event-based promotions require more flexible pricing rules.

(2) Management of Price Adjustment Strategies

The transparency of prices on cross-border e-commerce platforms makes it possible for us to automatically monitor the prices of similar products. We can use manual or automated web scraping methods to present the prices of competing products in the form of intuitive price curves, so that we can adjust product prices based on competitor dynamics.

Companies need to incorporate the management of price adjustment strategies into their daily management, set up dedicated personnel or even specialized positions for professional price management, and formulate price adjustment rules and calculation formulas for different scenarios. At the same time, they should adjust prices scientifically and flexibly based on the monitored price changes of competing products.

2. Multi-platform Price Management in Cross-Border Marketing

In cross-border marketing, multi-platform sales strategies are quite common among sellers. Different platforms have different commission settlement systems and different platform promotion activities, all of which increase the complexity of price management.

When sellers sell goods on multiple platforms, due to the different commission settlement systems of different platforms, they cannot adopt a unified pricing strategy.

Obviously, it is very necessary to formulate different pricing strategies for different platforms, as well as different price adjustment strategies. Moreover, due to the price transparency of cross-border platforms, monitoring the price changes of competing products is also part of daily management. It is also very necessary to adjust pricing strategies based on the price fluctuations of competing products. Therefore, the price management of multi-platform sales usually needs to formulate the following price management rules or systems:

- Pricing rules/systems for each platform
- Daily monitoring system for competitors on each platform
- Pricing adjustment rules/systems based on competitor prices on each platform
- Guidelines/rules for participating in major promotions on each platform
- Pricing rules/systems for store activities on each platform

9.3 Cross-Border E-Commerce Channel Management

In distribution channels, manufacturers can be seen as the starting point and users as the endpoint, with intermediaries and agent intermediaries in between. Cross-border marketing is no exception. In recent years, with the development of global trade and the popularity of the Internet, various Internet sales websites have become an indispensable part of the cross-border distribution channel architecture, such as the well-known Alibaba, Amazon and other cross-border e-commerce platforms.

Unlike the long channels common in offline distribution strategies, distribution strategies based on the Internet are believed to greatly reduce the length of distribution channels, and even support companies in establishing direct distribution channels, allowing goods to be sold to consumers without intermediaries. Plus, internet distribution does not require physical stores, which can greatly reduce sales costs, making cross-border e-commerce platforms the darling of cross-border distribution.

9.3.1 The Connotation of Distribution Strategy

Distribution is the establishment of sales channels. According to Philip Kotler's definition, a distribution channel (or marketing channel) refers to the process in which a commodity or service transfers from the producer to the consumer, and includes all businesses and individuals that help transfer ownership of this commodity or service.

International distribution channels refer to the routes and related series of institutions and individuals through which products or services are transferred from a manufacturer's audience in one country to consumers in the target country. In international distribution channels, it usually includes manufacturers, domestic intermediaries, foreign intermediaries, distributors, agents, wholesalers, and retailers.

Domestic intermediaries: Domestic intermediaries are in the same country as the enterprise, including exporters (distributors) and export agents. Foreign intermediaries: Foreign intermediaries are in the same country as the product consumers, including importers (distributors) and import agents. Distributors: Intermediaries who sell products in a designated area, characterized by owning the ownership of the product. Agents: The difference between agents and distributors is that agents do not own the goods, they are only commissioned by the producer to engage in commodity trading. Wholesalers: As the name suggests, they are intermediaries who import and export goods in bulk, and usually do not have direct contact with the end users. Retailers: Sales units that sell products to final consumers.

9.3.2 *Selection of Distribution Strategy*

International distribution channels are usually classified according to the degree of indirectness, length, and width. International distribution channels are divided into direct channels and indirect channels according to the degree of indirectness. Direct distribution in international markets refers to the process in which products flow from producers to foreign end consumers or users without any intermediaries, foreign consumers or users; indirect distribution in international markets refers to a form of distribution where products are sold to international market end users or consumers via foreign intermediaries.

International distribution channels are divided into first-level channels, second-level channels, third-level channels, etc., based on the channel levels that products or services pass through from the producer to the final consumer.

The breadth of international distribution channels refers to the number of intermediaries at a certain level of the channel through which a product or service passes from the producer to the final consumer. The more intermediaries there are at the same level, the wider the channel.

1. Choice of Distribution Channels

The establishment and maintenance of any distribution channel requires time and cost, so before formulating distribution strategies and choosing distribution channels, an analysis of the product should be carried out, such as the price, volume, weight and other basic factors of the product, as well as whether the product is fragile, perishable, customized, etc. At the same time, the market acceptance of similar products, the number of potential customers and their purchasing habits should also be considered.

The choice of distribution channels is a very important part of a company's sales strategy. The company needs to decide on the indirectness, length, and width of the distribution channels to meet the needs of the target sales market. The correct choice of distribution channels can help the company deliver products to users better, faster, and more efficiently.

(1) Degree of Indirectness

The choice between direct and indirect sales channels is usually based on the strength of the producer and the characteristics of the product. Especially in cross-border sales, cultural differences and geographical location differences need to be considered, and decisions need to be made carefully. Generally speaking, large equipment, proprietary tools, proprietary technology, virtual products, and some fresh goods are more suitable for establishing direct sales channels.

(2) Length Choice

As online sales account for an increasing proportion, many companies are advocating reducing the number of intermediaries. After all, the shorter the channel and the fewer the levels, the more conducive it is to compress costs and win more profit space or price advantages for the product. However, it should be noted that the sales channel is not the shorter the better. The existence of intermediaries is obviously not meaningless. Appropriately increasing the number of intermediaries may enhance the product's publicity, strengthen localized services, and allow the producing company to focus more on production.

In summary, the producing company should consider all factors, such as product characteristics, foreign trade conditions, target market capacity, intermediary business capabilities, the company's own situation, and user consumption habits, to determine the length of its distribution channels. Usually, when the producing company is in a strong position in the market or has outstanding capabilities, such as excellent marketing, publicity, organizational structure, and good logistics and warehousing capabilities, it can reduce the levels of distribution channels under the premise of benefiting the company.

(3) Width Choice

The strategy of choosing more same-type intermediaries (such as wholesalers or retailers) at the same level to distribute its products is called a wide channel strategy; otherwise, it is called a narrow channel strategy. Common width choices include extensive distribution strategies, selective distribution strategies, and exclusive distribution strategies.

An extensive distribution strategy refers to using as many intermediaries as possible at the same channel level to distribute its products. The company does not specify the geographical scope of each intermediary, nor does it have strict requirements for their qualifications. An extensive distribution strategy can maximize the exposure of the product to users and is often used for highly standardized products with high consumption frequency. The disadvantage of an extensive distribution strategy is that it is difficult to control the distribution channel, and price competition may occur between channels.

Select distribution strategy refers to the selection of a few intermediaries to distribute one's products in a certain period and specific market area. The select distribution strategy reduces the opportunities for contact between the company and users, but it enhances the company's control over the channel. It is suitable for specialized products or products with relatively fixed users. In cross-border distribution, the select distribution strategy is often used in conjunction with the extensive distribution strategy. When expanding the market for new products, the extensive distribution strategy is used to let users understand and accept the product as much as possible. When the product sales become stable, the select distribution strategy is adopted to purposefully reduce some low-quality intermediaries to facilitate the maintenance and management of distribution channels.

Exclusive distribution strategy refers to choosing only one intermediary to distribute its products in a certain period and specific market area. Adopting this distribution strategy can strengthen the connection between the company and the intermediary, provide a guarantee for the construction of the product brand, and enhance user service. The disadvantage is that the opportunity for users to come into contact with the product is low, which is not conducive to the promotion of new products. Those who want to build a good brand image or some special consumer goods are suitable for exclusive distribution strategies.

2. Online Distribution and Offline Distribution

With the rapid development of cross-border e-commerce today, online distribution has become a crucial part of corporate sales. More and more companies choose to carry out online and offline distribution at the same time, and some companies even focus on internet distribution and no longer spend costs to maintain offline sales channels.

Online distribution and offline distribution are essentially the same but often have certain differences in levels and structure. Relatively speaking, online distribution is easier to establish a short channel with fewer levels, reduce intermediate links, make product sales simpler and faster, and bring greater price advantages to manufacturing companies. Offline distribution is easier to establish a long channel with multiple levels. The increased intermediate links will indeed dilute product profits, but if the advantages of multi-level services can be played out, stable trading relationships with users can be established, and the brand image of manufacturing companies can be established, it is also conducive to enhancing the market competitiveness of manufacturing companies.

Overall, it is necessary to choose online and offline based on the characteristics of your products and the strength of your company. Whether it is single online or offline, or a focus on both online and offline, they are all part of the company's distribution decision. Those standardized, digital fast-moving consumer goods are suitable for focusing on online sales, while proprietary products, large equipment, and other long-cycle, high-priced products are more suitable for focusing on offline sales.

9.3.3 *Management of Distribution Strategy*

Distribution channels are not once and for all after they are established. The management and maintenance of distribution channels is a task that manufacturing companies cannot ignore. It should regularly check whether the distribution channels are smooth, efficient, stable, and controllable, and also coordinate and balance the relationships between various distribution channels, and timely increase or decrease sales channels to adjust the product distribution coverage area to maximize the role of distribution channels.

Cross-border distribution is usually slightly more complicated than domestic distribution, for example, it involves more transportation and warehousing links and may cause inventory backlog, difficulty in determining production scale, and product delivery time issues. Especially in the online sales link of the Internet, an information explosion point may mean billions of profits, and the logistics time and response speed directly determine whether the producer can catch up with the market hotspot and whether it can share the benefits of high-speed information dissemination on the Internet. Therefore, in today's market environment, the management of distribution channels should attract more attention from manufacturers.

1. Integration of Cross-Border Marketing Distribution Channels

There are many channels for cross-border distribution, and cross-border e-commerce platforms are just the most common, not the only one. Appropriate and diversified channel combinations can be chosen based on product and market conditions. Multi-channel distribution allows consumers to have more ways to access their products, which is more conducive to catering to consumers and target market preferences for channel diversity, increasing product display opportunities.

While multi-channel distribution brings more product competitive advantages, it also has inherent flaws, such as potential differences in user consumption experiences across channels, competition between channels, etc. These all require manufacturers to integrate and manage to balance the relationships between channels and construct an ideal channel structure. In the integration of multiple channels, the relationship between online and offline is considered difficult to coordinate, especially the contradiction between online sales and offline services often existing between online and offline channels. This can easily lead to competition and confrontation between the two channel merchants. If the horizontal competition between channels is not handled correctly, it may intensify channel conflicts and ultimately affect product sales.

At present, how to coordinate the relationship between online and offline is a topic that many companies are researching and trying. It is generally believed that promoting the combination of online and offline by leveraging strengths and avoiding weaknesses is an ideal way, such as building a partnership channel relationship between online and offline, attracting users online, collecting user information combined with offline user services, customer training, brand loyalty building to achieve a win–win situation for multiple channels.

2. Cross-Border Marketing Distribution Channel Management

Channel management refers to all activities to manage existing channels to achieve distribution goals, ensuring mutual coordination and cooperation between channel members and between the company and channel members. Its significance lies in jointly seeking maximum long-term benefits. Reducing conflicts, deepening cooperation, and maintaining good relationships between channels are the focus of channel management. This requires producers to have control and coordination capabilities that match the scale of the channel.

Common problems in channel management include: vicious competition between channel merchants, difficulty in managing overly large channels, arbitrary selection of intermediaries, lack of follow-up management, etc.

Vicious competition between channel merchants: This is one of the common management problems in cross-border sales. Cross-border companies choose multiple distribution channels to quickly enter the local market, causing price competition between channels, leading to consumers having multiple ways to access products but not forming purchases due to price confusion, service confusion, etc. In response to this, manufacturers should start building reasonable channel relationships from the stage of choosing distribution channels, and establish reward and punishment measures and patrol mechanisms, cultivate ideal channel relationships through humanized and institutionalized management.

Difficulty in managing overly large channels: When the distribution channel is too deep or too wide, it will make it difficult for the manufacturer to manage and increase management costs. For example, too many levels of distribution channels will increase product wastage, channel costs, etc. This requires companies to appropriately reduce distribution levels and shorten channel chains. Overly wide distribution channels can easily bring the problem back to vicious competition between channel merchants, causing internal consumption between channels, damaging product image, and reducing consumer goodwill.

Arbitrary selection of intermediaries: A cautious attitude should be adopted to formulate a set of comprehensive and complete standards for selecting intermediaries, such as financial strength and performance, market coverage, reputation, current business operations, cooperation attitude, etc.

Lack of follow-up management: Many companies believe that channel establishment is a one-time effort, which is a mistaken idea. The established distribution channels need to be managed and maintained. It should be noted that products, markets, and consumers are not unchanging, and it can even be said that every influencing factor in the distribution channel is changing at any time. Manufacturers need to communicate regularly with channel members, manage the channels according to the actual situation, and ensure that the distribution channels can meet the market requirements.

9.4 Cross-Border E-Commerce Promotion Management

In the digital age, people's attention is infinitely diluted, coupled with endless new ideas and products, forcing merchants to think of various ways to win user attention. Even well-known brands and mature products need promotions to maintain user interest, and new companies and products need even more promotions to enter the market.

The essence of promotion is to establish information channels between producers and consumers, strengthen the connection between the two parties, and producers and sellers use various means such as advertising, publicity, and sales to enhance consumers' understanding of products and stimulate their desire to purchase. There are various means of promotion, for example, advertising is the most common form of promotion, in addition, display, bundling sales, free giveaways, word-of-mouth publicity, etc. are all effective means of promotion.

9.4.1 The Connotation of Promotion Strategy

Promotion is to promote sales, which means to convey the information of the enterprise and its products to consumers and users in various ways, to promote their understanding, trust and purchase of the company's products, in order to achieve the purpose of expanding sales. The functions of promotion include shortening the market entry process, stimulating consumer purchases, improving sales performance, and consolidating the market position of products.

Shorten the market entry process: At the time of new product launch, reasonable promotion methods can let users understand the information of new products in a short time, establish a preliminary impression of new products, and shorten the process of users accepting new products.

Stimulate consumer purchases: When the user's intention to purchase a product is not clear enough, promotional activities can stimulate the user's purchase. For example, low-price promotion strategies are often used when promoting new products, encouraging users to try new products by reducing costs. For mature products, continuous promotion plans also help maintain users' long-term purchase intentions.

Improve sales performance: Long-term promotion plans can help manufacturers and users establish stable relationships, that is, improve brand awareness and user loyalty, and continuously promote user purchases.

Consolidate the market position of the product: Under the repeated reminders of promotional information, users will have a long-term brand impression of the product. With reasonable guidance, a good brand image can be established, the market position of the product can be consolidated, and a more advantageous position can be achieved in the market competition of similar products.

1. The Goal of Promotion

There are various ways of promotion, but they all follow the same principle. No matter how complex or novel the promotion plan is, it should not deviate from the goal of promotion, which is communication with the audience. We summarize the goals of promotion into three points: informing the target audience, reminding the target audience, and persuading the target audience.

Informing the target audience: The first purpose of promotion is to inform. It is responsible for conveying information related to the manufacturer and the product to the users. For example, in a new product promotion, the purpose, performance, principle, and selling points of the product are detailed. This is to inform the existence of the product and convey the product information to the users. In addition to informing and conveying product information, promotion can also suggest new uses for the product, promote the company's image, and increase product awareness. Typically, new companies and new products should focus on informing the target audience during promotion, allowing users to know and understand relevant information faster, and shortening the process of product entry into the market.

Reminding the target audience: Reminding the audience is the second purpose of promotion. In the promotion during the product maturity period, this purpose is often taken as the main task, responsible for reminding customers of the existence and value of the product, and maintaining customer awareness. In a buyer's market, products are extremely abundant, and users face multiple choices every day. If a product does not get the attention of users for a long time, it may be diluted or even forgotten. At this time, continuous promotional activities are needed to increase the presence of the product. In the process of reminding the target audience, attention should also be paid to the promotional activities of competitors, using their own promotional activities to offset the promotional effects of the other party, in order to maintain the market position of their own products among similar ones.

Persuading the target audience: Persuading the audience is the third purpose of promotion. In the growth and maturity stages of the product, persuasion can be used as the focus of promotion. It often focuses on persuading users to visit, influencing user purchase decisions, or improving user perceptions of the product, encouraging brand switching. Persuading the target audience requires a lot of skills. If not handled properly, it may cause the user's rebellious psychology and result in reverse marketing results. For example, hunger marketing can be seen as a persuasive promotional method, promoting the rarity of the product to users to promote purchases, and people may immediately complete the purchase under the psychological drive of "fear of loss". However, excessive hunger marketing may also cause people to feel annoyed, affecting users' liking for the product or even the brand.

2. Promotion Methods

With the guidance of promotional goals and strategies, effective promotional methods are also needed. For example, advertising is a very common promotional method. Its form is flexible and changeable, and it can achieve the three promotional purposes of informing, reminding, and persuading. Of course, promotional methods are not only limited to advertising. In today's unlimited creative thinking, the methods of promotion can be said to be unlimited, and even new promotional methods may be invented every day. Here we only briefly introduce some existing, common promotional methods.

Designated promotion: Designate products, such as buy product A get product B for free, or purchase designated goods at a low price; designate user objects, such as exclusive discounts for new customers, exclusive discounts for old customers, exclusive discounts for children under 12 on Children's Day, etc. Designated promotions are very beneficial for selling specific products and have good effects on launching new products or clearing backlog inventory.

Gift promotions: Buy one get one free is a promotion method that users love. Buy N items get N items free, buy goods get member points, spend a certain amount to get a gift, etc., all fall within this range. Gift promotions cater to users' pursuit of cost-effectiveness, are conducive to increasing product sales and positive reviews, and maintain or even increase the market share of the product.

Reward-based promotions: Reward-based promotions and gift promotions are similar in nature, including buying products to get free samples, discounts when you spend a certain amount, cash back when you spend a certain amount, and discounts when you buy N items. Discounts and cash back can be considered the most popular promotion methods for users, and they are also the most direct way for manufacturers to make concessions. They can greatly stimulate users' desire to purchase, but they will also cause manufacturers to lose some profit margins. Therefore, manufacturers need to carefully design when conducting reward-based promotions to ensure that their profits meet expectations.

Leverage promotions: When trying to capture users' limited attention, leveraging is a very good method. Various hot events, popular activities, and celebrities can all be used for leverage. In leverage promotions, celebrity endorsements and well-known event sponsorships are common. For example, internet celebrity styles and celebrity styles have a strong appeal in the fields of clothing accessories and beauty skincare. A recommended Weibo post can bring tens of thousands of sales. In recent years, with the improvement of internet communication capabilities, hot event marketing has also become a leader in leverage promotions. Following hot events can gain a lot of attention at a very low cost, and if handled properly, it can also promote the conversion from attention to purchase. However, this promotion method requires manufacturers to have the ability to capture hot spots, a quick response ability, and corresponding publicity ability, which cannot be achieved by simple planning.

Theme promotions: Theme promotions have some similarities with leverage promotions in specific operations. When manufacturers choose a popular theme, it will also form a leverage effect, such as public welfare theme advertisements, advertisements in line with sales platforms, etc. Theme advertisements usually attract users through a name, as long as they can form unified content and focus on hot spots, they can be tried as themes, such as global launches, local launches, etc.

Seasonal promotions: All products with seasonal characteristics can carry out seasonal promotions, such as winter promotions for down jackets, seasonal promotions for fruits and vegetables, and off-season promotions for various products.

Seasonal promotions are beneficial to match the manufacturer's products and user needs, encourage users who are in the hesitation period of purchase decision, and prompt them to make a purchase decision. Off-season promotions and seasonal promotions are not essentially the same. They use the unique features of the off-season to attract consumers and then use price advantages to reduce the inventory of off-season goods.

Special date promotions: Special date promotions, like seasonal promotions, give users a reason to buy to shorten their decision-making hesitation period and promote the occurrence of purchase behavior. Holiday promotions are the most typical special date promotions, but merchants obviously hope to use this promotion method at more times, so there are shopping festivals such as Double 11, Double 12, and 618. In addition, merchants designate some member special price days to attract users.

Add-on promotions: Adding extra value to a product to attract user attention and promote purchases is also an effective promotion method. In appliance promotions, trade-in for new ones, replacement without repair, free shipping in internet sales, and 7-day no-reason return and exchange are all service-based add-on promotions. Promoting a product after it has won some honor is also an add-on promotion, such as being the first in the XX award, recommended by the XX list, etc. In addition, another type of add-on promotion is to add cultural content to the product, such as special slogans, product stories, brand stories, etc.

Role Model Promotion: Establishing a role model during the promotion process can increase users' sense of authenticity and participation. For example, when recommending product performance, promoting the product as "the XX model that all colleagues have" or "friends have tried and said it's good" is equivalent to setting up a usage role model to narrow the distance between the product and the users. Many companies, when selling online, post screenshots of user comments on the display page, which also has a similar promotional effect. The key to role model promotion is to let users follow the role model in making purchase decisions.

Alternative Promotion: There are many unexpected or difficult to replicate methods in promotion, such as the no-discount strategy of many luxury brands, which is considered an alternative promotion. However, this type of promotion is difficult to apply to ordinary goods. Other examples include hunger marketing, limited edition promotions, etc.

9.4.2 Cross-Border Promotion Strategies

Promotion strategies can be divided into advertising promotion strategies, sales promotion strategies, personnel promotion strategies, and public relations promotion strategies, depending on the method of execution.

Advertising Promotion Strategy: Advertising promotion strategies usually aim to inform and remind, while also persuading users to purchase. Advertising promotion strategies are timely and can quickly arouse users' interest in advertisements and products. To achieve ideal advertising promotion results, companies need to analyze their own products and users, and choose suitable publicity channels and coverage within the budget. At the same time, the role of creativity in advertising promotion strategies cannot be ignored. Excellent advertising creativity can greatly improve promotion effects.

Sales Promotion Strategy: A direct and intuitive promotion strategy that promotes products from the business sales level. When planning sales promotion activities, consider the goal of the promotion, whether it is to increase product acceptance, enhance user goodwill, or clear product inventory. If the promotion activity is mainly for publicity and promotion, the expenditure budget can be appropriately relaxed, stimulate consumers to purchase at lower prices, let consumers understand the product advantages more deeply, and form a good brand impression. If the goal of the promotion is to clear existing product inventory, consider bundling sales, giving away promotions, etc., to let mature products drive new product sales and maximize the value of promotions.

Personnel Promotion Strategy: The value of people in promotions can never be ignored. A good sales team can ensure the best promotion effect. Understanding of the product, language skills, communication skills, and friendliness, etc., are all excellent qualities of sales personnel. It can be said that personnel are the basis for the successful implementation of all promotion strategies. Production companies need to establish strict sales team selection mechanisms to promote personnel capability improvement. For an already established sales team, it is important to maintain sensitivity, grasp market trends, perceive user needs, seize promotion opportunities, and assist in feedback on user opinions and maintain user relationships.

Public Relations Promotion Strategy: This is a long-term promotion strategy. It requires a long-term focus and slow results, but it is very beneficial for shaping the company's image and product brand. Companies can use news publicity, online publicity, public welfare publicity, list publicity, award publicity, etc., to improve their own popularity and reputation. In addition, holding speeches and exhibitions in public can also achieve the effect of publicity and expanding influence.

9.4.3 Cross-Border Promotion Management

Promotion management aims to increase sales through a series of plans, organizations, leadership, control, and coordination to attract and stimulate consumer spending. In other words, it requires managers to set promotion goals, develop promotion plans, and ultimately measure the effectiveness of the promotion plan execution.

Setting promotion goals: From a broad perspective, setting promotion goals involves choosing a focus between informing, reminding, and persuading; from a smaller goal perspective, choices can be made from directions such as increasing revenue, increasing turnover, increasing user numbers, increasing average customer spending, and increasing brand influence. If there are no clear promotion goals for the time being, manufacturers can analyze factors such as product cycle, market size, and user numbers to find the most pressing needs at present, which can guide the formulation of promotion goals. After setting the goals, manufacturers need to analyze the rationality of the goals to facilitate the next step of formulating a feasible promotion plan.

Formulating a promotion plan: According to the promotion goals and the scale of the promotion, choose the appropriate promotion means. If the scale of the promotion is large, a comprehensive promotion plan combining various promotion methods can be adopted. There are many factors that affect the promotion plan, such as activity ability, financial ability, production ability, technical ability, crisis handling ability, etc. In formulating the promotion plan, it is necessary to clarify the channels, methods, timing, and action plans for the promotion, compile a promotion budget, and finally arrange the specific execution process for the executors.

Promotion plan execution effect: After the implementation of the promotion plan, manufacturers need to check the promotion effect. According to the previously set promotion goals, compare the data performance after the promotion, such as whether the predetermined sales target has been achieved, whether more new users have been attracted, etc. Since the promotion plan usually takes into account multiple goals, multiple factors should also be considered when checking the effect.

Chapter 10
Cross-Border E-Commerce Risk Management

As a complex system engineering, cross-border e-commerce needs to integrate various services and knowledge such as internet technology, cross-border trade, cross-border electronic payment, cross-border logistics, customs declaration, law, foreign languages, etc. Enterprises involved in cross-border e-commerce are increasingly facing many new, covert, and not to be underestimated operational risk challenges in their transnational operations, such as information risks, credit risks, cross-border logistics risks and other endogenous risks, as well as legal risks, political risks, natural risks, infrastructure risks and other exogenous risks. On the other hand, due to the particularity of the main body and business model of cross-border e-commerce, there is a disconnection between the traditional management mechanism and the development of cross-border e-commerce. Its regulatory departments may face the risk of export tax refund in the tax link in their daily work, which is specifically manifested as enterprises fabricating deductible tax amounts, fabricating export business, irregular operations by intermediate agents, false customs declaration for export, and other risk events.

10.1 Sources of Cross-Border E-Commerce Risks

10.1.1 External Sources

1. Industry Rules and Supervision

Since the promulgation of the "United Nations Commission on International Trade Law Model Law on International Commercial Arbitration", there have been standards for adjudicating general trade disputes, but the trade model of cross-border e-commerce differs greatly from traditional trade. Cross-border e-commerce companies need to deal with consumers from various countries and confront policies and

X. Zhang, *Introduction to Cross-Border E-Commerce Ecosystem*,
https://doi.org/10.1007/978-981-96-1165-2_10

systems from multiple countries, dealing with various legal and regulatory systems, facing multi-level constraints formed by international trade rules, trade rules between major trading countries, internal trade rules of each country, and differences in trade rules between platforms. When transnational disputes arise, it is often difficult to determine jurisdiction. At the same time, product standards, inspections, and quarantines are essential links in international goods import and export. The relevant standards of each country vary in strictness and change from time to time, and cross-border e-commerce may also suffer losses due to these differences and changes in standards.

From the perspective of the importing country, the constant changes in the institutional environment and business environment can also bring significant operational risks to companies. While cross-border e-commerce complies with the traceability laws of the exporting country, it is also necessary to follow the traceability standards of the importing country. Export e-commerce that fails to comply with localized regulations is more likely to be involved in international commercial disputes and international arbitration, especially in after-sales and accountability links. International commercial disputes are not conducive to the normal operation and risk control of cross-border e-commerce companies. When the international trade liability tracing subject related norms of the target market accelerate the rectification or contradict the regulations of the country where the cross-border e-commerce company is located, it will be difficult for the export e-commerce company to quickly determine and accurately investigate the responsibility subject, and the accountability mechanism will also affect the realization of operating income and the guarantee of service quality for cross-border e-commerce companies.

2. Legal Aspects

Cross-border e-commerce is a commercial economic behavior, involving the consumer service field and the intellectual property field. The laws and regulations of these traditional fields will have many impacts on cross-border e-commerce activities, but whether the laws of traditional fields are applicable to cross-border e-commerce activities, and whether these laws have been updated according to the development of cross-border e-commerce. At present, the laws and regulations of these traditional fields have not yet established and improved the detailed rules for cross-border e-commerce behavior.

In the consumer field, China has formulated the "Consumer Rights Protection Law" (hereinafter referred to as the "Consumer Law"), "Product Quality Law", "Anti-Monopoly Law", "Anti-Unfair Competition Law", "Price Law", "Food Safety Law", etc. to protect consumer rights. Among them, the "Consumer Law" is the closest to consumers. In 2013, our country updated and revised the "Consumer Law", which increased the regulation of online transactions, and even formulated a seven-day no-reason return policy for online shopping. Unfortunately, it did not make relevant regulations for cross-border e-commerce consumption. In terms of intellectual property rights, China has formulated relevant laws such as the "Trademark Law", "Patent Law", and "Copyright Law". The relationship between the various laws has not yet been clarified, which is particularly evident in the application of the law in Article 2 and Article 56 of the "Consumer Law". The former is the priority application of the "Consumer Law", while the latter is the priority application of other laws and regulations. The legal positioning is vague and unclear, the legislative purposes intersect, and the adjustment ranges overlap, which not only cannot form the combined force of legal protection, but also hinders the determination of a unified guiding ideology for regulating cross-border consumption behavior.

3. Platform Rules

The rules and regulations of different cross-border e-commerce platforms vary. For example, Dunhuang.com adopts a commission system, free registration fee and EDM (Email Marketing) model, which has a lower cost; AliExpress insists on "price is king", sellers must have a lower price to have an advantage; eBay has stricter requirements for sellers, forming a strategy that emphasizes both quality and price; Amazon, which has the highest requirements for sellers, is product-driven, and while having a quality advantage, it must also build a brand. Companies need to juggle between the rules of different platforms, which can easily lead to an increase in the complexity of decisions such as product sales plans, and also put tremendous pressure on the platform management team. In the absence of understanding the rule system or difficulty in adapting to the rules of different countries and platforms, risk events are more likely to occur, leading to an increase in operating costs.

As the core link of cross-border e-commerce transactions, the responsibilities and obligations of e-commerce platforms are very important. The e-commerce platform is the first responsible person for the transaction activity and needs to assume the main responsibility. As the main body of commercial transactions, the e-commerce platform should carry out business qualification review, registration, and publicity for the operators on the platform. The e-commerce platform also needs to sign contracts or agreements with operators, clarifying the rights, obligations, and responsibilities of both parties in terms of entering and exiting the e-commerce platform, quality and safety guarantees for goods and services, and consumer rights protection. The e-commerce platform should establish and improve platform management rules and regulations, including but not limited to transaction rules, transaction security guarantees, consumer rights protection, and handling of bad information. The platform also needs to strengthen the inspection and monitoring system for the goods and service information published by the operators, take timely measures to stop violations of commercial administrative laws, regulations, and rules, and stop providing platform services when necessary. In addition, the e-commerce platform also needs to assume the following responsibilities, including the protection of registered product exclusive rights, corporate name rights, protection of business secrets and consumer personal information, consumer rights protection, stopping illegal activities, assisting and cooperating in investigating illegal activities, transaction information preservation, and regularly submitting online goods transactions and related service business statistics to the commercial administrative department. In addition, the trading platform also needs to consider many issues such as whether overseas merchants can settle in, the choice of website servers and data centers.

4. Logistics Infrastructure

In countries and regions where logistics channels are underdeveloped, cross-border e-commerce companies are prone to high logistics risks during their operations. Cross-border e-commerce companies that choose to develop these markets not only need to bear high logistics costs but also face troubles in terms of timeliness and safety. Cross-border logistics, due to the complexity of the logistics link, will generate many legal issues, including contract signing and performance, goods transportation safety, time and cost contradictions, disputes arising from returns and exchanges, information security and protection, etc., especially cross-border transportation and return and exchange logistics issues are more prominent. Establishing and improving the international transportation security system, including electronic payment, logistics security-related legal systems, while relying on laws and regulations, technology provision, and transportation goods information standardization construction. Because the return and exchange process is more complicated than domestic logistics, not only the logistics time is long, the logistics trace cannot be queried, the logistics cost sometimes exceeds the value of the goods, it also becomes a key area of consumer complaints.

5. Regional Intellectual Property Barriers

Different countries and regions have different intellectual property statuses and regulatory systems, which pose difficulties for the cross-border flow of goods. At the same time, there is also the problem of "patent trolls" who rush to register patents on major e-commerce platforms: these trolls take advantage of Chinese sellers' lack of understanding of the U.S. patent system, and rush to patent all or part of the details of the "hot-selling product categories" created by the sellers, and then immediately file infringement complaints with major sales platforms (such as Amazon). Because the incident happens suddenly, the platform and the seller are not clear about the ins and outs of the complaint, causing the complained seller to have to adjust according to the platform's infringement operation process, delist and "delete" the product.

In the current cross-border e-commerce transactions, the awareness of intellectual property protection and use is still weak, especially in the cross-border C2C transaction model, there are more counterfeit and imitation goods, and the improper use of product trademarks, pictures, text, etc. can easily trigger intellectual property risks. Brand registration has also become a problem in cross-border e-commerce transactions. When foreign merchants plan to enter a market, they find that their brand has already been registered, which can lead to intellectual property disputes.

6. Cultural Differences

In the context of economic globalization, cross-national operations and mergers and acquisitions of enterprises are becoming more frequent, and enterprises inevitably face foreign competition and the conflict of multiculturalism. All managers need to consider the operation and management of their enterprises with a global perspective, and consider the impact of cultural differences on enterprises. Cross-border e-commerce business makes enterprises face the difference between the host country's culture and the mother country's culture. This cultural difference directly affects the practice of management and constitutes a cultural risk in operation. The management method that is effective in a specific cultural environment, when applied to another cultural environment, may produce completely opposite results. There are often cultural differences between manufacturers and consumers in cross-border e-commerce, which can bring risks related to different cultural perceptions.

7. Uncontrollable Events

Cross-border e-commerce involves cross-national transactions and cannot avoid local political, regional customs, natural disasters, policy changes, and other factors. Such as the Ukrainian revolution, political instability in Vietnam, Southeast Asian xenophobic policies, and local protectionism, among many other factors. There are also major natural disasters that are unpredictable and destructive. When such disasters affect the quality of goods, cross-border e-commerce will also face sales difficulties. For example, the Japanese "311 earthquake" and the concurrent Fukushima nuclear power plant crisis have affected the sales of Japanese-produced ingredients, dairy products, and even cars and cosmetics in China. To this day, imported goods from Japan still need a certificate of radiation detection. Due to the inability to prove the origin, Kellogg's cereals and products from brands like Suntory, Orihiro, Rakuten, etc., have all been delisted from flagship stores on cross-border e-commerce platforms.

10.1.2 Internal Sources

1. Insufficient Awareness of Intellectual Property Rights

In traditional international trade activities, most foreign buyers complete their orders in large quantities. Importers usually conduct intellectual property investigations and risk prevention before importing goods, and control intellectual property rights. Although domestic exporters do not pay much attention to intellectual property issues, they will not store intellectual property infringement risks. Different from the traditional foreign trade model, in cross-border e-commerce, sellers are mainly small and medium-sized enterprises, and even many natural persons. They often lack professional knowledge about intellectual property rights, and the foreign buyers they face are also unspecified, so intellectual property issues become prominent. At present, disputes over intellectual property rights constitute the main problem of e-commerce. Under the situation of rapid development of e-commerce industry, infringements of intellectual property rights occur frequently, seriously affecting the international image of Chinese merchants and the healthy development of cross-border e-commerce industry. Cross-border e-commerce companies may face the risk of products being removed from shelves, links being deleted, inventory backlog, or becoming the target of intellectual property owners' litigation due to complaints of infringing others' intellectual property rights. The main reason for these intellectual property risk events is the weak awareness of intellectual property rights, lack of understanding of foreign intellectual property protection systems, and a fluke mentality towards infringement or not knowing how to deal with malicious litigation from competitors in cross-border sales.

2. Insufficient Ability to Defend Rights

Cross-border e-commerce transaction entities usually have difficulties in international rights protection when dealing with complex and changing international cross-border e-commerce activities. Some companies lack understanding of foreign laws and often cannot afford the high cost of transnational litigation when infringement issues arise, making it difficult to protect their rights. In cross-border e-commerce activities, a large number of small and micro enterprises, as well as many online stores and merchants on cross-border e-commerce platforms, usually do not have the ability to establish their own legal departments or afford the high cost of obtaining high-quality legal resources due to their small scale, incomplete organizational structure, and weak awareness of rights protection. When dealing with legal litigation and other issues, they often lack legal support and offline response mechanisms, which may lead to the company facing crises on multiple platforms at the same time.

3. Insufficient Market Analysis Ability

Most companies are not strong in product development and market analysis, are accustomed to imitation and copying, generally lack innovation consciousness and keen perception of blue ocean space, and few companies can allocate research and development and selection resources according to the specific consumer demand of the target national market, which leads to serious homogenization competition of Chinese goods in the target market. Cross-border e-commerce export companies often fail to complete sales targets as scheduled, leading to stockpiling and breaking the capital chain. The main reason for the risk of stockpiling in the sales link of export manufacturers is the lack of analysis ability of the target market demand at the selection stage, which leads to mismatched product development and serious homogenization of overseas warehouse stockpiling.

4. Improper Selection of Operating Platform

Cross-border e-commerce companies, especially small and medium-sized enterprises, often have inaccurate positioning of themselves when choosing third-party cross-border e-commerce platforms, lack understanding of the purpose of entering third-party cross-border e-commerce platforms, and blindly choose platforms, resulting in waste of company resources. Companies should focus on operating among various platforms, after all, the resources of the company are limited, and it is impossible to cover all aspects in cross-platform operation. How to determine their main battlefield and auxiliary battlefield is a core issue that cross-border e-commerce cross-platform operating companies need to pay attention to.

Cross-border e-commerce companies inevitably face the choice of which platform to join. Each platform mainly targets different countries and regions, and even the main industries are different. For example, AliExpress focuses on emerging markets such as Russia and the Middle East, while eBay, Amazon, and Wish all target the European and American markets. Among them, eBay has a larger market share in Australia, while Amazon has a greater advantage in the United States than eBay. In addition to the different geographical distributions of the platforms, there is also a trend towards market segmentation, with many specialized platforms beginning to occupy the market. Cross-border e-commerce companies, especially small and medium-sized enterprises, often have an unclear self-positioning and lack understanding of the purpose of joining a third-party cross-border e-commerce platform, which leads to blind platform selection and ultimately results in a loss of company resources. Improper platform selection may lead to various risks such as platform transformation risk, information security risk, and unsalable risk after the company chooses to join the platform.

10.2 Types of Cross-Border E-Commerce Risks

10.2.1 Operational Management Risk

1. Logistics Risk

Cross-border e-commerce logistics, due to its cross-border completion of item spatial displacement, often accompanies high package loss rates and long transportation times. For the complete supply chain of cross-border e-commerce export companies, the first and foremost operational management risk is logistics risk, mainly manifested as the "financial and goods loss" caused by the failure of cross-border logistics delivery. Common reasons include package loss caused by poor management of logistics companies, customs detention in the destination country, and package loss during domestic delivery in the destination country.

Cross-border e-commerce logistics involves many aspects and a wide range, and each node of the entire logistics chain will generate return and exchange logistics, which is a major problem for cross-border e-commerce. The inherent characteristics of e-commerce lead to a high proportion of returns and exchanges, long logistics cycles, product quality issues, loss of goods, risks of customs and commodity inspection, errors in delivery addresses, and a series of problems, all leading to the generation of return and exchange logistics. Especially in developed countries in Europe and America, the local "no reason for return" consumer habit and culture have led to a continuous increase in the return and exchange rate of Chinese cross-border e-commerce. Due to cross-border customs clearance and logistics, it is difficult for returns and exchanges to have a smooth channel to return to China, and various related costs increase, even resulting in the cost caused by returns and exchanges seriously exceeding the value of the goods, which is unacceptable to Chinese cross-border e-commerce, resulting in difficulty in achieving returns and exchanges.

2. Payment Risk

Payment is one of the important sources of operational risk in cross-border e-commerce, and it is very dangerous. Payment risk involves risks such as transaction authenticity identification, illegal fund flow, fund management and foreign exchange control. Exchange rate changes will also affect the payment process. Due to the timeliness of cross-border e-commerce transactions and the time difference between payment and receipt in cross-border payments, this will cause a large amount of funds of cross-border e-commerce companies to stay in third-party payment institutions, banks and other accounts for a certain period of time, thereby forming sunk funds. In cross-border payment services, payment institutions need to schedule funds between different reserve fund accounts, including domestic and foreign reserve fund accounts. Due to long settlement cycles and complex business operations, there will also be a large risk of fund flow. These sunk funds will be affected by exchange rate changes and will suffer financial losses due to exchange rate changes.

3. Stocking Risk

The current cross-border e-commerce model in China is mainly based on bonded import and overseas direct mail. Cross-border e-commerce represented by Tmall International adopts the model of official entry of brand owners into bonded imports. Cross-border e-commerce represented by Yangmatou mainly adopts the model of overseas direct mail, supplemented by bonded imports. Due to the flexible fluctuation of commodity sales prices, the impact of market changes on the overseas direct mail model is not very significant. The bonded import model is different. This model requires the goods to be transported to domestic warehouses in advance. Due to market changes, these goods reduce profits while maintaining the original price, increase the cost of import stockpiling, and thus lead to higher business risks caused by market changes. Cross-border e-commerce export companies often need to deal with the dilemma of stockpiling unsold goods due to the inability to complete sales targets on time after the goods are shipped to the overseas warehouse of the target country. In this case, the risk of stockpiling unsold goods often accompanies the breakage of the capital chain.

4. Exchange Rate Risk

Cross-border e-commerce operations cannot avoid the issue of exchange rate changes. The manifestation of exchange rate changes is the change in the currency exchange rate between different countries, which also represents the depreciation or appreciation of a country's currency. Chinese cross-border e-commerce faces the challenge of exchange rate risk in all aspects of the capital flow involved in commodity transactions. This type of business risk often occurs in countries or regions with large exchange rate fluctuations, such as Japan, Russia, the United Kingdom, and developing countries or regions such as Nigeria and Southeast Asia. Especially when the currencies of these countries or regions depreciate, it will lead to a decrease in sales and profits of Chinese cross-border e-commerce export companies, a decrease in consumer purchasing power, and a decrease in consumer demand. The change in the exchange rate between the payment and settlement currencies will increase the uncertainty of Chinese cross-border e-commerce operations.

In cross-border trade, the exchange rate is an important influencing factor. After the completion of sales, Chinese companies also need to face the challenge of exchange rate fluctuations. Exchange rate changes not only affect the profits, costs, and funds of cross-border e-commerce, but also bring exchange rate risks to the operation of cross-border e-commerce companies. Taking a domestic e-commerce platform as an example, the annual transaction volume is 30 billion yuan. Calculated at an 8% fluctuation, there is an exchange rate risk of 2.4 billion yuan, which is a considerable risk for the company. The fluctuation of the exchange rate may offset the company's annual profit, and may even cause losses. As the scale of cross-border e-commerce operations increases, the business risks brought about by exchange rate changes will also intensify, thereby restricting the development of cross-border e-commerce.

10.2.2 Information Risk

1. Corporate Credit Risk

Compared with traditional trading models, cross-border e-commerce relies on the Internet to carry out commodity trading activities. The trading entities belong to different countries and also reflect the virtuality and anonymity brought by the network environment. Different countries have different market environments, language barriers, different shopping habits, etc., coupled with the virtuality of the Internet, make the problem of information asymmetry more obvious. It is very difficult to identify the identities of the two parties to the transaction and trace their responsibilities. The lack of credit often triggers adverse selection and moral hazard issues in the trading market, which increases transaction costs and reduces market efficiency. According to data from China's E-commerce Complaints and Rights Protection Public Platform, in 2015 alone, the Shanghai Consumer Protection Committee accepted 1059 complaints about cross-border e-commerce, an increase of 368.6% year-on-year. In 2015, the number of complaints involving e-commerce in our country increased by 3.27% compared with 2014, and the fastest growing category was cross-border online shopping (7.53%). The complaints involved many issues such as online counterfeiting, online fraud, false shipments, order cancellations, overbearing terms, account freezing, difficulties in returning and exchanging goods, and poor after-sales service.

2. Information Security Risk

Different from traditional international trade models, cross-border e-commerce is based on advanced electronic information technologies such as the international internet and e-commerce platforms. While electronic information technology has become the basis for cross-border e-commerce services, the information security issues of computers and the internet have also become significant risks that foreign trade companies participating in cross-border e-commerce must face. The risks of information security mainly come from the compatibility and stability of computer and internet system software and hardware. Due to the short update and replacement cycle of computer and network software and hardware, and frequent upgrades, the software and hardware foundation of the entire cross-border e-commerce operation, including internet services, e-commerce platforms, network payment settlement systems, and the company's local operating environment, all have a mix of various software and hardware brands, models, and versions. Various compatibility issues, design flaws, and even system crashes are hard to avoid completely, leading to the interruption of the company's cross-border e-commerce business, and even the loss and leakage of transaction information and payment information.

3. Information Asymmetry Risk

In the agency relationship, cross-border brand agency e-commerce has a strong dependence on the brand's source of goods. The manufacturing and inspection of the goods are all the responsibility of the brand owner. Most cross-border brand agency e-commerce directly obtains goods from the brand owner, without the power to control or question the quality. Because cross-border e-commerce business involves different countries or regions, and different borders, it leads to high barriers to market entry and exit. For markets with large information changes, Chinese cross-border e-commerce will face the selective difficulty of entering or exiting. Especially in some countries due to political or economic reasons, it will exacerbate the information asymmetry risk between the subjects of cross-border e-commerce transactions, and the market operating environment will seriously deteriorate. Even in the short term, Chinese cross-border e-commerce companies can exit the market, but they still have to face significant losses, which may even lead to the company's income not covering expenses.

10.2.3 Structural Risk

1. Platform Entry Risk

For companies that simultaneously expand sales on multiple platforms, whether they can formulate a coordinated and efficient platform selection and team management plan at the beginning, and do a good job in follow-up work, is the key to the success or failure of the company's operations. For companies that gradually increase the number of platforms, each additional platform means breaking the original balance once, which is a reshuffle of the company's internal operations and product sales, and requires appropriate adjustments to return the company's operations to a balanced state. If you blindly increase the number of e-commerce platforms without adequate preparation, it may cause a lack of internal human resources, poor capital turnover, and chaotic team management, causing significant damage to the internal balance of the company.

2. Agency Relationship Risk

On the one hand, information asymmetry creates conditions for some poor quality overseas brands and even fake overseas brands to mix in. On the other hand, some brands have excellent brand appeal and a wide market span, but they have not yet formed a clear understanding of the cross-border electronic market, especially the lack of experience when they first enter the cross-border e-commerce industry, which may result in the risk that the cooperating agent cannot bring long-term cooperative benefits. Cross-border brand agency e-commerce often needs to start from scratch to establish a sales support system, conduct personnel training, and even product planning. It is this huge investment and hard work in the early stage of market development that makes the retention of labor results particularly important for agency e-commerce, which relates to a series of issues such as capital recovery. When the partner cancels the cooperation, these early investments become sunk costs.

10.2.4 Policy Regulatory Risk

1. Legal Regulatory Risk

Product standards, inspection and quarantine checkpoints are essential links in international commodity import and export. The relevant standards of various countries vary in strictness and change from time to time. Cross-border e-commerce may also suffer losses due to the differences and changes in these standards. From the perspective of changes in international customs clearance policies, policies related to international trade customs clearance are the results of the balance of various countries' customs to coordinate import and export trade and maintain their own trade interests. The risks of cross-border e-commerce operations caused by international trade laws and policies mainly focus on three aspects: ① Differences in trade laws and regulations of various countries. It has been reported that in recent years, buyers from the United States often chat with Chinese merchants on the pretext of buying counterfeit goods at high prices, obtaining their PayPal accounts, and the relevant brand merchants then file lawsuits in the United States based on the chat records. PayPal then freezes these Chinese merchants' accounts and funds, and even zeroes them out. PayPal's policy favors buyers, which is slightly different from our country's commercial law, economic law, and related practices. Therefore, there is a greater risk and hidden danger in cross-border operations before the export e-commerce is familiar with the relevant laws and regulations of the target market. ② Identification of the main body of product quality traceability. As a new engine of economic transformation, the cross-border e-commerce ecosystem itself has many weak links, and the relevant laws and management of different countries and regions are uneven, and cross-border business involves multiple parties, and there is a great difficulty and uncertainty in product quality traceability. ③ Inherent defects in the code and barcode mechanism. According to the management of the cross-border e-commerce platform, the logistics record method of inputting barcodes and codes is easy to be copied. The offender only needs to input the copied complete barcode and code at a certain terminal to form all the logistics information, which brings a huge right to the legally operated cross-border e-commerce enterprises and platforms. In addition, the "Hague Rules" maintain the interests of the carrier to a large extent, and the risk sharing is very uneven. Therefore, before the new shipping order is established, cross-border e-commerce companies have to face higher logistics accountability risks.

2. Intellectual Property Risk

Cross-border e-commerce companies may face the risk of product delisting or link deletion due to complaints that the products on sale infringe on others' intellectual property rights. Intellectual property risks can lead to inventory backlog, and in some cases, make the company the subject of intellectual property litigation claims. In the business practices of Chinese cross-border e-commerce companies, common intellectual property rights mainly include trademark rights (such as counterfeits), appearance patents or utility model patents, and product image theft infringement.

Theoretically speaking, cross-border e-commerce products that constitute intellectual property infringement need to be jointly responsible by the platform and the seller. However, in recent years, many precedents show that the platform will not be responsible for this. This means that the seller needs to bear the consequences of infringement independently, leading to the separation of interests between the platform and the seller. Therefore, the more platforms a cross-border e-commerce company enters, the greater the risk of infringement, and intellectual property disputes on larger platforms often affect the sales of related products on other platforms.

Essentially, cross-border e-commerce intellectual property issues are still e-commerce intellectual property issues, sharing the common attributes of e-commerce intellectual property issues. However, under the "cross-border" operating environment, it has significant uniqueness. These common and unique intellectual property issues pose higher requirements for the intellectual property capabilities and risk control construction of platform merchants and sellers. If the intellectual property is not done well, the result may only be temporary prosperity. Intellectual property issues are likely to affect the reputation and image of platform merchants and sellers in the international market, becoming a significant obstacle to the sustainable development of cross-border e-commerce.

10.3 Cross-Border E-commerce Risk Prevention

10.3.1 Prevention of Exogenous Risks

1. Legal Policy Regulatory Risk Prevention

Cross-border e-commerce companies may face simultaneous transactions from multiple countries, and it is essential to do your homework in advance. Understanding the target market country will be more beneficial for companies to analyze consumer preferences and then formulate corresponding marketing strategies to avoid potential operating risks. For the company's main target market, it is necessary to fully understand the intellectual property, tariffs, foreign exchange, and other policies of the relevant country. In the short term, international trade clearance policies vary from country to country, and it is difficult to influence their changing trends, but certain measures can be taken to deal with customs clearance, inspection and quarantine, positive list, and other problems.

On the one hand, cross-border e-commerce companies should strive to formulate new dynamic customs clearance strategies to mitigate the negative impact of policy regulatory risks. Specific measures include: ① Forming strategic cooperation alliances. For small and medium-sized enterprises in cross-border e-commerce, a certain level of integrated strategic cooperation alliance can be formed in terms of import and export customs clearance, integrating resources, sharing risks, and improving customs clearance efficiency. For export e-commerce and target market service providers, a localized strategic cooperation alliance should be formed. For cross-border e-commerce and multinational companies, a global strategic cooperation alliance can be formed at an appropriate level, leveraging the latter's resources and global influence to reduce policy regulatory risks. ② Establish a localized inspection team. Different target markets have different customs clearance policies for cross-border e-commerce, especially in the inspection and quarantine link. For example, Muslim countries prohibit the import of pork, but non-Muslim countries have a demand for pork imports. In the process of food production and inspection and quarantine, it is necessary to pay attention to the formation of differentiated inspections. In addition, different customs have different regulations on the upper limit of some chemical components. When the standards of the target market are different, cross-border e-commerce companies should form an adjustable product quality inspection system to adapt to the differences in customs inspection and quarantine rules and reduce customs clearance risks. ③ Keep up with the latest positive list in real time. The positive list has strict enforcement in each issuing country. When the strategy of cross-border e-commerce companies involves expanding the target market or expanding the business category, it is necessary to keep up with the latest positive list in real time. For example, China's import e-commerce prohibits the import of beef, and cross-border e-commerce platforms and companies should avoid the development of beef-related businesses when determining business categories.

On the other hand, cross-border e-commerce companies should also enhance their awareness of cross-border rights and responsibilities to improve their response speed to policy changes and their ability to prevent risks. This can be achieved by reducing the risk of cross-border e-commerce policy supervision. Specific measures include: ① Strengthening the awareness of rights. Companies should fully understand their own rights and interests, and legally protect their rights when conflicts of responsibility such as quality traceability occur, effectively reducing the difficulty of cross-border accountability and eliminating the risk of cross-border accountability. ② Strengthening the awareness of obligations. Cross-border e-commerce companies should actively undertake the obligations stipulated by international trade laws, fundamentally avoid the occurrence of unfulfilled obligations and inaction responsibilities, and reduce the risk of cross-border operations. ③ Strengthening the awareness of responsibility. The subjects of responsibility under international trade regulations are not the same, and the scope of responsibility that cross-border e-commerce companies should bear is relatively wide. Cross-border e-commerce companies should take the assumption of statutory responsibility as the primary principle, strengthen the awareness of cross-border responsibility, formulate management and business strategies, and reduce the risk of cross-border accountability.

2. Prevention of Platform Rule Risks

(1) Choose the Platform Carefully

Cross-border e-commerce companies, especially small and medium-sized enterprises, often have inaccurate self-positioning when choosing third-party cross-border e-commerce platforms, lack understanding of the purpose of entering third-party cross-border e-commerce platforms, and therefore blindly choose platforms, resulting in a waste of company resources. Companies should prioritize their operations among various platforms, after all, company resources are limited, and it is impossible to cover all aspects when operating across platforms. How to determine their main battlefield and auxiliary battlefield is a core issue that cross-border e-commerce companies need to pay attention to when operating across platforms. Choosing a platform involves two aspects of assessment, one is to start from a single platform, and the other is to pay attention to the cooperation between platforms, that is, the overall effect of multiple platforms. In terms of single platform selection, the first thing to note is to analyze and evaluate the platform, understand whether the platform model and positioning are consistent with the company's business goals. Secondly, companies also need to pay attention to the platform's customer base and reputation, for example, customers in emerging countries such as Russia and Brazil are mostly price-sensitive customers, while customers in Europe and America mostly value the quality and transportation time of products. In addition, the current charging models of various cross-border e-commerce platforms are different, so the cost of entering the platform also needs to be considered. In cross-platform operations, the most important thing for companies to choose a platform is to fully combine the advantages and geographical locations of various platforms, and formulate the platform entry plan according to the company's overall development strategy. The first thing to consider is the match between the product and the platform, and select the appropriate platform based on the price characteristics of the product, the target consumer group, etc. Secondly, it is necessary to match the company's positioning according to the platform rules and regulations, and choose the appropriate number and specific platforms. Finally, it is necessary to allocate management teams and other company resources according to the selected platforms.

(2) Detailed Operation Strategy

After deciding on the platform to settle in, companies need to formulate detailed and meticulous operational strategies for customs clearance, commodity inspection, tax declaration and refund, foreign exchange collection and settlement, bonded warehousing and logistics, risk monitoring and management, etc. On the one hand, from the perspective of the product sales process, logistics account for 20% to 40% of the cost of cross-border e-commerce companies. Therefore, logistics and warehousing pay more attention to the diversified product demand of cross-border consumption during the operation process, which is precisely the advantage of the overseas direct mail model. Companies can make trade-offs between the bonded warehouse and overseas direct mail models based on factors such as the characteristics of their own products, the international market conditions of the products, and the fluctuation trend of the RMB, and choose the operating model corresponding to different platforms to ensure their own operational safety. How to efficiently and flexibly coordinate and plan among different logistics channels has become a key part of affecting the efficiency of cross-platform operations. On the other hand, cross-border e-commerce companies need to think about how to build a management team to achieve the highest efficiency in the process of cross-platform operations, and take corresponding measures to reduce management costs and labor costs according to their own development needs and positioning. The management problems faced by cross-platform operations are more about the management of "people" rather than the daily business operations themselves. The company's leadership does not need to understand every detail, but it needs to ensure that the team understands its own goals in order to maximize efficiency. In addition, under normal circumstances, the data of any two platform malls does not support direct interconnection, which requires the company to flexibly handle it based on its own platform database. When operating on different platforms, try to arrange a dedicated team to ensure sufficient focus and professionalism, and try to ensure a high correlation of product categories in cross-platform operations, and do not over-expand SKU (stock unit) to avoid management problems. Due to the increased management difficulty of cross-platform operations, cross-border e-commerce companies need a powerful intelligent system to support the overall operation management, and can consider introducing a supply chain management system suitable for cross-platform operations, but need to weigh the pros and cons in advance.

(3) Grasp the Policy Rules Orientation

In the process of cross-platform operations, companies may face simultaneous transactions from multiple countries. Doing homework in advance is essential, understanding the target market country will be more conducive to companies analyzing consumer preferences, and then formulating corresponding marketing strategies to avoid potential operational risks. For the company's main target market, it is necessary to fully understand the intellectual property, tariffs, foreign exchange and other policies of the relevant country, as well as some execution habits of the corresponding platform, such as Amazon's US site only supports returns to US addresses, etc. At the same time, before companies start cross-platform operations, they should spend some time familiarizing themselves with the back-end operations and basic rules of each platform, and understand the differences and special features between each platform. The rules of cross-border e-commerce platforms may change once a week, or even once a day. Companies need to arrange a dedicated team to follow up on rule changes, start from registration, release, transaction, loan, evaluation, after-sales, etc., thoroughly understand the rules of the relevant platform, and clearly define the active areas and forbidden areas of each platform. After understanding the business scope defined by different platforms for the company, the company can then conduct systematic thinking and summarization, establish its own cross-border thinking framework, and carry out strategic expansion.

(4) Achieve strategic Cooperation and Mutual Assistance

In dealing with intellectual property disputes, most domestic sellers do not choose to actively litigate, which may potentially impact the operation of the business on other platforms and the overall image of Chinese enterprises. Especially for small and medium-sized enterprises with limited funds and less developed organizational structures, they often lack legal support and offline response mechanisms when dealing with issues such as intellectual property infringement. This could lead to a crisis on multiple platforms, with the will but not the power to respond. In such cases, strategic alliances or industry associations can provide necessary legal aid to small and medium-sized enterprises, such as assisting in seeking the best solution when encountering intellectual property disputes, and guiding small and medium-sized enterprises in making choices between active litigation and seeking reconciliation. At the same time, when small and medium-sized enterprises encounter legal disputes that lead to product detention, large enterprises can assist small and medium-sized enterprises in implementing emergency response measures such as goods transfer, such as providing free warehousing for a period of time or assisting in finding other sales channels, to jointly cope with the risks in cross-platform operations. A feasible suggestion is to establish a specialized organization for dealing with cross-border intellectual property litigation under the guidance of government departments, to achieve information sharing and collective litigation in cross-border litigation. At the same time, enterprises can also exchange operating experiences on various platforms through strategic alliances, providing guidance and further learning opportunities for small and medium-sized enterprises and novice sellers. Establishing a strategic alliance is an important measure to jointly avoid risks such as intellectual property infringement in cross-platform operations. 3. Prevention of Logistics Risks Cross-border e-commerce enterprises should familiarize themselves with and respond to changes in international logistics and freight policies. It is necessary to improve cross-border logistics operations as a major direction, integrating the best resources of the supply chain to balance logistics costs, timeliness, accuracy, and safety. Cross-border e-commerce enterprises need to improve the management information system of node enterprises in the supply chain, fully realize information sharing, enhance their own intelligent monitoring and coordination capabilities, enhance the response capability of international logistics services, ensure the rapid circulation of information flow and commodity flow, and reduce cross-border e-commerce logistics risks. Specific measures include: ① Establish an international logistics service capability assessment system to clarify the main body responsible for cross-border freight. The revision of the "Rotterdam Rules" reminds cross-border e-commerce enterprises that only by establishing a sound enterprise capability assessment system for international logistics service providers can they comprehensively locate the main body responsible for freight from the source and reduce logistics risks. ② Improve the ability to control international logistics costs and reduce the risk of goods compensation. After the logistics outsourcing agreement is reached, comprehensive supervision of the contractor should be carried out considering factors such as delivery, risk control, and insurance premiums. If necessary, the latter can be required to provide a complete alternative plan or emergency plan to cope with the new compensation policy adjusted by the "Hague Rules" and "Hamburg Rules", reducing the cost of goods compensation and operating risks. ③ Provide differentiated international logistics services to enhance policy adaptability. Cross-border e-commerce enterprises should provide differentiated international logistics services based on reality, especially focusing on the localization of logistics for export products in the target market, enhancing the enterprise's dynamic adaptability to international freight policies, and reducing logistics risks in the target market. For export e-commerce, enterprises need to adapt to different logistics models on various platforms. Although the bonded model ensures delivery speed and user experience, it neglects the more diversified product needs of consumers in cross-border consumption, which is precisely the advantage of the overseas direct mail model. Enterprises can make choices between the bonded warehouse and overseas direct mail models based on factors such as their own product characteristics, international market conditions of the product, and the trend of RMB fluctuations, choosing the logistics model that corresponds to different platforms to ensure their own operational safety. In terms of import e-commerce, the current delivery modes mainly include overseas direct mail and bonded stock, among which the import retail bonded stock mode has great advantages in terms of transportation cost, tax cost, delivery efficiency, return cost, etc. Import e-commerce not only needs to directly undertake the "B2C" responsibility of overseas brands selling directly to consumers, but also has the "B2B" function of mastering regional supply and expanding offline stores. Compared with the "direct mail collection" of small quantities and many kinds, the demand for the volume of goods and the flexibility of the supply chain in import e-commerce is obviously more in line with the bonded stock mode. Therefore, import e-commerce can try to use this mode to adjust the supply of goods.

3. Prevention of Intellectual Property Risks

In order to deal with intellectual property risks, it is urgent to establish a strategic alliance or industry association mainly aimed at handling legal affairs in the field of intellectual property and providing necessary legal assistance to small and medium-sized enterprises. Large-scale cross-border e-commerce companies in the strategic alliance or industry association have accumulated rich experience in dealing with the increasing intellectual property trade frictions, gradually gained the right to speak, and can assist in seeking the best solution when encountering intellectual property infringement disputes, guiding small and medium-sized enterprises in actively responding to lawsuits and seeking settlements. At the same time, when small and medium-sized enterprises encounter legal disputes leading to product detention, large enterprises can assist small and medium-sized enterprises in implementing emergency measures such as goods transfer, such as providing free warehousing for a period of time or assisting in finding other sales channels, to jointly cope with business risks. In addition, companies can also exchange operating experience on various platforms through strategic alliances, providing entry guidance and further learning opportunities for small and medium-sized enterprises and novice sellers.

4. Prevention of Payment Risks

The changes in international payment policies and the development of cross-border e-commerce promote and influence each other. Cross-border e-commerce companies need to actively respond to changes in international payment policies, achieve a healthy transition between traditional payment methods and cross-border e-commerce payment systems, improve cross-regional and cross-cultural electronic payment systems, ensure the security of complex transaction environments and the smooth flow of funds, so as to prevent cross-border e-commerce payment risks. Specific measures include: ① Expanding import payment platforms. While expanding international business, import third-party payment platforms should fully refer to international norms to deal with international risks such as exchange rate fluctuations and payment legality. ② Creating an export payment system. At present, cross-border e-commerce companies exporting to other countries (regions) in the world have not yet formed a localized cross-border electronic payment system. Overseas consumers mainly use foreign payment platforms such as PayPal. The fund flow of China's export e-commerce is restricted by the third-party payment platform chosen by target market consumers, and the problem of fund precipitation is becoming increasingly acute, and the funds in transit are difficult to turnover. Creating an export payment system is conducive to the integration of cross-border e-commerce business and the reduction of business risks. ③ Promoting the integration of import and export payment platforms. After the development of cross-border e-commerce to a certain stage, it can form the integration of domestic and international business of third-party payment platforms. For example, Alipay can divide its business into domestic import e-commerce enterprise sector and export e-commerce enterprise sector, serving domestic consumer payment and overseas consumer payment respectively, which is conducive to overall coordination, improving cross-border payment efficiency and reducing business risks.

5. Prevention of Exchange Rate Risks

(1) Macro Level

Firstly, financial policy. The country is accelerating the promotion of financial system reform, relying on the advantage of the Renminbi entering the direct withdrawal rights, and accelerating the internationalization of the people. From the national level, the coverage of bilateral local currency swap agreement countries and regions is accelerated. With the launch of the Renminbi cross-border payment system, the coverage and utilization of this system should be accelerated globally, encouraging settlements in Renminbi, and actively promoting the transition from the US dollar to the dual currency pricing of the Renminbi and the US dollar.

Secondly, exchange rate policy. In terms of exchange rate management, it is recommended to manage exchange rate changes in a small and gradual manner. The implementation of this measure is conducive to enhancing exchange rate flexibility and to some extent stabilizing market expectations for currency. In the long run, it is beneficial to promote cross-border e-commerce companies, especially small and micro enterprises, to slowly adapt and cultivate awareness and ability to prevent risks brought about by exchange rate changes.

(2) Industrial Level

Firstly, scale structure. Vigorously develop the industrial cluster strategy, accelerate the integration and improvement of the existing industrial chain of cross-border e-commerce, and accelerate the optimization and upgrading of the existing industrial structure and industrial reorganization. Relying on the cross-border e-commerce platform, actively promote enterprise alliances within the same industry or related industries, forming a cluster effect of small and medium-sized enterprises. The aim is to achieve scale effects and industrial cluster effects, to improve industrial competitiveness and market concentration, and to improve the ability to respond to exchange rate risk.

Secondly, production mode. With the advantage of traditional labor-led, through research and development and design within the industry, it transforms into the emerging industry advantage led by emerging technologies. Actively develop cross-border service businesses, such as education service import and export, medical service import and export, etc., focusing on micro-innovation of goods, achieving differentiation, customization, and flexibility. Through the transformation of industrial production methods, increase the added value of goods, and reserve enough profit space for goods. With the production method as the starting point, return to the essence of business, return to the goods themselves.

(3) Enterprise Level

Firstly, business strategy. Cross-border e-commerce companies focus on the transformation of business strategies. While improving product quality, they should also pay attention to the expansion of the mid-to-high-end market, especially markets with stable economic environment, high market acceptance, and high profit margins, to ensure high market competitiveness. According to actual market needs, adjust the product structure of cross-border e-commerce companies in a timely manner, strive to implement brand strategies, increase the profit space of goods through brand premiums, increase the proportion of high value-added goods, and thereby achieve the purpose of transferring exchange rate losses. Cross-border e-commerce companies can also diversify their operations, diversify industries, products, markets, platforms, etc., to disperse exchange rate risks. Pay attention to exchange rate changes, enhance awareness of exchange rate risk control and hedging, and build a mechanism for preventing and warning against exchange rate risk.

Secondly, management strategy. Starting from improving corporate production efficiency, scientifically manage and control product quantity and quality, reduce indirect costs of goods through a process-oriented, scientific, and systematic management system. Use scientific methods to quantify exchange rate risk. Establish an internal risk control department within the company, or rely on cross-border e-commerce platforms or banking institutions, establish an exchange rate change linkage mechanism, and achieve exchange loss transfer. Incorporate exchange rate risk assessment into the management mechanism, incentive mechanism, and financial personnel assessment mechanism of senior management, and enhance the awareness of exchange rate risk prevention of relevant personnel in the enterprise.

6. Prevention of Uncontrollable Event Risks

Major natural disasters, political and public opinion turmoil are the most serious and unavoidable risks for cross-border e-commerce. Once the "black swan" takes off, cross-border brand agency e-commerce will face great difficulties. Considering the inevitability of risks, cross-border e-commerce should actively use insurance tools to spread risks, and should also adhere to compliant operations, comply with the laws and regulations of the country where the business is located, and actively and reasonably "hedge" through comprehensive risk prevention measures. 10.3.2 Endogenous Risk Prevention (1) Risk Prevention for Platform Entry Companies should prioritize their operations among various platforms, after all, the resources of the company are limited, and it is impossible to cover all aspects when operating across platforms. How to determine their main battlefield and auxiliary battlefield is a core issue that cross-border e-commerce cross-platform operating companies need to pay attention to. The choice of platform entry involves two aspects of assessment, one needs to start from a single platform, and the other should pay attention to the cooperation between various platforms, that is, the overall effect of multiple platforms. In terms of single platform selection, the first thing to note is to analyze and evaluate the platform, to understand whether the platform model and positioning are consistent with the company's business goals. Secondly, companies also need to pay attention to the customer base and popularity of the platform. For example, customers in emerging countries such as Russia and Brazil are mostly price-sensitive customers, while customers in Europe and America mostly value the quality of products and the timeliness of product transportation. In addition, the current charging models of various cross-border e-commerce platforms are different, so the cost of platform entry also needs to be considered. In multi-platform operations, the most important thing for companies to choose to enter the platform is to fully combine the advantages and geographical locations of various platforms, and formulate the platform entry plan according to the company's overall development strategy. The first thing to consider is the match between the product and the platform, and select the appropriate platform according to the price characteristics of its own products, the target consumer group, etc. For example, when the company's products are more popular, they can lean towards platforms and customer groups that focus on price advantages, while the product strategy of the high-end route is just the opposite. Secondly, it is necessary to match the company's positioning according to the platform rules and regulations, and choose the appropriate number of platforms and specific platforms. Finally, it is necessary to allocate management teams and other company resources according to the selected platforms. For example, small and medium-sized enterprises can concentrate products and human resources on the main operating platform to ensure the product sales of their main platform. (2) Prevention of Stockpiling Risk On the one hand, in response to the risk of stockpiling, cross-border e-commerce should establish a sustainable brand concept, actively abandon unfair competition, and resist "low price and low quality" dumping activities. In response to the risk of supply and demand fluctuations, we should pay attention to the scientific statistics of sales and inventory, improve the accuracy of booking and picking up goods, and leave a reasonable flexible supply margin. It can also negotiate with suppliers on the "quick response" supply chain to improve the turnover speed of goods. On the other hand, a considerable part of the reason for the risk of stockpiling in the sales link of export manufacturers is the lack of analysis ability of the target market demand at the selection stage, which leads to mismatched product development and serious homogenization of overseas warehouse stockpiling. For this reason, cross-border e-commerce should pay attention to cultural factors, improve the pertinence of products, carefully select goods before selling them, and evaluate their cultural acceptance; pay attention to the localization of goods marketing, advertising promotion, etc., and pay attention to combining local cultural factors and following consumer habits when marketing. For example, the rise of NetEase's strict selection is precisely because of its precise and unique positioning, which has achieved a balance between ordinary consumers' pursuit of the quality and price of daily necessities. (3) Prevention of Agency Relationship Risk.

To reduce the quality risk of the brand itself, e-commerce agents should fully understand the background, strength, financial status, reputation, etc., of the brand to prevent fraud or infringement, and avoid becoming an agent of "fake foreign brands" through brand investigation. For overseas brands with chaotic offline distribution channels and vague market positioning, cross-border brand e-commerce agents can also prepare for future online sales conditions and possible online sales strategies through investigation. Cross-border brand e-commerce agents should fully understand the level of support the represented brand provides to the e-commerce agent, and be vigilant towards overseas brands that provide less support to prevent taking on a "hot potato".

Regarding unreasonable responsibility allocation clauses in the agency contract, cross-border brand e-commerce agents should carefully review the contract content and be wary of the authorizer setting traps through the contract. If the company has difficulty reviewing the contract alone, it can also consider connecting with a specialized legal institution for assistance. Cross-border brand e-commerce agents should also carefully examine the hierarchical agency relationship in brand authorization to guard against potential risks. In the event of agency termination, cross-border brand e-commerce agents should seek more help from the "exit mechanism" related clauses in the contract confirming the commission-agency relationship, strive to first ensure that their own rights are not damaged in the exit mechanism, and further fight for their rights.

As the brand's influence expands, market recognition improves, and customer loyalty rises, cross-border e-commerce should focus on cultivating its own user group. While cultivating consumers' acceptance of the brand, it should also cultivate consumers' stickiness to the e-commerce's own reputation and its own platform.

7. Corporate Credit Risk Prevention

The virtuality, networked, and non-physical characteristics of cross-border e-commerce make this trading model more reliant on credit support than traditional trading models. Establishing and improving a credit assessment system can to some extent reduce the degree of information asymmetry, reduce the risk and transaction cost of both parties, increase the willingness to trade, and improve market efficiency. Specifically, appropriate credit assessment methods should be adopted to accurately and scientifically screen and process the required indicators, efficiently establish a credit assessment model, accurately assess the company's credit status and monitor the credit subject in real-time and dynamically, timely reflect the credit changes of the credit subject and propose solutions, improve the accuracy of the company's default probability measurement to reduce the default probability of trading activities, reduce the cost of credit risk management for all parties involved in cross-border transactions, improve the timeliness and accuracy of cross-border e-commerce credit risk management, and effectively prevent credit risks in cross-border e-commerce.

Among them, the cross-border e-commerce big data credit evaluation system needs to be constructed and further improved by combining internet, Internet of Things, mobile technology, and big data technology, through accurate evaluation, efficient modeling, real-time monitoring, and reducing the probability of default. The first is big data mining. Cross-border e-commerce, as a new type of trade method, has generated and accumulated a large amount of diverse user network behavior big data. It should obtain data through the internet to make up for the shortcomings of traditional evaluation methods, aggregate massive data generated from social networks and e-commerce behaviors, provide lateral support for the evaluation results, achieve multi-source data fusion; monitor the credit changes of the credit subject in real time, come up with solutions in time, and avoid risks; use massive data to obtain strong correlations between factors, avoid the impact of accidental factors, and achieve efficient modeling. The next is simulation, based on the collection of multiple comprehensive indicators of enterprises and the big data mining of important indicators of the meso and macro environment, to achieve as accurate as possible restoration of the actual market situation through the Monte Carlo algorithm and machine learning, reflecting the different default situations of the same enterprise indicators under different external environments, providing enterprises with a reference for opportunistic decision-making, and reducing the probability of default. Finally, there is the artificial intelligence model, which mimics the human brain's information processing process, intelligently processes information, and achieves big data risk control. Using an artificial intelligence machine learning platform, through data analysis, processing, mining, the model is built to more accurately assess the probability of enterprise default.

MIX
Papier aus verantwortungsvollen Quellen
Paper from responsible sources
FSC® C105338

If you have any concerns about our products,
you can contact us on
ProductSafety@springernature.com

In case Publisher is established outside the EU,
the EU authorized representative is:
Springer Nature Customer Service Center GmbH
Europaplatz 3, 69115 Heidelberg, Germany

Printed by Libri Plureos GmbH
in Hamburg, Germany